the riddle of
ROMAN
CATHOLICISM

the riddle of
ROMAN
CATHOLICISM

JAROSLAV
PELIKAN

ABINGDON PRESS—NEW YORK—NASHVILLE

THE RIDDLE OF ROMAN CATHOLICISM

Copyright © MCMLIX by Abingdon Press

Library of Congress Catalog Card Number: 59-10367

Scripture quotations unless otherwise noted are from
the Revised Standard Version of the Bible and are
copyright 1946 and 1952 by the Division of Christian
Education of the National Council of the Churches of
Christ in the U.S.A.

TO SYLVIA

. . . sicut et Christus dilexit ecclesiam
—Eph. 5:25

CONTENTS

I. Introduction. The Problem of Roman Catholicism 11

    The Puzzle.   The Audience.   The Perspective.

PART ONE THE EVOLUTION OF ROMAN
               CATHOLICISM 17

II. How Christianity Became Catholic 21

    *The Missionary Enterprise. Church Organization. Church
    Life. Theology. A Modus Vivendi with the State.*

III. How Catholicism Became Roman 34

    *Primacy in the Early Church. Rome in the Early Church.
    The Prestige of the Roman Name. The Orthodoxy of the
    Roman Bishop. The Primacy of the Roman Patriarch. Holy
    Rome and the Holy Roman Empire.*

IV. The Tragic Necessity of the Reformation 45

    *The Catholicity of the Reformers. The Reformation Gospel.
    The Roman Catholic Reaction. Christendom Divided. The
    Disintegration of Catholic Europe.*

V. The Roman Church in the Modern World 58

    *The Modern State. Modern Society. The Modern Mind. The
    Modern Church. Bulwarks Against Modernity.*

PART TWO THE GENIUS OF ROMAN
CATHOLICISM 73

VI. The Keys of Peter 77
The Establishment of the Church. Authority in the Church.
Obedience to the Church. The Jurisdiction of the Church. The
Church as Mother.

VII. The Two Swords 94
Twin Realms. A Twofold Law. Dual Citizenship. A Divided
Loyalty? A Double Standard.

VIII. Mystery and Magic 110
Baptism. Confirmation. The Eucharist. Penance. Extreme
Unction. Marriage. Holy Orders. The Sacramental System.

IX. Ave Maria 128
Holy Mary. Mother of God. Pray for Us! Blessed Among
Women.

X. The Angelic Doctor 143
The Origins of Thomism. The Enthronement of Thomism.
The Appeal of Thomism. The Revolt Against Thomism. The
Future of Thomism.

XI. Cultus and Culture 159
The World Community. The Worshiping Community.
Worship and the World. Worship and Community.

PART THREE A THEOLOGICAL APPROACH
TO ROMAN CATHOLICISM 173

XII. The Unity We Have 177
The Church Is One. The Church Is Holy. The Church Is
Catholic. The Church Is Apostolic.

XIII. The Unity We Seek 190

The Testimony of the Scriptures. The Heritage of the Fathers. The Witness of the Reformation. The Tradition of the Liturgy. The Ministry of Reconciliation.

XIV. The Way of Conversion 202

A Two-Way Street. The Roads to Rome. A Short Cut to Reunion? A Blind Alley.

XV. The Burden of Our Separation 214

Mutual Responsibility. Gentle and Firm Testimony. Honest Self-Examination. Assessment of Needs and Debts. Concern for the Total Church.

XVI. The Challenge of Roman Catholicism 227

A Comprehensive World View. An Inclusive Appeal. An Urban Ministry. A Living Tradition. A Sacramental Worship. A Policy for Reunion.

Notes 241

Index 259

I

The Problem
of Roman Catholicism

✠ CAN A ROMAN CATHOLIC be a loyal President of the
United States? Why must the Roman church maintain a competitive
school system in this country, with over four million pupils in the
elementary grades alone? Is it true that Roman Catholics worship
saints and have made a goddess of the Virgin Mary? Do they seriously
believe that those little statues on their dashboards will help prevent automobile accidents? How can the church defend its absolute
stand against birth control and divorce? What actually goes on behind the high walls and before the high altar?

The Puzzle

These questions, which are only samples, suggest that most Americans look at Roman Catholicism with a mixture of suspicion and
fascination. They are not quite sure it really belongs on the American

11

scene, and yet they find they cannot ignore it. In fact, they write about it and talk about it, alternately praise it and denounce it. Books like *People's Padre* and *A Nun's Story* reach a wide audience, and so do the meditations of Thomas Merton. Even as they read such books, many Americans are very poorly informed about the Roman church. They often know more about the batting averages of the Yankees or the marriages and divorces of Hollywood than they do about the life and workings of the most formidable religious institution in the history of America and of the world.

There are many reasons for this ignorance. For one thing, the Roman Catholic Church is so complex that the outsider does not know where to start if he wants to understand it or even to criticize it. Insiders have not been of much help either. The best interpretations of Roman Catholicism in English are, almost without exception, translations from French and German writers or works of penance by converts from Protestantism. Neither type of literature meets the need of the American reader. The obverse type of literature, the exposé by Protestant converts from Roman Catholicism, has even less to commend it.

Small wonder, then, that the prejudices and clichés of past generations continue to dominate the image of the Roman church current in America. Though their prose would be less high-flown, most American Protestants would still describe Roman Catholicism with Macaulay as: ". . . a complete subjection of reason to authority, a weak preference of form to substance, a childish passion for mummeries, an idolatrous veneration for the priestly character, and, above all, a merciless intolerance." [1] When news commentators suggest that a good Roman Catholic layman may be a good President, even those for whom 1928 is only a childhood memory confess to an uneasiness. Let someone propose that government aid should apply also to parochial schools, and committees are formed to pass resolutions and write letters to Congressmen. Resentment of Roman Catholicism is as strong in some parts of the United States today as it was when nativism was agitating against Irish, Polish, and Italian immigrants half a century ago.

12

Much of the resentment now is aimed at Roman Catholicism rather than at Roman Catholics. Most Americans today have some Roman Catholic neighbors and friends. They have learned to live with them, if only by declaring a moratorium on the discussion of religious differences. Yet they often wonder how people can swallow all that Roman Catholicism represents. If one were to ask specifically what Roman Catholicism does represent, the answer would be a vague puzzlement. To the non-Roman observer in America, the Roman church remains what Winston Churchill once called the Soviet Union: "a riddle wrapped in a mystery inside an enigma." [2] He cannot fathom it; and yet when he hears that the church has increased its membership by one million in a single year and that it represents a fifth of the population of the United States, he must acknowledge that this is a force to be reckoned with. What he needs is information and interpretation, so that he can grasp the riddle of Roman Catholicism and come to terms with it.

The Audience

Such information and interpretation is what this book is intended to provide. It is addressed, first of all, to Protestants who are interested in Roman Catholicism—and that should include most Protestants! Interest in Roman Catholic Christianity is becoming increasingly fashionable today. Among some sophisticates this interest has become a fad. But even the more sober-minded pay more attention to Roman Catholicism than they used to. In this area, as in so many others, Paul Tillich speaks for many of us:

The [Roman] catholic church . . . has manifestly been able to preserve a genuine substance that continues to exist, although it is encased within an ever hardening crust. But whenever the hardness and crust are broken through and substance becomes visible, it exercises a peculiar fascination; then we can see what was once the life-substance of us all and what we have now lost, and a deep yearning awakens in us for the departed youth of our culture.[3]

Motivated by such a fascination, this book aims at an interpretation of Roman Catholicism that is sympathetic and critical.

13

Protestants cannot get by with the repetition of Reformation slogans today. In some ways Roman Catholicism has improved since the Reformation; in other ways it has deteriorated; but it is with modern Roman Catholicism that we have to deal. An outstanding Protestant churchman, Bishop Hanns Lilje of Hannover, has made this clear:

Each generation of Protestants must re-think the decision of the 16th century. We must be able to say why we today are not Roman Catholics. We want the truth—even if it is unpleasant. . . . We want relationship with the Roman Catholic Church. We want to discuss not only the points at which we differ but the polemics of our faith.[4]

In the interests of the truth—"even if it is unpleasant"—this book seeks to act as an antidote both to the slanders by certain Protestants and secularists and to the precious description of Rome by certain aesthetes, apologists, and recent converts. Neither group is doing justice to its material or performing a service for its audience.

This book would also like to reach a Roman Catholic audience. Their picture of Protestantism is frequently as distorted as the Protestant picture of Rome, but there are other books on this. Even more alarming is the ignorance of many Roman Catholics about Roman Catholicism. Coming from national backgrounds where it was unnecessary to be well informed about the church, many American Roman Catholics have not kept their religious information on a par with their information in other fields of thought and life. There is an increasing number of books to enlighten them, but perhaps a book by an interested outsider has something to contribute, too. As long as the relation between Roman and non-Roman Christians in the United States remains on the level merely of "human relations" or of "intergroup tensions," the witness of the two to each other, and of the Holy Spirit through them, will be muffled. This book wants to speak to Protestants and to Roman Catholics who have heard the summons of the Spirit to responsible membership in the church of Jesus Christ.

14

The Perspective

It would be possible to study Roman Catholicism from many perspectives. One of the most important interpretations of it, that of Friedrich Heiler, sets it against the background of the world religions and seeks to isolate within it those features that show an affinity to religion in general.[5] The influence of Heiler's book and the replies to it from both Protestants and Roman Catholics are testimony to the success with which it has penetrated into the religion of catholicism. But for readers who are unacquainted with the history of religions, Heiler's interpretation is not as fruitful as it should be, and much of its point is lost on them.

This volume is written from the standpoint of a theology which has its roots in the Reformation and therefore—not nevertheless, but therefore—feels obliged to take the church of Rome seriously. It will first attempt to understand the origins and the evolution of Roman Catholicism by means of historical review. Secondly we shall make an effort to grasp its genius by looking at some of its most central features, practices, and teachings as they are seen and apprehended by Roman Catholics themselves. Thirdly we shall try to formulate a theological approach to Roman Catholicism by examining the relation between it and the rest of Christendom and considering the responsibilities of Roman and non-Roman Christians to one another.

Throughout this discussion we shall be attempting to fathom the riddle of Roman Catholicism. How can one institution include (to stay only in North America) both the Pontifical Institute of Medieval Studies in Toronto and the shrine of Our Lady of Guadalupe near Mexico City? How is it possible for Rome to call marriage a sacrament, as very few Protestants do, and then to say that celibacy is a higher estate than marriage? Sometimes the ancient paganism of devout people is covered by so thin a veneer of Christian piety that even the friendly observer is puzzled. The movements of the church organization are likewise difficult to understand. Its critics are ready to believe the worst about its political involvements and ambitions, and some of its bishops seem bent upon proving the critics right. In very few other churches does the minister kiss the Bible as part of a worship service, and yet this is the church that bypassed the Bible to proclaim the assumption of the Virgin Mary simply on the authority of an infallible pope. At a time when liberal Protestantism was humanizing the picture of Jesus Christ, sometimes at the cost of the divine in him, Roman Catholicism insisted upon his full divinity—and then seemed to lose him in a cloud of saints. At a time when fundamentalist Protestantism was insisting upon creation in six days of twenty-four hours each and damning Darwinism, Rome permitted considerable academic freedom and spoke of how the Spirit had accommodated himself to the world view of the biblical writers. Yet Rome requires all the theologians and philosophers to submit to the authority of the church and all historians to make sure that the results of their research do not conflict with the official teachings of the church.

How can all this be? What is it that holds this complex of opposites together? Is there anything—Protestantism, for example—for which Rome does not have room somewhere? Does the church mean it seriously when it issues "an invitation to the separated communities" of Christendom to attend an ecumenical council aimed at a discussion of differences? And what are we to do about Roman Catholicism? Even when we close our eyes, it refuses to go away. The least we can do is to make an effort to understand it.

PART ONE

———

THE EVOLUTION
OF ROMAN CATHOLICISM

✠

Roman Catholicism as we know it is the product of twenty centuries of history. To understand it, we must try to understand this history. Not only is it the product of history, but it involves a distinctive attitude toward history. A Roman Catholic looks upon the history of the church as an organic whole; he is proud "that catholicism cannot be identified simply and wholly with primitive Christianity, nor even with the gospel of Christ, in the same way that the great oak cannot be identified with the tiny acorn." [1] And yet he must insist that the church is the institution of Christ, that Peter was the first pope, and that the seven sacraments all go back to the Lord himself.

This attitude toward history makes it essential that we examine the historical evolution of Roman Catholicism. In the following chapter we shall attempt, first, to determine how the primitive Christian movement acquired the comprehensiveness and variety we associate with catholic Christianity. Within catholic Christianity one sector became more powerful and influential than the others, and therefore we shall have to study the process by which catholicism became Roman. Since most non-Roman churches would insist that they are still catholic without being subject to Rome, we turn next to the Reformation, which made such a distinction possible and necessary. Finally we shall look at the situation of the Roman church in the modern world. Although such a survey must be only a survey, it is probably the best device for getting to understand and to appreciate the genius of Roman Catholicism, which we shall examine at some length in Part Two of this book.

II
How Christianity
Became Catholic

✠ How DID CHRISTIANITY become catholic? How did it
happen that from the simple message and unpretentious life of Jesus
of Nazareth, as we find these described in the gospels, there came an
international organization, fully equipped with priests and bishops
and patriarchs, with rites and sacraments and pomp, with the power
of discipline for this world and the control over grace for the next?
Surely the contrast is a striking one, even for a person who believes
that it was Jesus' intention to establish catholic Christianity. This
chapter seeks to isolate some of the factors responsible for that development. It is in many ways the most crucial chapter in the book;
for once a person concedes that the development of catholic Christianity was valid, he is obliged to look at Roman Catholicism differently.

Let me set down an oversimplified formula for what I mean by catholic Christianity: identity plus universality. By "identity" I mean that which distinguishes the church from the world—its message, its uniqueness, its particularity. By "universality," on the other hand, I mean that which impels the church to embrace nothing less than all mankind in its vision and in its appeal. "Identity plus universality" is not a logical definition, and it is not intended as one. Indeed, catholic Christianity is probably as incapable of logical definition as is the taste of cheddar cheese or the music in the closing scene of *Don Giovanni*. One famous definition finds the essence of catholicism in this, "that it does not distinguish between the church in the religious sense of the word (the church of Christ) and the church in the legal [or institutional] sense of the word." [2] A better description is that of the Russian theologian, Aleksiei Khomiakov (d. 1860):

The church is called one, holy, universal (or catholic), and apostolic: because she is one and holy; because she belongs to the whole world, and not to one particular locality; because through her all humanity and all the earth are hallowed, not one particular nation or one particular country; because her being consists in the agreement and unity of spirit and life of all her members on the whole earth, who acknowledge her; because, finally, the whole of her faith, her hope, and her love is contained in the writings and the teachings of the apostles. [3]

Throughout its life, then, catholic Christianity means identity plus universality. The combination appears in catholic piety, churchmanship, theology, and liturgy; and the narrative of how that combination came into existence is the history of the rise of catholic Christianity.

Of course, no enumeration of factors and events can be an adequate explanation of any phenomenon in history. There is too much complexity in the phenomenon, and too much ignorance and prejudice in the historian. But an enumeration of factors can help the present-day reader to understand and appreciate how catholic Christianity arose. Each of the elements we shall examine here involves some combination of identity and universality, but in different proportions. Each was present, at least seminally, in the work and message of

22

Jesus and in the early church. In the words of a liberal Protestant historian, "Catholicism is . . . as old as the Church if we include its rudimentary form; there is hardly a single one of its elements which was not present" [4] in the first century. Where these elements appear together, be it East or West, there is catholic Christianity.

The Missionary Enterprise

One of the most important factors in the rise of catholicism was the missionary enterprise of the early church. Only when Christians began to realize the implications of Jesus' life, death, and resurrection for the rest of humanity beyond the confines of God's ancient people, did the possibility of a church catholic arise. According to the New Testament, it was with Jesus himself that this realization began. Most of his explicit references to evangelization among the non-Jews belong to "the gospel of the forty days," the commands and promises which the disciples received from their risen Lord and which are partially preserved in the closing chapters of the four gospels. But the accounts of Jesus' ministry show that his was not a narrow nationalistic message, but one whose invitation extended beyond his own people. In this sense it is certainly valid to say that the work of Jesus led to the missionary enterprise of the apostolic church, and that the "great commission" recorded in the gospels is the consistent climax of what he had said and done all along.

The ministry of Jesus was catholic, for he maintained his identity with Judaism, but not at the cost of the universality of his message beyond Judaism. In this respect, too, he was carrying out a basic conviction of Jewish history itself. According to the New Testament, he came to repair the loss of universality, symbolized by the Tower of Babel. What was lost there in a welter of identities was recovered at Pentecost, when the Spirit of the risen Christ came down upon "Parthians and Medes and Elamites and residents of Mesopotamia, Judea and Cappadocia, Pontus and Asia, Phrygia and Pamphylia, Egypt and the parts of Libya belonging to Cyrene, and visitors from Rome, both Jews and proselytes—we hear them telling in their own tongues the mighty works of God."

23

Yet the catholic implications of the Pentecost experience did not dawn upon the church all at once. During the first generation after Pentecost, the ideal of identity came into conflict with the ideal of universality. Peter opposed universality in the name of Judaeo-Christian identity, insisting that the only way to Christianity was through Judaism. Consistently carried out, such an insistence would have prevented the church from becoming catholic. So (if one may put it sharply, in the light of later history), to become catholic the church had to oppose Peter! Not by following Peter, but by following Paul in opposition to Peter, the church safeguarded the catholic vision of Pentecost. Then Peter, too, caught the catholic vision. The meeting referred to in Acts 15 has sometimes been called the first catholic council. The decisions to which it came do incorporate the catholic principle of "identity plus universality"; for they require converts to set themselves apart from the world (identity), but they refuse to make it impossible for gentiles to join the Christian cause (universality). These decisions put the seal of apostolic approval upon the mission work of Paul, which was, in turn, the pattern for the mission and expansion of Christianity during the following centuries.

Through the meticulous scholarship of historians we are in a position to trace that expansion in the Roman empire.[5] During the second and third centuries, little pockets of Christians appear in various parts of the empire. The church laid claim to the name "catholic" [6] as early as the beginning of the second century, but only after three centuries of missionary activity could Augustine say that the church was called "catholic" in Greek "because it is scattered throughout the world." [7] The message of the missionary movement guaranteed the church's identity, its converts guaranteed the church's universality. Sometimes the conversions seem superficial to us, and universality seemed sometimes to obscure identity, as it has in the missionary movement again and again. But the church preserved its identity, as it had preserved its universality during the first century. Neither exclusive nor inclusive alone, but catholic—such was the church that emerged from the missionary activity of the early Christians.

24

So the Christian movement caught up and fulfilled the catholic ideal of the world around it.[8] Catholicism is older than Christianity, for the age into which Christ came was longing for a universal community. Stoic philosophers like Seneca (d. A.D. 65) announced the principles of world brotherhood; Gnostic seers invited men to participate in a cosmic process whose outcome was the restoration of primal harmony; and Jewish writers envisioned the gathering of all the peoples before the throne of the Lord. But the church catholic rejected these alternatives because none of them incorporated "identity plus universality." The Gnostic intoxication with universality destroyed identity, while the Jewish preoccupation with identity made universality well nigh impossible. Nevertheless, catholic Christianity took up into itself whatever it could of these opposing systems, and thus it could present itself in its mission work as the fulfillment of these catholic visions and the representative of One who was "the desire of all nations" (Hag. 2:7).

Church Organization

A church that could mount the offensive of the missionary enterprise had to be organized. Part of being catholic, therefore, has always been a form of organization within the church. So much is this so that the episcopal form of church government and the priestly view of the ministry are perhaps the first characteristics that come to mind when we think of catholic Christianity. The church became catholic when it acquired an ordered episcopal ministry.

Here again the question of origins is controversial. Just as the church traced its missionary enterprise to the command of Jesus, so it found the origins of the episcopate in the institution of Jesus.[9] But what Jesus instituted, according to the New Testament, was the apostolic office. There are references to this institution in the gospels, but once more we must look to "the gospel of the forty days" for the most explicit warrant. Here Jesus is portrayed as vesting authority in the apostles to bind and loose, to feed his lambs and his sheep.[10] That apostolic authority, acknowledged and shared by Paul, was the basis of church organization in the first century. If the church was to continue

25

for only a generation, as some passages in the New Testament seemed to say, it needed no further organization. But when it became evident that the church might have to remain in the world for some time to come, the apostolic office also had to find a way of perpetuating itself. This it did through the establishment of the threefold ministry of bishop, deacon, and presbyter. These do not appear to have been distinguished until later—just how much later is a matter of debate— but the ministry itself is a creation of the first century.

This means that the catholic church, too, was a creation of the first century, since the threefold ministry is one of the constitutive elements in it. At first this ministry existed alongside the free visitations of the Spirit. Gradually those visitations diminished in intensity and in frequency. They never disappeared completely; in fact, the monastic orders seem to have been the place where they continued to appear. But the church could not depend for its existence upon these sporadic and ofttimes eccentric manifestations. The ordered ministry became the link between the original institution of Christ and the later ages of the church. In the pastoral epistles the apostle Paul is portrayed as having transmitted his office to Timothy and Titus, and as charging them, in turn, to ordain others.[11] A century later Tertullian spoke for the entire church when he said: "The church is from the apostles, and the apostles from Christ, and Christ from God." [12]

As time went on, the threefold ministry was divided into the offices of deacon, presbyter, and bishop. To the bishop the task of transmitting the church's continuity with the apostles was finally entrusted. When the city congregations grew into dioceses, some of the bishops had large groups of clergy under them. Those dioceses which could claim to have been founded by apostles were accorded special honor in the chain of apostolic authority. The church was catholic by virtue not only of its geographical extension, but of its apostolic origin. The locus of authority in the catholic church, therefore, were the bishops, individually and collectively. Because of the apostolic succession, the episcopate was a means of assuring the catholic character of the church. It represented the apostolic character of the church's message and ministry, and thus it helped to maintain the church's identity. At the same time, it also symbolized the continuity of the church in every age with the apostles of the first age; and thus it helped to maintain the church's universality in time as well as in space. Apostolic and therefore catholic in both its identity and its universality, the church's ministry was a guarantee that the church would continue in the apostles' fellowship.

Church Life

"Catholic" is more than a way of describing the outreach of the church and the structure of its organization. It is also a way of speaking about the special forms of church life developed by the church in the process of becoming catholic.

The most significant stage of that inner process is the growth in the importance of the sacraments. Biblical scholars today are less inclined than they were half a century ago to question the institution of baptism and the Lord's Supper by Jesus. Yet this does not permit us to read back into the gospels all the later theories regarding the sacraments.[13] When it moved into the Hellenistic world, the church found in baptism and in the eucharist as a "medicine of immortality" [14] a way of meeting and satisfying the longing for forgiveness, immortality, and fellowship with the Divine which was so prominent in that world. Both baptism and the Lord's Supper helped to make the church universal in its appeal and significance; but by being rooted in the life and death of the historical Jesus Christ, these sacraments also helped to preserve the church's identity and to keep it from losing itself in the sacramentalism of the mystery-religions. So it was that the sacraments helped the church to become catholic.

With the growth in the prominence of the sacraments came the development of the church's liturgical worship. The rather simple rites reflected in the New Testament and described by the earliest fathers were not adequate for the needs of a church that was becoming catholic.[15] The evolution of the ministry into a priesthood was both a cause and an effect in this shift.[16] Valuable though the spontaneous outbursts of ecstatic speech may have been as demonstrations

27

of the Spirit's presence and functioning, they were also a threat to the universal character of the church's message and worship. The ordered liturgies that established themselves in the churches still allowed considerable room for spontaneity and freedom, but they insured the catholicity of a worship which was never uniform throughout the church but which was nevertheless universal in its basic content and its fundamental appeal.

A sacramental system and a liturgical worship both became necessary because of a shift in the standards of church membership. At least part of the early church set its standards in passages like this:

> It is impossible to restore again to repentance those who have once been enlightened, who have tasted the heavenly gift, and have become partakers of the Holy Spirit, and have tasted the goodness of the word of God and the powers of the age to come, if they then commit apostasy, since they crucify the Son of God on their own account and hold him up to contempt. (Heb. 6:4-6.)

These standards were gradually eroded away in the course of the second and especially of the third century. An epitome of this erosion is the career of Cyprian, bishop of Carthage (d. 258).[17] From a rigid insistence that Christians could not be forgiven if they committed a mortal sin after baptism he moved to a qualified approval of such repentance on the deathbed, and eventually he had to relax even this. Thus the primitive image of a pure church was replaced by the comprehensiveness of piety we usually associate with catholic Christianity. The catholic church still inculcated the stringent discipline of its original message, but it had room also for the more casual worshiper. The spiritual athletes became the founders of the monastic orders, and their saintly life was set before all the faithful as an ideal. But the church had learned to take people as they were, to enfold them in its all-embracing membership, and then to educate them toward a higher and deeper spiritual life. Universality was thus preserved, and the church proved that it was comprehensive. It took a long time for this comprehensive church to purge itself of all that it had absorbed, and thus to clarify its identity, and thus to establish its true catholicity.[18]

Theology

In order to become catholic, Christianity had to develop the intellectual forms of its message as well. This took time, and it took reflection. Theology became possible only when the church, in Emil Brunner's apt phrase, got down to "thinking it over" and clarifying its message for friends and enemies.[19] During these early centuries the church also acquired the raw materials of creed and biblical canon upon which theology has continued to draw. In these, as well as in the theology that was based upon them, catholic Christianity articulated both its identity and its universality.

This dual aspect of catholicity corresponds to the twofold function of theology, that of definition and defense. The church assigned to theology the task of definition, which was a means of clarifying its identity by combating heresy and defining the true catholic faith in opposition to heresy. In this way theology helped to set the church apart from the perverters of the faith and to establish the equation: catholic=orthodox. It is significant that most of the major theologians in the ancient church whose works have been preserved composed a treatise with some title like *Against All Heresies* or *Defense Against Heresies* or *Condemnation of Heretics*. This was not because the theologians of early Christianity were unusually combative people, but because the primitive Christian movement recognized that its best weapon against the distortion of apostolic faith was a precise definition of its identity. The heretics, in turn, did the church the favor of not attacking some notion on the fringe of its teaching, but of centering their attention upon the pivotal doctrines of creation, redemption, and revelation. In response to such attacks the theologians of the church were required to sharpen its identity at the very points at which that identity could so easily be blurred. Irenaeus of Lyons (fl. 180) is perhaps the best illustration of how the attacks of the heretics compelled a theologian to define both the form and the content of the church's teaching and thus to maintain the church's identity.

At the very same time, the church also called upon the theologians to defend the faith against misinterpretation from the outside and

29

thus to guarantee its universality. Their defense of the faith against the Roman empire took as its thesis that catholic Christianity was the perennial philosophy for which Greeks and Romans had vainly sought. Clement of Alexandria (d. 220) could thus invite the pagan philosophers and Gnostics to forsake the partial truth of their sectarian systems and to find the universal Truth in Christ.[20] His pupil Origen (d. 254), greater than his teacher, combined such defense of the faith with deep study of the Scriptures.[21] He deserves, if anyone does, the title "catholic theologian"; for nothing fine or noble was alien to him, whatever its source, and yet he probed into the particularity and identity of biblical faith as few men before or since. He was also the most influential theologian of the ancient church, at least until Augustine, and helped to put this catholic mark upon those who were shaped by him and even upon those who condemned him.

Despite his virtuosity, Origen was the church's man, and so were the other catholic theologians of the time. This meant not only that they put their theological talents at the church's disposal, but also that they drew their theological insights and judgments from the church's teachings. To become catholic the church needed theologians to define her identity and to defend her universality. They, in turn, needed the church to set down the data of the faith. This she did in her creeds, whose importance for the development of catholicity is difficult to exaggerate.[22] They were a basis for theology and a link between theology and liturgy. In them catholic theology had a neat summary of both its identity and its universality. The God of the creeds was universal—the Maker of heaven and earth and of all things visible and invisible; the Judge of all men living and dead through his Son Jesus Christ; and (as the term "Father" came to be interpreted) the Father of the world. The creeds served also to establish the identity of Christian faith, for their core was a series of events that happened—and happened only once—to One who suffered under Pontius Pilate. When heretics like Marcion (d. ca. 160) tried to limit the universality of the faith and when Gnostics tried to blur the identity of the faith, it was to the creeds that theologians had recourse as the warrant of their catholicity.

30

Even more significant for the rise of catholic Christianity was the establishment and eventual canonization of the Christian Scriptures, both Old and New Testament. No less an authority than Adolf Harnack called this the most important event in the history of the church.[23] By retaining the Old Testament as a Christian book when it moved from the Jewish to the Greek world, the Christian movement equipped itself with credentials that traced its ancestry all the way back to the creation of the world and thus proved its universality. By assembling and accepting a collection of Christian writings as a second Testament alongside the Old, Christianity incorporated into its system of authority a means of identification by which missions and church organization and church life and theology were all to be judged. By combining Old Testament and New Testament in a single Bible, the church declared its intention to safeguard both its universality and its identity through what came to be called "the Scriptures of the catholic church." These books were the Scriptures because the catholic church said that they were, and the church was catholic because the Scriptures proved that it was. Such was the case for catholicity which the theologians propounded on the basis of creed and canon.

A Modus Vivendi with the State

There is one more historical factor involved in the rise of catholic Christianity, the establishment of a *modus vivendi* with the state.[24] Catholicism as a historical force is unthinkable without some agreement between the church and the state as to the respective provinces of their jurisdiction. The agreement need not be voluntary on both sides; indeed, it seldom has been. From one side or the other, as we shall see in Chapter VII, pressure has usually dictated the terms of agreement. Later theories could explain that all this was providential, or even in conformity with natural and revealed law. But the arrangement gives every appearance of being a makeshift, and the theories of being rationalizations after the fact. Yet some arrangement and some theories there had to be for catholicism to come into existence.

For a segment of the church it may be possible to live temporarily without such an arrangement, especially if it is charged with a fervent

31

expectation of the world's end and the Lord's return. But if the church was to assume the role in culture and in individual life which the word "catholic" implies, it needed to build some bridges to the state. By the fourth century the Roman state found itself in a position where it had to come to terms with the Christian movement. And in the catholic church of the fourth century the Roman state confronted a Christian movement with which it could deal. Its organization was stable, its program was clear, and its continuity was assured. This is more than could be said of the empire. Ignoring the church was no solution, and persecuting it only made things worse. So the state first tolerated, then favored, and finally established the Christian religion as the religion of the empire. The church moved from catacomb to throne in less than a century—a great opportunity and a great temptation.

The urge to universality made the church capitalize on the opportunity, the urge to identity made it resist the temptation. Only a catholic church could have done both. It capitalized on the opportunity by its missionary program and by adjustments in the standards of its membership; thus the church could absorb the people who joined it because that was the thing to do in the fifth century. It resisted the temptation by strengthening its organization; otherwise the illusion of a "Christian empire" might have cost the church its identity and freedom. Because the church had become catholic through the processes we have been describing here, it was ready when recognition came. Through its bishops the church met the empire, pagan or Christian, as well as the empire's enemies. It was Leo the bishop (d. 461) who met Attila the Hun at the city's gates, and it was Ambrose the bishop (d. 397) who excommunicated the emperor Theodosius the Great. Although their actions may have became the pretext for extravagant papal claims in later centuries, their original purpose was to show the power of the church and its freedom from domination by any secular power.

For this position, as for its catholicity generally, the Christian movement had to pay a price. By its alliance with the state the church was tempted to use the power of the state as a weapon against heretics

32

and infidels. By the adoption of a pedagogical attitude toward human weakness, the church was tempted to become cynical about the possibilities of improvement and to leave people in virtual paganism for centuries. In these and in many other ways, the catholic church had to give hostages to fortune as the price for becoming catholic. But it is a testimony to the continuing identity of the church's Christian witness that the most severe denunciations and warnings regarding this situation continued to come from the spokesmen of the church. The proof of the Spirit's presence in the church is not that the church is pure, but that the church is willing to confess its impurity.

How did Christianity become catholic? It became catholic by a complex variety of factors, some of which have been outlined in this chapter. During the first two or three centuries of its existence, the church acquired characteristics that have marked it ever since. It is to this catholic church that, humanly speaking, we owe the preservation of our Christian Scriptures, even if we repudiate the development of the catholic church and do so in the name of the Christian Scriptures. The reformers and the revolutionaries of church history have looked to this period to diagnose "the fall of the church," while Christians of catholic persuasion, Roman or not, have looked to it as the time when the main lines of catholic history were set. To be catholic today means to affirm the essential correctness of the development we have been summarizing here. But to the average American, "catholic" means more—or less. It means to acknowledge the primacy of the bishop of Rome. Therefore we must turn to the question of how the catholicism we have been describing in this chapter became the Roman Catholicism we are studying in this book.

III

How Catholicism
Became Roman

✠ OUR DISCUSSION of how Christianity became catholic has purposely omitted one factor from consideration—the role of the Roman church. In analyzing and interpreting that role in the present chapter, we must go over some of the ground we have already covered. Christianity did not become catholic and only then Roman Catholic; in the process of becoming catholic Western Christianity became Roman Catholic. To understand the riddle of present-day Roman Catholicism, therefore, we must turn to a consideration of the factors that contributed to the unique position of Rome within the catholic church. Here again we shall select certain factors that seem crucial, and try to account for that unique position on the basis of history.

Primacy in the Early Church

Supporters of Roman Catholic claims sometimes give the impression that the primacy of Rome was an acknowledged fact in the church

34

of the first century. Our sources from the first century do not substantiate this impression. They say much less about primacy at all than one might expect or wish. And what they do say about such matters deals less with the primacy of Rome than with the superior rank of two other forces in the early church—the congregation at Jerusalem and the apostle Peter.

The congregation at Jerusalem enjoyed a position unique among apostolic congregations. Here the Holy Spirit had appeared in a way unmatched by any other church. Here not merely one or two apostles, but the twelve had worked. The earliest Christian martyr was Stephen in Jerusalem. It was to Jerusalem that Mary returned after the events of Good Friday and Easter. These and many other prerogatives helped to make Jerusalem the headquarters of the Christian movement and "the home town [*metropolis*] of all the citizens of the New Testament." [1] Its high rank can be gleaned from the story of Paul. Even though the authorization for his ministry and his missionary work had come by way of Antioch, it was to Jerusalem that Paul seems to have looked as the seat of apostolic authority. The apostolic community in Jerusalem had the right to preface its decisions with the awesome formula: "It has seemed good to the Holy Spirit and to us." (Acts 15:28.) When Jerusalem had spoken, the issue was settled, at least for the time being. Paul acknowledged the congregation at Jerusalem as the capital of the church; he was silent in an epistle addressed to the church at Rome about any similar honor for Rome. The primacy among the churches belonged to Jerusalem.

The primacy among the apostles belonged to Peter. In the first part of the Book of Acts, which describes the life and activity of the early church before Paul, Peter is the dominant figure. Peter is the spokesman for the church; Peter must be persuaded by a heavenly vision that the gospel belongs to gentiles too; Peter is jailed when the church's enemies want to cripple it. The order of the names in the catalogues of the apostles varies from list to list, but there is one constant element. In every list of these names, Peter's name comes first. Early Christian tradition has amplified this picture of Peter's place in the apostolic community, and from both Scripture and tradition it

35

seems almost incontestable that among the apostles Peter was "the first among peers." It was, after all, to Peter that the words of Jesus preserved in the gospel had been addressed: "I tell you, you are Peter, and on this rock I will build my church, and the powers of death shall not prevail against it." (Matt. 16:18.) Later on, in Chapter VI, we shall discuss the meaning of these verses in a little more detail.[2] In the present context the passage is an additional indication of Peter's rank in the apostolic church.

Rome in the Early Church

Peter's rank was ultimately transferred to the church at Rome, but only after considerable time had elapsed. At the middle of the first century Rome appears to have been one of the most important congregations of the growing church, but not more than that. Paul's letter to the Romans commends them for the reputation they have acquired throughout the church, but it does not ascribe any special prerogative to them. (See Rom. 1:8.) Other references in early Christian literature bear out the impression that the Roman congregation was thriving and active.[3] It was admired for its size and wealth, and it was praised for its generosity. Its location in the capital city kept it in the eye of Christians throughout the empire. When Jerusalem was destroyed by the armies of Titus in A.D. 70, that city's hold upon the loyalty of the churches was relaxed. When, at about this same time, both Peter and Paul suffered martyrdom for the faith in the city of Rome, the capital city of the empire began to grow into the capital city of the church.

The martyrdom of both Peter and Paul in Rome is not a part of the biblical narrative but belongs to tradition. It has often been questioned by Protestant critics, some of whom have even contended that Peter was never in Rome. But the archaeological researches of the Protestant historian Hans Lietzmann, supplemented by the literary study of the Protestant exegete Oscar Cullmann, have made it extremely difficult to deny the tradition of Peter's death in Rome under the emperor Nero.[4] The account of Paul's martyrdom in Rome, which is supported by much of the same evidence, has not called forth similar skepticism. As the resting place of these two apostles—one of them the prince of the apostles, the other the apostle to the gentiles—Rome was the natural choice to take over the spiritual headship originally ascribed to Jerusalem.

The Prestige of the Roman Name

We have already suggested that part of the splendor of the Christian congregation at Rome was reflected light from the brilliance of the eternal city itself. Three fourths of a millennium of Roman history had passed before Peter ever came to Rome. During those centuries the city had acquired a halo—first for the citizens of the city itself, then for the inhabitants of Italy, ultimately for the entire empire. What Cochrane has aptly termed "Romanitas: the apotheosis of power" added the aura of a religious symbol to the natural beauty and political might of Rome. Patriotism and religion, both of them strong wines, were thus blended into a heady potion. Pagan Roman writers who otherwise seem quite blasé become rhapsodic when they speak of Rome.

The Christian congregation located in Rome had a curious relation to this. On the one hand, Christianity was violently opposed to Roman claims of divinity. The harlot of the Apocalypse was an appropriate symbol of the perversion which such claims represented. The establishment and growth of a Christian church right in the harlot's city was a triumph. Christians could attach to the Roman congregation some of the emotion which their pagan neighbors expressed for Rome itself. A theologian like Tertullian could denounce Rome and the empire in strong language, and yet laud the Roman congregation: "How happy is its church, on which the apostles poured forth all their doctrine along with their blood! where Peter endures a passion like his Lord's! where Paul wins his crown in a death like John's!" [6]

Such loyalty to Rome became much easier for Christians in the fourth century. Because the emperor himself was Christian now, piety and patriotism did not need to be in conflict any longer. In fact, Christians could contend now that by their prayers they were the

37

best support for a righteous government. Now it was the pagans who threatened the common weal. To symbolize this change and to resist the centrifugal forces at work in his realm, the emperor Constantine moved the capital of the empire from Rome to "new Rome," Byzantium, in 330. The name of the new capital was changed to Constantinople. It was to replace the old Rome in the hearts of Roman citizens and to strengthen the unity between the eastern and the western halves of the empire.

Politically, the shift to Constantinople was a failure; the empire could not be united. Religiously and ecclesiastically, however, it helped to hasten the elevation of the Roman church to its hegemony over the West. Loyalty to the empire was loyalty to the city. When the capital of the empire was transferred, some of the loyalty went with it, but much of it remained attached to Rome. Capital or not, it was the eternal city. Now that the city no longer had the emperor as the emblem of its position, it needed someone or something else to represent the true Rome. The mantle of the emperor fell upon the shoulders of the pope. When Leo turned back the Huns, he was acting in the name of the church and in the name of the city. The prestige of the Roman name joined with that of Peter and Paul in supporting the authority of the Roman bishop. It was an acknowledgment of this role when the bishop of Rome took over the old sacerdotal title of supreme pontiff, *pontifex maximus*.

The Orthodoxy of the Roman Bishop

The same Pope Leo reinforced the power and prestige of the Roman see in other ways as well. When the church, torn by conflict over the doctrine of the person of Christ, met at Chalcedon in 451, the formula of union came largely from Leo. "Peter has spoken through Leo" the delegates are supposed to have exclaimed.[7] Leo's papal moderation—which, as Father Rahner has said, "mediates between a unity based upon primacy and a pluralism of bishops" with no head—helped to gain the support of the delegates for his moderate doctrinal position.[8] The decree of Chalcedon has, in turn, been the basis of the orthodox Christian doctrine of the person of Christ throughout the

38

church for the past fifteen centuries. This attestation of the orthodoxy of the Roman bishop is by no means an isolated instance. Throughout the history of ancient dogma the occupants of the Roman see manifested an astonishing capacity to select and formulate—or to take credit for—the orthodox solution to thorny theological questions.

Such questions generally arose in the Eastern half of the church as part of a continuing conflict between Alexandria and Antioch. Repeatedly the theologians of these two sees came into conflict over the doctrine of the Trinity and the doctrine of the person of Christ. Central though these doctrines are to Christian faith and thought, the impression is unavoidable that in the conflict Eastern theologians sometimes performed the same function of bringing glory to their diocese that football players perform for an American university. When the theologians of Antioch and Alexandria had brought the debate to a standoff, either Rome or Constantinople or both would frequently intervene in an effort to settle the argument and to provide the orthodox answer. Constantinople had done just that in 449, and it had guessed wrong. The council which legislated for it in that year came to be called "the robber synod of Ephesus," and at Chalcedon two years later the adoption of Leo's formula was also the repudiation of Constantinople's intervention at Ephesus.

Gradually this came to be a habit—this ability of Rome to be on the winning side in doctrinal disputes. Prudence and good timing undoubtedly helped along, but it would be wrong to ascribe Roman victory to strategy alone. There is an intrinsic validity to the theological formulas which Rome put forward, and the orthodox acceptance of them is a testimony as much to this as to Rome's influence. Chalcedon was typical in many ways. The Roman answer reduced the theological issues to their importance for the faith, life, and worship of the church, and thus succeeded in assigning secondary importance to the merely speculative elements. Once this reduction was effected the common ground between the two sides came into view and the extremists at either end could be identified. Support for this common ground also came from Scripture and tradition, which often said "both-and" where the extremists on both sides insisted upon an

39

"either-or." Because a particular answer was in harmony with Scripture and tradition and therefore orthodox, Rome supported it. Invert this and you have the foundation of papal infallibility. Because Rome supported an answer, it was in harmony with Scripture and tradition and therefore orthodox. Rome was always right—or almost always.

There are two celebrated cases in the first six centuries of church history when Roman bishops seem to have been on the wrong side in a theological debate. Both of them have occasioned much controversy since the promulgation of papal infallibility at the Vatican Council in 1870. The first concerns the Roman bishops Zephyrinus (d. 217) and Callistus I (d. 222). According to the theologian Hippolytus (d. ca. 235), both these men were guilty of the "modalistic" heresy. They did not distinguish between the "persons" of the Father and the Son, but made the Son a mere mode of manifestation of the Father.[9] Roman Catholic theologians and historians have accused Hippolytus of slander and have defended the orthodoxy of the bishops.[10] The most recent Protestant scholar to discuss the question comes to the conclusion that Zephyrinus, at least, should be exonerated of the charge of modalism.[11] In the second case Roman Catholic theologians have even greater cause for embarrassment.[12] The sixth ecumenical council of the church, meeting at Constantinople in 680-681, solemnly condemned Pope Honorius for heresy in the doctrine of the person of Christ. Although our sources on Zephyrinus and Callistus are not reliable enough to substantiate a final judgment either way, the evidence regarding Honorius' teachings, and especially regarding the council's action, is very incriminating.

Of course, even one case is sufficient to provide historical refutation for the claim of papal infallibility, which is suspect on so many other counts as well. But all this must not be permitted to obscure the consistency with which the Roman bishops of the early centuries supported orthodox teaching. Anyone who cherishes that teaching as a valid expression and defense of Christian doctrine is paying tribute to Rome's espousal of the orthodox cause. That espousal also helps to explain the high rating accorded to Rome by sister churches, East and West, during most of the church's history.

40

The Primacy of the Roman Patriarch

When Christianity became catholic, it organized itself around several apostolic patriarchates as seats of authority. Four (originally three) of these were in the East—Alexandria, Jerusalem, Antioch, and "as one born out of due time," Constantinople. Only one was in the West—Rome. Although by definition an apostolic patriarchate was one which could trace its establishment to an apostle, Constantinople acquired the rank for political reasons when it became the new capital city of the empire in the fourth century. At some of the ecumenical meetings during the fourth and fifth centuries, Constantinople succeeded in having itself acknowledged as the second in rank among all the apostolic patriarchates, second only to Rome, "because it is the new Rome." [13] Then someone discovered that, with remarkable foresight, the apostle Andrew had founded the church in Constantinople.

A glance at the map of the Mediterranean will show that of these five apostolic patriarchates, four are grouped rather closely together, while Rome stands in occidental isolation at the opposite end of the sea. Added to the other factors we have been describing, this geographical position enhanced Rome's power in many ways. It was to the West that the great migration of the nations came. Except for the Slavs and the Bulgars, most of the new tribes who entered Europe occupied territories belonging to Rome's patriarchate. Even in the case of the Slavs, Rome assumed patriarchal authority over some dioceses that had originally belonged to the East and it founded others, with the result that the Slavic peoples of present-day Poland, Czechoslovakia, and part of Yugoslavia are part of the Western rather than of the Eastern half of the church. Thus Rome's territory grew very rapidly with the migration of the nations, just as a country church on the crossroads in the United States today may suddenly find itself the center of a new suburb and of an entirely new population.

While Rome's territory was increasing, the province of the other patriarchs shrank. During the seventh and eighth centuries, Islam began to make huge inroads into Christian lands. The Western church lost its ancient stronghold, North Africa, which had given it

41

Tertullian, Cyprian, and Augustine. The Eastern patriarchs lost vastly more. By the time the expansion of Islam was completed, Constantinople itself had fallen (1453). As Athanasius (d. 373) and others had fled to Rome when there was a heretical emperor in Constantinople, so Rome stood as a haven for those who fled the Moslems. The Moslems tolerated Christianity in the lands they conquered, and the churches continued to exist. But obviously they could not have the right of self-determination which the patriarch of Rome enjoyed. Even in the "Dark Ages," therefore, the Roman see had a unique position among the apostolic patriarchates—unique because of its primacy, because of its orthodoxy, because of its location, and because of its freedom.

The occupants of the Roman see were not reluctant to articulate that unique position. The period when the West was expanding while the East was contracting was also the time when the far-reaching claims of the Roman papacy were being promulgated. From his position as "first among peers" in the college of apostolic patriarchs, the Roman patriarch evolved into the supreme pontiff of all Christendom. Within his own patriarchate he extirpated the independent creative development of the churches in Milan, in France, in Germany, in Spain, and in Great Britain. Their jurisdictions were severely curtailed, their native liturgies Romanized, their clergy forced to conform to Roman custom and law. In his relation to other patriarchs, the Roman bishop likewise increased his assertions of jurisdiction and authority. Thus Pope Nicholas I (d. 867) deposed the patriarch of Constantinople, Photius (d. 891), and invalidated his ordination. Nicholas justified this intervention in the internal affairs of another patriarch with this declaration, addressed to the Byzantine emperor: "The privileges of this see or church [Rome] are, I say, perpetual. . . . They existed before your regime, and thank God they still exist unchanged. And after you they will not cease to exist unimpaired as long as the Christian name is preached." [14]

Perhaps the most brazen such intervention was the "Latin patriarchate of Constantinople" established after the conquest of that Christian city by the crusaders from the Christian West in 1204.

42

Here the West convinced the East that it would be satisfied with nothing short of total hegemony over the entire church. Many Eastern Orthodox writers assert that the events connected with the Crusades had more to do with the schism between Rome and the East than any other action from either direction.[15] In modern times, leaders of the Roman church have admitted the excesses and mistakes in the "Latinization" of Eastern liturgical rites, and present policy strictly forbids the mutilation of these rites when communion is re-established with Rome. In both policy and action, the Roman bishops of past ages demonstrated their unwillingness to be merely prime among the patriarchs. Primacy came to mean the centralization of authority. The patriarch of the West assumed ever greater authority over the bishops, clergy, and people of the West, and he laid claim to ever greater authority over the rest of the apostolic patriarchs. Without that centralization of authority there would have been no papacy, but because of it catholic Christianity today is identified in many minds exclusively with its Western, Roman form.

Holy Rome and the Holy Roman Empire

With Rome's rise to power over the rest of the church there came a new relation to the state. A *modus vivendi* may have been enough for Christianity to become catholic, but for Western catholicism to become the Roman Catholicism we are studying here, a very special interpretation of relations between church and state came into being. The empire whose capital was established at Constantinople also had an interpretation of the right relation between church and state. So characteristic is that interpretation that it has acquired the nickname "Byzantinism" or "caesaropapism." Because the Byzantine emperor was a Christian anointed for his divinely instituted office, he was, as the art of Ravenna makes clear, a latter-day Melchizedek, both king and priest.[16] Under the protection of such a Melchizedek the church enjoyed a preferred position in society, but had little freedom to make its own decisions.

Rome wanted a better arrangement. Isolated in the West, with only an "exarch" in Ravenna to worry about, Rome did not have to suffer much interference from the emperor, but it could not influence governmental policy either. What it needed was an emperor closer to Rome—closer in distance and simultaneously closer in obligation. Such an emperor it found with the establishment of the Holy Roman Empire. Ecclesiastically, the coronation of Charlemagne in 800 was a device by which the patriarch of the West declared his independence of the Byzantine "Roman" emperor. The Holy Roman Empire, through which medieval feudal Germany declared its continuity with ancient Rome, depended for its legitimacy at least partly upon Christian Rome. Just how much, was a hotly debated issue. What the history books describe as the "investiture controversy" was not merely the church's defense of its own right to select and install its bishops. It was also the state's defense against the claims of the church. The pope claimed the right to depose the emperor, and in the investiture controversy he tried to do just that. Repeatedly pope and emperor clashed over the limits of their respective jurisdictions. The zenith of papal power under Pope Innocent III (d. 1216) was followed less than a century later by the exile of the pope in Avignon and by the humiliating history of the papacy in the fourteenth and fifteenth centuries. Through it all the pope claimed authority over the state as well as the church, but conditions within the church seemed to many to prove that he could not rule even the church.

The rise of the papacy and the decline of the papacy are still useful boundary markers for the history of medieval Europe. They also serve to demarcate the period when catholicism became Roman. The riddle of Roman Catholicism is insoluble without the history of that period. What Roman Catholicism is today that period made it. Yet between that period and the present there is "a great gulf fixed," which prevents Roman Catholicism from becoming what it once was. That gulf is the Protestant Reformation and the rise of the modern world. To fathom the riddle of Roman Catholicism, therefore, we must move now to an analysis of what the Reformation did to the catholicism that had become Roman.

IV
The Tragic Necessity
of the Reformation

✠ In our effort to see how the riddle of Roman Catholicism
has evolved historically, we have examined the processes by which
primitive Christianity produced the catholic church and those by
which the Roman church achieved its unique status within the catholic church. A third stage in the history of Roman Catholicism also
requires our attention, for what we call Roman Catholicism today
is the form which this section of the church has taken after its conflict with the Reformation. If the equation for the earlier situation
ought to read: catholic church=Roman Catholicism + Eastern Orthodoxy, then the equation for the new situation ought to read:
Roman Catholicism=Western church − Reformation. It will be evident that in these two equations the term "Roman Catholicism"
is not being used the same way. In the first instance it means the
entire undivided Western church, of which all of us, Roman Catho-

45

lies and Protestants, are descendants. In the second instance it means one segment—the largest segment, to be sure, but still only one segment—of the divided Western church. The source of this ambiguity is the Reformation.

For that reason and for others the Reformation was a tragic necessity. The tragedy of the Reformation consists in the loss by both sides of some of the very things each claimed to be defending against the other; its final outcome was not what either Rome or the reformers had wanted. Yet the necessity of the Reformation consists in the loyalty of the reformers to the best and the highest in Roman Catholic Christianity and their obligation to summon Rome back to it. Partisans on both sides have difficulty acknowledging that the Reformation was indeed a tragic necessity. Roman Catholics agree that it was tragic, because it separated many millions from the true church; but they cannot see that it was really necessary. Protestants agree that it was necessary, because the Roman church was so corrupt; but they cannot see that it was such a great tragedy after all. As Chapter XIII will point out, an honest assessment of the Reformation belongs to any theological effort at meeting the present situation between Protestantism and Roman Catholicism. Without such an assessment neither the tragedy nor the necessity of that situation can be clearly seen or courageously met.

The Catholicity of the Reformers

"The revolt from the church began because the German people could not and cannot but be devout." [1] This winged word of the nineteenth century Roman Catholic saint, Clemens Maria Hofbauer (d. 1820), aptly summarizes the tragic necessity of the Reformation. In fact, recent research on the Reformation entitles us to sharpen it and to say that the Reformation began because the reformers were too catholic in the midst of a church that had forgotten its catholicity. That generalization applies particularly to Luther and to some of the Anglican reformers, somewhat less to Calvin, still less to Zwingli, least of all to the Anabaptists. But even Zwingli, who occupies the left wing among the classical reformers, retained a surprising amount of

46

catholic substance in his thought, while the breadth and depth of Calvin's debt to the heritage of the catholic centuries is only now beginning to emerge.

It is important to make clear what we man by "the heritage of the catholic centuries." The reformers were catholic because they were spokesmen for an evangelical tradition in medieval catholicism, what Luther called "the succession of the faithful." [2] The fountainhead of that tradition was Augustine (d. 430). His complex and far-reaching system of thought incorporated the catholic ideal of identity plus universality, and by its emphasis upon sin and grace it became the ancestor of Reformation theology. Even though the features of Augustine's thought which sired Roman Catholicism were more prominent than Protestants once recognized, he remains the church father of the Reformation; this receives negative support from the condemnation of certain Augustinian tenets by Pope Clement XI in his *Unigenitus* of 1713.[3] All the reformers relied heavily upon Augustine. They pitted his evangelical theology against the authority of later church fathers and scholastics, and they used him to prove that they were not introducing novelties into the church, but defending the true faith of the church.

Not only Augustine could serve to substantiate the claim of the reformers to be truly catholic. Throughout the centuries they found substantiation. Although they spoke of the "fall of the church" in the post-apostolic era, they seized upon individuals and groups in every epoch of Christian history who had opposed Roman domination or who had taught evangelical doctrine. Bernard of Clairvaux (d. 1153), for example, had done both. For this he was highly revered by both Luther and Calvin. John Huss (d. 1415) was practically canonized by the reformers for his opposition to Rome. They also managed to find more obscure figures in medieval history. To prepare books like the Magdeburg *Centuries* they combed the libraries and came up with a remarkable catalogue of protesting catholics and evangelical catholics, all to lend support to the insistence that the Protestant position was, in the best sense, a catholic position.

Additional support for this insistence comes from the attitude of the

47

reformers toward the creeds and dogmas of the ancient catholic church. The reformers retained and cherished the doctrine of the Trinity and the doctrine of the two natures in Christ which had been developed in the first five centuries of the church. They symbolized their continuing catholicity in other ways as well. England and Sweden kept the apostolic succession of ordaining bishops even after their break with Rome. Various Reformation liturgies served to manifest the continuity between the Reformation and the catholic centuries. Although the Swiss Reformation was more radical than either the Anglican or the Lutheran in repudiating elements of the catholic past, here too, the piety of the people and the systems of the theologians both maintained more continuity with catholicism than is evident at first glance. Even among the Anabaptists and other radical reformers there were strange vestigial remnants of the catholicism out of which they had come, as for example, in the "innerworldly asceticism" [4] which transplanted many of the ideals of medieval catholic monasticism into the life of the congregation.

Hence the Reformation was indeed a catholic movement. If we keep in mind how variegated medieval catholicism was, the legitimacy of the reformers' claim to catholicity becomes clear. With men like Augustine and Bernard on their side, the reformers could well protest against the usurpation of the name "catholic church" by their opponents. A leading irenic and orthodox theologian of the seventeenth century, Johann Gerhard (d. 1637), spoke for all the reformers when he said:

If the papists want to prove the truth of the name "catholic" as applied to their church, let them demonstrate that the dogmas of their church are catholic, that is, that they are in conformity with the catholic writings of the prophets and apostles! . . .

If the papists want to deny us the name "catholic," let them demonstrate that we have seceded from the catholic faith and that we deny the mystery of the Trinity! [5]

The Reformation Gospel

Not a new "Protestant" gospel, then, but the gospel of the true church, the catholic church of all generations, is what the Reformation claimed to be espousing. Substantiation for this understanding of the gospel came principally from the Scriptures; but whenever they could, the reformers also quoted the fathers of the catholic church. There was more to quote than their Roman opponents found comfortable. Every major tenet of the Reformation had considerable support in the catholic tradition.

That was eminently true of the central Reformation teaching of justification by faith alone. For the reformers this teaching stood or fell with the question of the biblical support for it; but because it was so important to the very life of the church, the reformers could expect to find it being taught by theologians between Paul and Luther, too. That the ground of our salvation is the unearned favor of God in Christ, and that all we need do to obtain it is to trust that favor— this was the confession of great catholic saints and teachers. Justification by faith alone really means justification by grace alone, "grace" understood not as something in man which wins God's good will, but as something in God which makes man pleasing to him. Without this teaching, the reformers maintained, there was no church, catholic or otherwise, but only a human institution built upon human merit. The target of their critique was only one strand in the development of the medieval teaching on justification, and with other strands of that development the reformers had a definite affinity. What they saw in the teaching of the Roman Catholic Church was the undue stress upon works, and the answer to this was the justification of the sinner by divine grace through faith alone.

"Faith alone" did not ignore the necessity of the good works that come from faith. Nor did it exclude the divinely appointed means for arousing and sustaining faith, the word of God and the sacraments. On the contrary, the theology of the reformers was a theology of the word because they assigned a central place to the preaching and teaching of the word of God. This, too, was intended to be a defense of true catholicity; for the church was truly catholic and apostolic when it relied upon biblical teaching, and it became sectarian when it admitted human opinions into the body of its teaching. In actual practice, of course, the stress of the reformers upon the

49

authority of the Bible as the word of God did clash with the ideal of catholicity. Using the Reformation privilege of private interpretation, many Protestants found it possible to discard essential elements of catholic Christianity—the priesthood, private confession, the real presence in the Lord's Supper, infant baptism, the sacraments as such, even the doctrine of the Trinity. Nevertheless Luther and Calvin claimed the support of the best in the catholic tradition for their elevation of the Scriptures over tradition. Loyalty to the catholic fathers consisted in subordinating them to the Scriptures, as they had subordinated themselves to the Scriptures.

In their own way, therefore, the reformers not only retained but actually restored the ancient Christian definition of catholicity as identity plus universality. Because the identity of the Christian faith was under threat from the emphasis upon works and upon man's natural knowledge of God, the accent of the Reformation fell less upon universality than upon identity. But it would be a mistake to conclude from this that the other pole of catholicity, the vision of the church universal, was absent from the thought of the reformers. Luther's idea that the true church was "hidden" and Calvin's doctrine of the church invisible did seem to lose that vision in the abstraction of the unattainable. But these doctrines were the polemical expressions of the reformers' deep conviction that true religious identity had been sacrificed to a false organizational universality, and they do not exhaust the meaning of catholicity in either Calvin or Luther. According to both of these reformers, the church had been Christian and catholic before the papacy; therefore it could be both Christian and catholic without the papacy. In the name of such Christian catholicity they were willing to challenge Rome.[6]

The Roman Catholic Reaction

To this challenge Rome replied in a series of actions, which began with the excommunication of Luther in 1520 and climaxed in the Council of Trent of 1545-63. The basic reaction of Roman Catholicism to the Reformation must therefore be classified as a rejection of the Reformation protest. Nothing so illustrates the tragic character of the Reformation as this: the Roman church excommunicated Luther for being too serious about his catholicism, while it retained within its fellowship the skeptics and the scoffers who did not bother to defy its authority. In keeping with this action, Roman Catholics ever since have displayed an astonishing incapacity to understand the Reformation, and an unwillingness to admit that the religious convictions of the reformers were animated by their fidelity to catholic ideals. Instead they have perpetuated the reaction of the sixteenth century, a qualified but decisive no.

The no was qualified, then and now, by the admission that the reformers had a point in their criticism of moral and institutional conditions in the church. This was not the fundamental criticism to come from the reformers, but it has figured prominently in the lampooning of Rome by Protestant pamphleteers. These same pamphleteers have not been as ready to grasp and to admit that on this score the Roman reaction of the sixteenth century did produce far-reaching reforms. Under the leadership of popes like Paul III (d. 1549), Rome instituted moral and canonical reforms to correct many of the fearful abuses that had crept into the clergy and hierarchy of the church. Trent's legislation against these abuses and the work of the newly created Society of Jesus enabled the papacy to clean house. Anyone who based his support of the Reformation primarily on moral grounds, therefore, lost half of his case as a result of these reforms. He would lose much of the other half if he studied the similarity between moral conditions in Roman Catholic lands and those in Protestant lands since the Reformation. By its reactions on this front, the reform movement in Roman Catholicism has substantiated the Reformation claim that the church was in need of a house cleaning.

All the more tragic, therefore, was the Roman reaction on the front which was most important to the reformers, the message and teaching of the church. This had to be reformed according to the word of God; unless it was, no moral improvement would be able to alter the basic problem. Rome's reactions were the doctrinal decrees of the Council of Trent and the Roman Catechism based upon those decrees. In these decrees, the Council of Trent selected and

51

elevated to official status the notion of justification by faith plus works, which was only one of the doctrines of justification in the medieval theologians and ancient fathers. When the reformers attacked this notion in the name of the doctrine of justification by faith alone—a doctrine also attested to by some medieval theologians and ancient fathers—Rome reacted by canonizing one trend in preference to all the others. What had previously been permitted (justification by faith and works), now became required. What had previously been permitted also (justification by faith alone), now became forbidden.[7] In condemning the Protestant Reformation, the Council of Trent condemned part of its own catholic tradition.

Yet Trent was acting as the defender of the catholic tradition. As it said "faith and works" in response to the Protestant "faith alone," so it reacted to the Protestant "Scripture alone" with "Scripture and traditions." By "traditions" it meant in the first instance "apostolic tradition," which was reflected by the New Testament but not exhausted by it. But the Tridentine Confession of Faith makes clear that "traditions" also include the tradition of the church through the centuries.[8] Thus Trent ruled out the theological method of the reformers, which had pitted the Scriptures against the traditions and had declared its intention to reject even the most hallowed traditions if they conflicted with the Scriptures. Speaking for the reformers, Martin Chemnitz (d. 1586) wrote a detailed and balanced refutation of Trent, in which he accused Roman Catholicism of forsaking the tradition in the very act of defending the tradition; for tradition was on the side of biblical authority.[9]

Chemnitz' interpretation of the doctrinal decrees of the Council of Trent has been criticized by some modern Roman Catholic scholars.[10] These revisionists have attempted to show that on the doctrine of justification and on the authority of Scripture the formulations of Trent are actually a compromise between the Reformation extreme and the opposite extreme of certain fifteenth century theologians. Only when they are read in the light of both extremes, rather than merely in the light of the reformers, are these formulations said to come into proper perspective. There is undoubtedly something to be

52

said for this interpretation, and it deserves more careful attention than Protestant theologians have been willing to give it. But it does not appear to have demonstrated its fundamental contention; for the explicit target of Trent's anathema is consistently the Reformation position—or "extreme"—while some fairly subtle and sophisticated historical scholarship is often necessary to unearth the opposite "extreme" also included in the condemnations.

The very effort to revise the usual interpretation of Trent accentuates the importance of Trent as the line of demarcation between "Roman Catholicism" as we used it in the preceding chapter and "Roman Catholicism" as it is usually used and as it will be used throughout this book. The Roman communion with which modern Christians must deal is Rome after Trent, post-Tridentine Roman Catholicism. It is vain to try to roll back the basis of discussion to some *status quo ante*, for Trent is still the line. Because there would have been no Trent if there had been no Reformation, the protest of the reformers helped to make necessary the tragedy of the Council of Trent. This recognition, compounded of historical judgment and theological reflection, would appear to be an indispensable condition on both sides for reopening the discussion between Roman Catholicism and Protestantism. We shall return to this in Chapter XIII.

Christendom Divided

When the dust had settled after the Reformation, the scene was quite different from the expectations of either Rome or the reformers. Rome had hoped that the prodigals would return, but had been left waiting. The reformers had sought to reform the entire church, but had been forced to settle for part (or rather, parts) of the church. Neither side had intended to divide the church, both sides claimed to be defending the very thing that would unite the church. But ever since the Reformation the church has been divided, and divided more deeply and irrevocably than ever before in the long and painful history of Christian schism.

Everyone has lost something by the division of the church. It has made a travesty of the word "catholic" in the title "Roman Catholic."

53

Roman Catholicism has never been universal; the presence of the Eastern churches has served as a reminder of that. But in the centuries before the Reformation it could at least take pride in being coextensive with Western Christendom and therefore *the* catholic church for the Christians of the West. Now things are quite different. "The church is catholic": the predicate "catholic" may have remained the same; but the subject of the sentence, "church," has been fundamentally altered. Roman Catholic writers may draw graphs to show Roman Catholicism as the mainstream going back to Christ and the apostles, with various branches forsaking the mainstream. The graphs are not as convincing as their authors would wish, simply because of the facts reviewed in this chapter. Some measure of catholic Christianity has continued in the West through non-Roman channels. It is interesting, for example, that the main seed plot of Christian mysticism in the West since the Reformation has been Protestantism rather than the Roman Catholicism which had permitted earlier mystics to sprout. Jakob Böhme (d. 1624), George Fox (d. 1691), Emanuel Swedenborg (d. 1772), and many others illustrate the perpetuation in Protestantism of an element of catholic Christianity.

To save itself from its own distortions, catholic Christianity has repeatedly needed prophets, who have been born of Mother Church but have grown up to denounce her for her harlotry. Tertullian, Bernard of Clairvaux, Savonarola, Luther—all these were sons of the catholic church whose devotion to the church compelled them to speak a prophetic word against the church as it was. By its reaction to the Reformation, Rome has not entirely muffled such prophetic words in its midst, but it has certainly made them more difficult to speak and to hear. Thus, while the fragmentation of Western Christendom gives the lie to universality, the separation from Protestantism also deprives Rome of one impulse that had helped it to maintain its evangelical identity. If catholicity means universality plus identity, it is much more difficult for Roman Catholicism to be really catholic than it was before the Reformation.

Protestants also lost something through the Reformation. The re-

54

formers had good biblical warrant for proclaiming that in order to be "built upon the foundation of the apostles and prophets" (Eph. 2:20) the church had to be faithful to apostolic teaching, and that no external succession with the apostles could guarantee its fidelity. But that fidelity, and consequently that claim to catholicity, has suffered in the history of Protestantism no less than in the history of Roman Catholicism since the Reformation. After it had lost the continuity of its organization with the catholic tradition, Protestantism also began to lose the continuity of its message with the tradition. Does "after" here imply "because"? The churches that came out of the Reformation have indeed experienced great difficulty in defining and in preserving their Christian identity.

They have experienced even greater difficulty in defining and in preserving any genuine Christian universality. Their separation from Rome, which was in turn separated from the East, made this difficult enough. But when a separated Protestantism itself began to divide with the apparent speed and ease of an amoeba, the classic Protestant defenses of Protestant catholicity against Rome made even less sense. The church was universal, but only in faith; or it was universal in hope, so that the achievement of its universality awaited the Lord's second coming; or it was universal only in the sight of God, but divided to human eyes. All such formulas would seem to be counsels of despair, which had to do something about the unity and universality predicated of the church and promised to the church in the New Testament. Neither identity nor universality, then, has kept its integrity in Protestant Christendom since the Reformation.

Protestant Christendom and Roman Christendom are both hard put to define identity and universality and thus to manifest their catholicity. Catholicity is possible in a divided church. In Chapter XII we shall seek to show that it is both possible and necessary. But it is a difficult and complex goal to achieve in a divided church. The tragic necessity of the Reformation finds its most dramatic reflection in the divisions of the church and in the efforts of both Protestants and Roman Catholics to make the best of a bad situation.

55

The Disintegration of Catholic Europe

When Christendom was divided, this did not mean only that the church was replaced by churches. It also meant that the invisible but powerful ties binding the nations of Europe to one another were severed. As Chapter III pointed out, Holy Rome and the Holy Roman Empire were both unitive factors in medieval Europe; it is symptomatic that the challenge to the authority of the former was accompanied by a significant decline in the prestige and power of the latter. The period of the Reformation was also the time of the disintegration of catholic Europe, symbolized by the Thirty Years' War of 1618-48. After 1648 all the king's horses and all the king's men could not re-establish the unity of catholic Europe as the *corpus Christianum*, the Christian commonwealth of the West.

In place of the *corpus Christianum*, the sixteenth century saw the beginnings of the national state in the modern sense of the word. In England, Scandinavia, and Germany espousing the cause of the Reformation was a means by which kings and princes could assert their national independence against both Holy Rome and the Holy Roman Empire. On the other hand, the growth of Spanish national consciousness in the fifteenth and sixteenth centuries was not accompanied by a break with Roman Catholicism. All the major reformers were also spokesmen for the burgeoning nationalism of the time. Zwingli died in a battle for Swiss independence. Nationalism used the Reformation and the Reformation used nationalism, but the outcome was to unleash the centrifugal forces in Western culture whose effects for both good and evil are with us yet. By the end of the sixteenth century the unity of catholic Europe was shattered forever, and the Reformation had taken its part in bringing this about.

The Reformation also took part in the emergence of modern secular culture. The independence of modern culture from domination by the institutional church makes it "secular," but this has often meant that it is also free from the influence of the Christian faith and is thus "secularistic." The second does not necessarily follow from the first. On the contrary, the Reformation sought to cultivate

56

a lay Christian culture—"secular" in the sense that an artist or a states-man was in a divine calling even when the institutional church did not control his art or his statesmanship; but not "secularistic" in the sense that art and statesmanship are beyond the purview of the Christian faith. This idea does involve a considerable gamble for any church, Protestant or Roman Catholic. The secular may slide imperceptibly into the secularistic, confronting the church with a culture that assigns to religion only the cultivation of individual piety but bars religion from the vital centers of cultural activity. That was the gamble which the Reformation took. Did it win or lose?

Upon the answer to that question depends part of our assessment of the Reformation. It must be only part of our assessment; for the Reformation stands or falls as an interpretation of the Christian gospel and not as a solution of the problems of culture. As Stringfellow Barr says: "Civilization would be one of the things added unto us if we sought first the Kingdom of God." [11] Nevertheless, we dare not ignore the cultural issue when we evaluate the outcome of the Protestant Reformation. It did involve the loss of values and insights without which all of us are poorer. It also meant the recovery of values and insights which have enriched both the church and the culture. Was the recovery worth the loss, and was the loss necessary to achieve the recovery? For both church and culture, this is the question that makes the Reformation a tragic necessity.

V

The Roman Church in
the Modern World

✠ During the centuries since the Reformation, the Roman Catholic Church has been engaged in a continuous process of facing up to the problems of modern culture and life. It has chalked up both gains and losses in its series of contests with modernity, but the final score is not in yet. Our effort to use history as a means of probing the riddle of Roman Catholicism must turn now to this unique period in its development. From the stand which Rome has taken in response to the challenges of the modern world we can better understand the postures it has felt obliged to take today.

The Modern State

Perhaps the most dramatic aspect of the conflict between Roman Catholicism and the modern world has been its running conflict with the modern state, whether in the form of the monarchy, the republic, or the totalitarian state.

Monarchy was the form which the new national states of Europe adopted after their emergence from feudalism and their declaration of independence from the Holy Roman Empire. In Protestant lands like England and Sweden, the new monarchy sought to use the churches for its own purposes, and often succeeded. In Roman Catholic lands like France and Spain, the monarchs were no less ambitious and often equally successful. But when the king of France attempted to control the church in France as part of his campaign to establish his country's power and independence, he met opposition not only from the church within France, but from Rome. When many leaders of the Roman Catholic Church in France felt inclined to go along with the monarch's ambition and to establish the church upon a national foundation in the movement known as "Gallicanism," Rome struck against both the monarchy and the hierarchy. Remembering the church's loss of independent action under Byzantine "caesaro-papism," Rome opposed the pretensions of the absolute monarchs and their attempts to wean the churches in their country away from their mother beyond the Alps. The Kulturkampf with Germany showed the church's firmness on this question even and especially in a land where Roman Catholicism did not have a virtual monopoly upon the loyalty of Christians.

Although Roman Catholicism has therefore been wary of absolute monarchy in the modern world, it has managed rather better with monarchy than with either democracy or totalitarianism. For one thing, the monarchs have usually needed the church to supply them with divine sanction for the monarchy, a sanction which democracy sought in the people and which totalitarianism sought, if at all, in the race or class or nation. The inherently hierarchical organization of the monarchy, even of an "absolute" monarchy, made it easier for a hierarchical church to deal with it than with the diffused centers of power in a democracy or the single concentration of power in a totalitarian state. In addition, the post-feudal monarchy bore a distinct family resemblance to earlier forms of royal or oligarchical government with which Rome had had long experience. But as the codification of the church's relation to feudalism and the Holy Roman Empire during the fourteenth century was followed almost immediately by a near collapse of the church, so the church managed to identify itself with the monarchy at just about the time when the monarchy was undergoing a serious challenge—indeed, a fatal challenge—from the rising forces of democracy.

The identification of the church with the monarchy, and with the *ancien regime* generally, made the church one of the principal targets of the rising opposition to monarchy, aristocracy, and Christianity during the eighteenth century. The old regime had been a benefactor of the church; the church took a stand as a defender of the old regime—and almost went down with it. Many of the church's criticisms of democracy were theologically sound. As preached by the *philosophes*, the democratic gospel was indeed a glorification of man rather than of God, a substitution of progress for Providence as the basis of human hopes, and a concentration upon what Becker has called "the heavenly city of the eighteenth-century philosophers" at the expense of the City of God.[1] The church would have been remiss in its duty if it had not struck out at the heresy of this false gospel. But the hand with which the church struck was even less clean than usual, so that it was easy for both the church and its despisers to identify the gospel with a reactionary political philosophy.

With the rise of a democratic ideology less hostile to Christianity than the French form had been, Roman Catholic political action became the victim of its own declarations. As Professor Nichols has shown, the political theory of the Roman communion has restricted its maneuverability in democratic countries.[2] The ghost of the French Revolution has proved to be very hard to exorcise even under a form of government that is friendly to the church. It is ironic that a church which has been able to justify its relation to the empires of Constantine, Charlemagne, and Napoleon should have so much trouble finding a *modus vivendi* with the democratic form of government, under which it has achieved the notable successes of the past century. Where the standard notions of the proper relationship between church and state have proved impossible in the modern world, Roman Catholicism has had difficulty formulating new notions for a new relationship.

This very difficulty stood the church in good stead when totalitarianism arose in the twentieth century. Differ though it did from ancient tyrannies in other ways, totalitarianism represented a threat which the Roman church understood on the basis of past experience with other forms of absolutism. At the same time, even the totalitarian state had de facto, if.not de jure legitimacy, and the church had to face the facts. The story of how Roman Catholicism used both condemnation and concordat to negotiate with Nazi Germany, which is only now being unfolded through the publication of documents and of memoirs, presents the best case study for the dilemma of the Roman church in its contacts with the modern total state and for the way the church is equipped to handle the dilemma. On the other side of the coin is the church's record in Falangist Spain, where Roman Catholicism has not been under pressure from a large and well-organized Protestantism as it was in Germany. There concordat has been much more evident than condemnation in the church's approach; and the church has permitted itself to be exploited—to a degree that some Roman Catholics in America have vigorously denounced—for the benefit of a Fascist totalitarianism.

Fascist totalitarianism in Italy formed a special case, as had relations with previous Italian governments, because of the church's involvement in Italian politics. Particularly thorny has been the problem of the papal states, to which the church laid claim on the basis of historical records—some genuine, some forged—and on the basis of precedent. In the stormy decades surrounding the unification of Italy, the same time when it was carrying on the Kulturkampf against Bismarck, the papacy was also defending its right to be an independent political entity and to stay out of any unified Italian state. With Mussolini the church made better headway in this defense than it had with the leaders of Italy's drive for nationhood, and in the Treaty of the Lateran on February 11, 1929, Pope Pius XI finally achieved recognition from the Italian dictator of his right to the

61

papal states. This did not muffle the church's attacks upon Fascist ideology, but it did affect the practical relations between church and state under Fascist rule.

Thus the problem of what to do with the modern state has proved to be an epitome of the church's problem in modern culture as a whole. Individual successes and achievements are counterbalanced by serious losses in prestige and influence. So often has the church been on the defensive that defensiveness has become natural for it in political life even when this was not the appropriate attitude. Economic power and political ambition have often added their discordant note to the voice of the church in the defense of the gospel. But Roman Catholicism has made it possible for the faithful to take part in politics, also in the politics of the modern state, with the assurance of the church's blessing. A group portrait of Roman Catholic Senators who have died during the past twenty-five years would have to include (in alphabetical order), Patrick McCarran, Joseph R. McCarthy, Brian McMahon, and Robert F. Wagner.

Modern Society

The same embarrassment which such a group portrait suggests has characterized the history of Roman Catholic attitudes toward modern society generally. The labor movement, for example, put the social ethics of the church to a severe test.[3] In the discussions leading up to Leo XIII's encyclical *Rerum novarum* of May 15, 1891, many of the most influential members of the hierarchy manifested a deep hostility and suspicion toward the organization of laboring men into unions, partly because of the anticlerical bias of many leaders in the labor movement, evident, for example, in the Knights of Labor.[4] Encouraged by *Rerum novarum*, Roman Catholics in both Europe and America entered the ranks of labor unions and assumed positions of responsibility and leadership, sometimes over the opposition of their parish priest and even their bishop. The militant and positive strategy of these men helped to defeat Marxism in the labor unions of the United States. But the merely permissive language of *Rerum novarum* and of other papal pronouncements has deprived

62

Roman Catholic labor leaders of the detailed ideological foundation they have wanted for their battle against Marxism.

Specifically, many leaders of the labor movement in Europe and some in the United States have wanted papal approval for a program of Christian socialism. When capitalism arose in Europe during the age of the Reformation, the church was so firmly entrenched in feudalism that it had difficulty adjusting its economic and ethical theories to the new system. But the statements of the church on the morality of risk capital and of economic competition showed that the ethic of Roman Catholicism could be applied to an economy different from the one in which the ethic had originally been composed. In socialism, however, the church confronted not merely a new system for production and distribution, but a system whose opposition to its predecessor was based upon ethical judgments. Hence the initial reaction of the church to this opposition was an ethical validation of the existing economic system. These condemnations of socialism are still the law of the church and an effective weapon against Communism. Many responsible laymen in Europe have felt that the church has leaned too far in one direction and is now unable to right itself, for they believe that in Central Europe Christian socialism is the only alternative to both Communism and capitalism.

The inertia of tradition is hard to overcome, even when the welfare of the church is at stake. During the past two decades a group of Roman Catholic priests in France have made an admirable effort to build a bridge between the church and labor.[5] These "labor priests" have taken jobs as manual laborers, while retaining their priestly status and performing their priestly functions. Their heroic efforts and their failures illustrate the dilemma we have been describing in this chapter. Roman Catholicism has recognized the need of relating itself to the vital centers of modern society, but it has lacked both the ideological and the organizational apparatus to do so. The definition of the priest which the church has inherited from its tradition is irreconcilable with the way of life adopted by the labor priests, and the church was right when it pointed this out. The history of Roman Catholic dealings with modern society, symbolized by the record of

63

the labor priests in France, illumines the tragedy of the Reformation. Roman Catholicism has had the will to build such a bridge, and Protestantism has had the freedom to build it; but neither has had both.

The Modern Mind

On no other front has the church battled as hard or lost as much as on the intellectual. The Roman church was the mother of the universities. Whatever learning there was in medieval Europe served the church. Music and painting were centered in the cathedrals. Even the scholarship of the Renaissance often owed its existence to the patronage of the church and its leaders. Since the sixteenth century, however, one area of intellectual and cultural life after another has slipped out of the church's hands and become autonomous, and the leaders in these areas have come to regard the teaching and tradition of the church as hostile—or, even worse, as irrelevant—to their thought and work.

All this did not start with Galileo (d. 1642), but his story is perhaps the most celebrated instance of the change. Galileo's study of the universe through his telescope brought him into conflict with the *Physics* of Aristotle, which enjoyed the approval of the church.[6] The basis of his conclusions was an induction from what he had seen, while the basis of the church's position was a written authority. By condemning him, the church put itself on the side of reaction in the intellectual sphere, just as it did by its pronouncements in the political and social spheres. Each successive advance in the development of modern science has met with similar opposition from Roman Catholicism. Protestantism has been no less vociferous and no more discerning, but it has a convenient way of changing its mind without the complex rationalizations that are necessary in Rome.

How complex such rationalizations are, can be seen in the status of the Darwinian hypothesis in Roman Catholicism. On the books, the condemnation of the hypothesis stands. The Roman church theoretically maintains a historical exegesis of the first chapters of Genesis no less opposed to science than the fundamentalist exegesis is.[7] But it is evident even from papal declarations on the subject, and especially

64

from books that have received official approval, that there is room within Roman Catholic teaching for the evolutionary theory—provided that it does not question the divine origin of the human soul. As in the case of Galileo the practice of the church eventually permitted what the theory of the church had seemed to rule out, so in the case of Darwin there has been an "evolution" in the church's own position. But in the meantime much irreparable damage has been done to the church's standing.

Yet in its attitude toward science the church has not tied its own hands as tightly as it has in philosophy. The authoritative status accorded to the theology of Thomas Aquinas (d. 1274) will concern us at length in Chapter X. Significant here is the way this status has insulated the thought of Roman Catholicism from the impact and influence of modern philosophy. In canonizing not merely Thomas, and not merely his theology, but his philosophy as well, the church has committed itself to a particular theory of knowledge, according to which intellect and reason are superior to will. Whether or not this theory is true, it certainly is subject to serious question; and much of the history of modern philosophy has consisted in subjecting it to such question. The two outstanding continental philosophers to raise these questions were Descartes (d. 1650) and Kant (d. 1804). Against both of them the church reacted violently through its theologians and philosophers and then through official condemnation of their principles.

As a consequence, Roman Catholic thought in its center has not heard the fundamental word of criticism directed at it by modern philosophy. Instead of re-examining its view of faith and reason on the basis of Kant's *Critique of Pure Reason*, the church has made the philosophical demonstrability of the existence of God an article of religious faith.[8] This refusal to listen has brought on also an inability to communicate. Roman Catholic philosophers live in a world of their own, with their own vocabulary, their own terms of reference, and their own unexamined presuppositions. The very definition of "philosophy" is different. Two of the most frustrating experiences I have ever had were sitting in a course on Kant offered by a Roman Catholic professor, and watching a discussion between a Thomist and a logical positivist at the meeting of a local philosophical discussion group. In both cases Roman Catholic thought needed the criticism its bête noire had to offer, and it also had some telling criticism to give in return. But in both cases the cleavage of the centuries made communication almost impossible.

It is ironic that such a cleavage should have come between catholicism and culture. For Roman Catholicism has insisted upon an organic view of the entire history of the church. The life and teaching of the church are not static, but dynamic; the church grows through the centuries. Even the period of the New Testament is not a golden age to which the church tries to return. Nevertheless, the very church that has incorporated the principle of change and growth into its view of authority has taken a reactionary stand against change and growth, and has made the medieval period in the history of thought a sort of golden age. Scientists and philosophers have gone into exile from the church, which once had been their patron. A like fate has befallen artists and men of letters. Once the church harbored artists who beautified not only its worship, but the entire life of the secular community. The secular community strove to match the cultural standards being set by the church. It has succeeded, and then some. As the standards of the secular community have gone up, the standards of the church have gone down. Madonnas acquired a saccharine smile, and pious doggerel infested religious poetry in all the languages of Europe. The guilt here is an ecumenical one. Rejected by the churches, both Protestant and Roman Catholic, cultural leaders struck off for themselves, leaving much of the art of the church in the hands of hacks and sentimentalists.

The twentieth century has seen some reversal of this trend, as the field of modern literature illustrates. An impressive number of names would fall within the Roman Catholic tradition, a considerable number of them being converts to Roman Catholicism: Francis Thompson, Sigrid Undset, Evelyn Waugh, Graham Greene, Edith Sitwell. Still the church feels strange in modern culture. Many of the conversions to Roman Catholicism among intellectuals and artists have

66

been protests against one or another extreme in modern culture, and the church has been more successful in attracting disenchanted writers than in motivating its own obedient children to become creative in an artistic or literary way. Thus Roman Catholicism has performed a role closer to that of Protestantism than to its own genius and history. The motto "Christ and culture in paradox" would in many ways be the most appropriate for that role, rather than the traditionally Roman Catholic one of "Christ above culture." [9]

Tragic as this consequence is for modern culture, it has also crippled Roman Catholicism. Coming simultaneously with the church's isolation from modern political and social movements, the alienation of the intellectuals has given Roman Catholics the sense of living in a ghetto—a very large ghetto perhaps, but still an enclave separated from the centers of power where the decisions are made and the directions are indicated in modern life. In America the ghetto mentality has been accentuated by the sociology of the European immigrants who have made up the bulk of Roman Catholic membership in the first part of the twentieth century. Their efforts to preserve Old World customs against the incursion of Yankee ways have coincided with the church's resistance to modern thought, and the church which produced Thomas Aquinas has had to bear the charge of antiintellectualism. When the second generation rebelled against what Evelyn Waugh has called "the smell of garlic and olive oil and grandfather muttering over the foreign-language newspapers," [10] the church, too, seemed old-fashioned and reactionary. What the second generation rejected, the third generation is trying to repossess; but the intellectual difficulties are great, largely because of the chasm between the Roman church and the modern mind.

The Modern Church

If the losses of Roman Catholicism in the political field have been the most dramatic and its losses in the cultural and intellectual field have been the most severe, the most important of its losses have been in the religious sphere. The development of the Roman church since the Reformation has brought about changes not only in its relation to "the world," but also in its relation to "the church." One of the factors that makes modern Roman Catholicism such a riddle is its curious position in modern Christendom.

That position is the result of the stance which Rome adopted at the Council of Trent. During the two centuries after Trent scarcely a decade passed without some effort at reunion.[11] Meetings like the Polish Conference of Thorn in 1645 tried to bring Roman, Lutheran, and Reformed theologians together. Theologians like Bossuet (d. 1704) from the Roman Catholic side and Calixtus (d. 1656) from the Protestant side tried to find formulas upon which both sides could agree, but Rome remained cool to all proposals that did not start from its premises. Protestantism had separated itself from the true church, and reunion really meant Protestantism's return to the true church. In the theology of the prominent Jesuit thinker Robert Bellarmine (d. 1621) these premises were the explicit basis for the entire problem of reunion.[12] Thus even when individual Protestants or entire Protestant churches came to the admission that they needed the testimony and the fellowship of their separated Roman brethren, Rome's response was to demand of them that they disavow their church and confession and come over all the way.

In other words, as we shall see again in Chapter XII, Roman Catholicism after Trent refused to treat its separation from Protestantism in the same light as its separation from Eastern Orthodoxy. Despite their schism, the churches of the East remained churches, with which Rome could carry on its discussions as with dissident younger sisters.[13] But the churches of Protestantism were not churches at all, and with them Rome could carry on its discussions only as with disobedient children—children whom it loved and for whom it grieved, but to whom it could not listen and whom it could not accept as adult equals. Lutherans and Reformed in the seventeenth century, Anglicans in the nineteenth, discovered that their protest against the Roman position had frozen that position on all the crucial questions from justification and tradition to the ministry and apostolic succession. The church of Rome has said no to all the other churches of the West.

68

It has likewise said no to the theological trends within those churches. Influences there have been in both directions; but when Rome has discerned in its own midst the presence of theological tendencies that appeared Protestant, it has struck out at them. Jansenism is a good example.[14] Carrying out to their logical conclusions some of the philosophical and theological teachings of Augustine, Jansenism attracted the attention and support of some leading French Roman Catholic thinkers, including Blaise Pascal (d. 1662). In some of its tenets regarding sin and free will Jansenism sounded like Calvinism, and with good reason; they were both derived from a certain reading of Augustine. When Pope Urban VIII in 1642 and Pope Innocent X in 1653 condemned Jansenism, they were also condemning part of the theology of Augustine.[15] Jansenism was, of course, a distortion of Augustine, because it removed statements from their context and did not recognize that Augustine's extreme statements on the bondage of the human will were part of a larger and more complex position. For this reason Rome's condemnation is understandable. But the condemnation of Jansenism meant that the voice of the theological tradition itself had to be muffled if it sounded too Protestant. The moral and doctrinal theology of the seventeenth century badly needed the corrective of Augustinian theology, for they were overemphasizing human capacity at the expense of divine grace. But the papacy acted against the corrective in a direct way, and only indirectly did it scold the excesses which had made the corrective necessary.

Bulwarks Against Modernity

In its more recent history Roman Catholicism has once more manifested its hostility to any theological revision that appeared to be Protestant in its origin or its direction. The modernist movement in Roman Catholic theology endeavored to employ within Roman Catholicism some of the historical and critical methods of scholarship that had been developed in the Protestant theology of the nineteenth century. It also made some concessions to modern science, especially to the evolutionary hypothesis. In the Roman church, it may be argued, modernism represented less of a threat than it did in the

69

Protestant churches; for these claimed to be built upon an infallible Bible which had to be defended at all costs, while Rome drew upon the tradition and did not have to be troubled by particular literary or scientific theories.[16] Nevertheless, Pope Pius X denounced modernism as a "synthesis of all heresies," [17] carrying out the attitudes previously voiced by Pius IX and Leo XIII. It was the official teaching of the church, which no son of the church dared to deny, that Paul was the author of Hebrews, I and II Timothy, and Titus; that the creation story in Genesis is a historical account; and that the gospel of Matthew was the first of the four gospels to be composed, albeit in an Aramaic original, with Mark and Luke following in that order.

Now these are literary and historical questions with theological implications. By its condemnation of modernism and its elevation of certain literary-historical theories to the status of church teachings, Rome closed the door to the historical study of Scripture, church, and dogma as this was being carried out by Protestant theological scholarship. There were many assumptions in that scholarship that needed condemnation from the standpoint of Christian teaching—its naïve idealism, its theory of progress, its negative attitude toward the Old Testament, its moralistic picture of Jesus Christ. But Pius' encyclical *Pascendi* of 1907 made no distinction between these assumptions and the critical method of men like Harnack and Loisy. Although Roman Catholic historians and biblical exegetes have found considerable room to maneuver, the result of the church's attitude has been a calamitous separation between the theological work of Protestant scholars and the thought of Roman Catholics.

It was likewise a bulwark against modernity when the Vatican Council of 1870 promulgated the dogma of the infallibility of the pope.[18] Pope Pius IX, under whose aegis the council met, had made clear his own hostility to modern thought in the condemnations voiced by his Syllabus of Errors of 1864.[19] The council made many of these condemnations its own in its Dogmatic Constitution *De fide catholica* and thus put itself squarely on the side of reaction. The embarrassment of liberal Roman Catholics with the Syllabus and with the Vatican Council is even greater than their uneasiness about the

Council of Trent. In everything the church does in modern world, this need to erect bulwarks against modernity is painfully evident. Even when Rome promulgated the dogma of the assumption of the Blessed Virgin Mary in 1950, the real motif was the glorification of the church, as a discerning Protestant theologian has made clear:

This is, in effect, a magnificent reconstruction of the doctrine of the church. The authority of the church is historically anchored not only in Christ and in the apostolic succession that comes from Peter, but simultaneously and even more deeply in Mary. The doctrine of Mary becomes the real basis for the doctrine of the church. . . . The worship of Mary makes it permissible, without making it obvious, for the church to be transformed from the place of worship to the object of worship.[20]

Thus a new separation and alienation has come between Rome and the modern world, including the modern church.

Separation, alienation, ghetto—these are the words one is constrained to use in describing the history of modern Roman Catholicism as it has separated itself or been forcibly separated from much of modern life. If medieval catholicism ran the danger of losing its identity in its achievement of universality, the modern temptation has been the obverse one; so constrained has modern Roman Catholicism been to defend and define its identity that its claim to universality has acquired a hollow sound. Only in memory or in hope can the Roman church of the present day speak of universality, but the definition and defense of identity which the modern world has called forth from Rome still includes the claim to universality. Separated from Protestantism and isolated from modern culture, Rome still claims to be universal, even though the only way to recover universality is by acknowledging some sort of legitimacy in both Protestantism and modern culture. Out of the tragic necessity of the Reformation has come a Roman Catholicism that cannot recover and yet cannot forget what it was before the Reformation. What makes it that way, and what are we to do about it? This is the riddle of Roman Catholicism.

71

PART TWO

———

THE GENIUS
OF ROMAN CATHOLICISM

☩

As he passes a Roman church on a Sunday morning, many a Protestant asks himself, "I wonder what it's like to be a Roman Catholic!" It is hard for him to imagine what it must mean to belong to this mysterious and powerful institution—to obey its laws, to live by its sacraments, and to die in its fellowship. He may shudder at the thought of adoring the saints, and he may think that the dominion of the clergy is undemocratic. But unless he is a very unusual Protestant, he is fundamentally ignorant about the genius of Roman Catholicism.[1]

That is what these next six chapters try to examine. After utilizing some of the resources of history to learn how Roman Catholicism became what it is today, we turn to a consideration of its inner life. Several crucial areas of that life will claim our attention. In each we shall endeavor to be both sympathetic and critical, trying to understand before we criticize and trying to criticize from within the framework of an "evangelical catholicity."[2] We can understand only to the extent that we love, Augustine said. The exposition that follows claims to understand the forms which the genius of Roman Catholicism has taken; for it loves the Christian and catholic dynamic which expresses itself in those forms, even when it feels obliged to reject the forms themselves. For such an understanding, history is not enough. The evolution of Roman Catholicism may illumine its genius, but does not explain it. Perhaps nothing can explain it, but the subject is important enough to justify the effort.

VI

The Keys of Peter

✠ Perhaps the first thing that impresses the outsider about Roman Catholicism is the sheer size and power of its organization. Businessmen frequently comment on the efficiency of its administrative methods, lawyers on the complexity and smoothness of its appellate procedure. What amazes the Protestant, accustomed to think of churches and denominations as voluntary associations of human origin, is the religious devotion of Roman Catholics to their ecclesiastical organization, as manifested, for example, during the election of Pope John XXIII. The combination of identity plus universality, of which we spoke in Part One, manifests itself here too. A loyalty which Protestants reserve for the "kingdom of God" Roman Catholics are able to attach to their particular form of the church. They find universality in identity. This visible ecclesiastical institution is the church of Jesus Christ on earth, as he said:

I say . . . unto thee, that thou art Peter, and upon this rock I will build my church; and the gates of hell shall not prevail against it. I will give unto thee the keys of the kingdom of heaven; and whatsoever thou shalt bind on earth shall be bound in heaven; and whatsoever thou shalt loose on earth shall be loosed in heaven. (Matt. 16:18-19 K. J. V.)

The Establishment of the Church

What do these words of Jesus mean? From the play on words between "Peter" and "rock" and from the phrase "gates of hell," it seems that the quotation was originally spoken in Aramaic, the native language of Jesus. Interpreters of the New Testament have suggested a host of meanings for the passage. As Roman Catholic scholars now concede, the ancient Christian father Cyprian used it to prove the authority of the bishop—not merely of the Roman bishop, but of every bishop.[1] Peter here is the representative of the college of bishops, who are united in him; the church can withstand the gates of hell as long as it holds to the bishop. Earlier Protestants often followed the Reformers in making the "rock" refer to Peter's confession rather than to Peter's person.[2] The foundation of the church is Christ, to whom all the members of the church bear witness in their confession just as Peter did. Some modern exegetes have questioned the authenticity of the statement because of the appearance of the word "church" in it. Since Jesus expected the end of the world to come very soon, he did not envision anything like a church; therefore the two passages in the gospels where he uses the word "church" are both the pious invention of later Christians.[3]

An intriguing suggestion has come from some recent interpreters: that these words originally belonged to the (now lost) ending of Mark's gospel. In reworking the material from Mark, Matthew changed its sequence and order to suit his purpose in writing and to match the other sayings he incorporated from his other source or sources. As a result, what had originally been a saying of the risen Lord to his apostles, with parallels in the last chapter of each gospel, was read back into the story before his passion. From the resurrected Christ these words would be more intelligible than from the Jesus who, as the next paragraph in Matthew says, "began to show his disciples that he must go to Jerusalem and suffer many things from the elders and

78

chief priests and scribes, and be killed, and on the third day be raised." (Matt. 16:21.) Addressed to Peter after his denial and restoration, they would be a parallel to the command in John's gospel, "Feed my lambs. . . . Tend my sheep." (21:15-16.) Thus the rock upon which the church was to be built would be Peter and the other apostles in their function as shepherds of the church, feeding it with the gospel message.

Whatever their original intention may have been, these words have become the charter of Roman Catholic Christianity. Its official interpretation of them is that here Christ founded the church upon Peter and his successors, the bishops of Rome, to whom he thus accorded a primacy of jurisdiction over all other priests and bishops; that, moreover, the church which he established was a visible, external organization, membership in which was necessary for salvation. The establishment of such a church thus belongs to the explicit intention of the historical Lord himself. He is still the head of the Church, still the chief cornerstone. The only ultimate authority is his authority. Anyone who defies the lordship of Christ or seeks to arrogate it to himself thereby excludes himself from participation in the blessings of Christ. Despite the extravagance of certain Roman Catholic statements on the power of the pope, this fundamental assertion of the lordship of Christ precedes and qualifies any such statements. "I will build my church" means that the source of the initiative and dynamic in the life of the church is Jesus Christ, not anything human—neither Peter nor any other apostle nor any pope or bishop. Christ builds the church.

He builds it on the rock, that is, on Peter. Christ is the sole agent, but Peter and his successors are the means. What the Lord intended by these words was to establish a living and continuing office of teaching and administration in his church, so that when his own visible presence had been withdrawn, the church would not be left without an authoritative expression of his will and purpose. Therefore he could not have meant Peter in his person alone, but must have envisioned Peter as the first in a succession (an interpretation which the Protestant scholar Stauffer regards as "not impossible" according to the text).[4] That succession is perpetuated in the occupants of the see of Peter at Rome. If the gates of hell are not to prevail against Christendom, therefore, it must cleave to the see of Peter. Obedience to Peter and his successors is obedience to Christ himself. As he said to the seventy, "He who heareth you heareth me," and he who rejects you rejects me.[5]

Such an interpretation of the mind of Christ as set down in the statement to Peter enables Roman Catholicism to surround the external ecclesiastical institution with the aura of sacredness. The organizational church is not merely our effort to obey Christ's will and command as well as we can under the limitations of historical existence. Nor is it merely an agency through which the Holy Spirit creates the true church. The organizational church *is* the true church, established by Christ and kept in the truth by his Spirit, who acts through Peter and his successors. Hence it can be and must be the object of religious devotion and loyalty. The church is the mystical body of Christ; and "those who are divided from one another in faith or in government cannot live in the unity of such a body, and in its one divine spirit." [6] On the basis of this conviction that his church is the direct creation of Christ himself, the Roman Catholic, whether layman or cleric, regards obedience to the authority of the church as identical with obedience to the authority of Christ. Failure to understand this identification will make it utterly impossible to fathom the riddle of Roman Catholicism.

Authority in the Church

If it was Christ's intention to establish an external ecclesiastical organization as his church in the world, he must also have provided that organization with a system of authority to preserve it against error and perversion. The Roman Catholic view of the church does not merely ascribe its origins to the Lord himself, but also locates such a system of authority within the church as a guarantee of its continuing fidelity to its divine origin. Submission to this system of authority is submission to Christ as he continues to speak to the church and through the church.

80

A primary locus of that authority is the Bible. It is the written repository of the word of God and, as such, requires obedient acceptance by all the members of the church. The church has buttressed this authority of Scripture by requiring of its members that they accept the inspiration and inerrancy of all its books. During the controversy over modernism, mentioned in Chapter V, the inerrancy of Scripture in matters of science and history came under serious question by some Roman Catholic theologians. But through papal declarations and through official pronouncements by the Pontifical Biblical Commission the church insisted that the Scriptures were without error. Although the polemic of Roman Catholicism against the reformers stressed the insufficiency of Scripture alone to establish articles of faith, this must not be permitted to obscure the high position of authority accorded the Bible in the teaching and practice of the church. In the theology of Thomas Aquinas, for example, Scripture speaks the decisive word on doctrinal matters. Even the authority of a church father like Augustine must be subordinated to this decisive word of Scripture. The Bible is the keystone of religious authority for the Roman Catholic theologian.[7]

For the layman, too, the word of Scripture is decisive. The twentieth century has seen a resurgence of Bible reading among Roman Catholic laymen, enthusiastically supported by certain bishops and priests and endorsed by the papal encyclical *Divino afflante Spiritu* of September 30, 1943.[8] In most Western lands there have been new translations of the Scriptures (many of them based upon Greek and Hebrew rather than merely upon the Latin text) as well as other helps for the lay reader of the Bible.[9] Roman Catholic high schools and colleges have expanded their courses in Bible study, and many parishes have likewise established groups who meet to read and discuss sacred Scripture. To a degree probably unmatched in the history of Roman Catholicism, both theologians and laymen are giving attention to the Bible as a source for their devotion and an authority for their doctrine.

Neither as a source for devotion nor as an authority for doctrine, however, does the Bible stand alone. Indeed, according to Roman

81

Catholic interpretation, the Bible does not even claim to be the sole authority in the church, but points beyond itself to the continuing activity of the Spirit through the tradition of the church.[10] The teachings of Jesus are not exhausted by the gospels, for "the world itself could not contain the books that would be written" (John 21:25) to record them all. Alongside what the New Tesetament has preserved of the teachings of Christ, then, there is an unwritten tradition, which has assumed written form as time and necessity have required. The authority of Scripture is not the authority of a naked book, but the authority of a book in the process of being interpreted. Tradition is that by which Scripture is continually being interpreted. Therefore the Council of Trent puts the authority of traditions on the same level with the authority of Scripture,[11] and the Profession of Faith of the Council of Trent affirms:

The apostolic and ecclesiastical traditions and all other observances and constitutions of that same Church I most firmly admit and embrace. I likewise accept Holy Scripture according to that sense which our holy Mother Church has held and does hold, whose [office] it is to judge of the true meaning and interpretation of the Sacred Scriptures; I shall never accept nor interpret it otherwise than in accordance with the unanimous consent of the Fathers.[12]

Who determines what this "unanimous consent of the fathers" is? On many issues the fathers are anything but unanimous, and often the same father can be quoted to support both sides of a crucial question. Medieval theology puzzled over the solution of this problem. It harmonized positions that seemed contradictory, and it appealed from the teachings of individual church fathers to the official decisions of the church councils.[13] Even the Council of Trent did not clarify the procedure by which the theologian or the believer was to reconcile the disparate elements in the tradition; nor did Trent itself completely reconcile such disparate elements in the very doctrines it was defending against the Reformation. It remained for modern Roman Catholicism, in erecting the bulwarks against modernity of which we spoke in Chapter V, to articulate the method of harmonizing the tradition. The infallibility of the pope provides the church with a living tradition. Whether or not it is true that Pope Pius IX declared, "Tradition? I am the tradition!" it is certain that by introducing this new authority into the teaching of the church modern Roman Catholicism has found a way to substitute clear and distinct doctrines for the ambiguous statements of Scripture and tradition. "Together with these sacred sources of Scripture and tradition,[11] wrote Pope Pius XII, "God has given a living *magisterium* to His Church, to illumine and clarify what is contained in the deposits of faith obscurely and implicitly." [14]

In the process this magisterium has virtually suspended the authority of tradition. As the authority of Scripture loses its power when Scripture is co-ordinated with a tradition which originally sought to be only an interpretation of Scripture, so the authority of the tradition, in turn, is neutralized when the bishop of Rome acquires the right to edit it or set it aside. So traumatic was the effect of the dogma of papal infallibility that the pope did not avail himself of this privilege for eighty years. But when he finally did, by proclaiming the assumption of the Blessed Virgin Mary on November 1, 1950, he confirmed the suspicions and misgivings of the dogma's critics. Not only is Scriptural proof obviously lacking for this notion, but the tradition of the early Christian centuries is also silent about it. At best, the argument from silence is the only one with which tradition supports the dogma of the assumption. If the graves and relics of lesser saints were marked by early Christians and were the occasion of great miracles, how much more careful would they have been to note the grave and to preserve the relics of the Blessed Virgin; since there is no mention of these in early Christian literature, she must have been assumed into heaven.[15] This dogma also illustrates how, in a church where clerical celibacy is the rule, lay piety has access to the highest reaches of the church and its theology; for every theologian and prelate came from a lay home.

Of course, the authority of the pope is still fundamentally ecclesiastical rather than theological. He is the visible head of the church, capping the vast pyramid of its organization. He may speak infallibly

ex cathedra only once in eighty years, but every day he both symbolizes and exercises the church's hold upon the hearts and lives
of men. Because of the equation between the mystical body of Christ
and the ecclesiastical institution, the pope's everyday actions as head
of that institution—his practical decisions about matters of policy,
his pastoral instructions about questions of morals, his warning pronouncements about international affairs—all carry the sanction of
his divine office. When the word "church" is mentioned, a Protestant
will think of a building, perhaps with some people in it; but a Roman
Catholic will think of the organized church, with its bishops and
priests and with the Holy Father as its head and symbol. If the
church as the body of Christ is the representative of Christ in the
world, then the pope as the vicar of Christ is the representative of
the church in the world. At times the maze of dioceses, congregations, religious orders and such, may seem almost impenetrable to an
ordinary layman or priest; but he knows that finally all other authority
in the church is subordinate to the authority of the pope and subject
to correction by him.

Ordinarily the authority of the church reaches the layman through
his priest, as it reaches the priest through his bishop. Protestant objections to the centralization of religious authority in the papacy often
overlook the great latitude enjoyed by a Roman Catholic bishop.
According to official Roman doctrine, a bishop's powers belong to
his episcopal office as such and are not merely delegated to him by
the pope, although the pope does confirm the election of the bishop.
The bishop has considerable authority in the interpretation and administration of the church's regulations on marriage, in the education, assignment, and discipline of the parochial clergy, and in many
other practical matters of diocesan responsibility. Within the borders
of his own diocese, the bishop is, as the people say, "a little pope."
This designation is more accurate than the people realize. For as
bishop of the city of Rome the pope has a special status there which
he does not have in Strasbourg or in Cincinnati, just as his status as
patriarch of the West endows him with prerogatives that do not apply in Istanbul or in Moscow. When a bishop confirms a child or

ordains a priest, he does so by virtue of his episcopal office. Thus the experience of the average Roman Catholic layman with his church is largely restricted to his own diocese. Whatever lies beyond does not affect him directly, but he knows that it is there when he needs it.[16]

Even the diocese and the bishop remain quite remote for many believers. They know the authority of the church as it takes parochial form, and specifically as they meet it in the person of their own parish priest. The mobility of modern population has caused a loosening of the ties between parish priest and people, but the parochial clergy are still the front line of the church in the community.[17] Where their relations to the people are good, the entire life of the church prospers; where these relations degenerate, the church is sick. Anticlericalism as a political movement is often directed against the leaders of the hierarchy, the bishops and the cardinals. But anticlericalism as an individual attitude is more often the outgrowth of tensions between a person and his pastor.[18] What seems to the outsider an intimidation of the laity by the clergy is likewise the product of a certain relationship between pastor and people. Anticlericalism and intimidation are both consequences of the authoritarian role played by a priest in his parish. In a society which is itself authoritarian and in a population which has a low cultural and educational level, this role has often carried the priest into areas of life that are not properly his business; hence the reaction by the people, and the consequent reaction by the church.

Many parishes in Western Europe and in America today are proof that priestly authority is not irreconcilable with pastoral concern. Throughout the life of such a parish, neither anticlericalism nor intimidation, but mutual regard is the rule. The devotion of the faithful to their priest is a beautiful thing for any Christian to behold. It is a devotion born of sharing with him the most crucial experiences of life, yet it is characterized by a relaxed good humor and a salty wit. Laymen in such a parish learn to distinguish between the man and the office. They acknowledge the authority of the priestly office regardless of the man; but when the man is dedicated and helpful, they develop a relationship with him that goes beyond the official one.

85

Then he is the bearer not only of the church's authority, but also of its parental love; and his people find it altogether natural to call him "father."

Obedience to the Church

Yet devotion, however tender it may be, is not the correlate of authority. Where there is authority, the appropriate response is not merely devotion, but obedience. This is a concept often met with in Roman Catholicism, and one that is difficult for the outsider to comprehend. Men of high intelligence and an emancipated mind subject their thoughts and actions to the church, obeying its authority even when it apparently makes no sense. There is undoubtedly a salutary moral discipline in obedience, but to many an outsider it seems that the Roman communion has carried this discipline to extremes and has lost the distinction between the voice of the church and the voice of God.

In principle at least, the Roman church has maintained this distinction. The voice of God is expressed in the divine law, whether natural or revealed, while the voice of the church is expressed in the canon law. The natural law is binding upon all men, Christian or not, and the church has the obligation to announce it; more of this in Chapter VII. The revealed law is binding upon believers in an absolute way, for it is divine law; it is immutable. The regulations of the church, on the other hand, are acknowledged to be human law, and do not possess the same authority as either the natural law or the revealed law. They may be changed and adapted, and the church has the right to suspend them when it sees fit. But as long as they are in force, the members of the church are in duty bound to obey them. Recently, for example, the Holy See introduced extensive changes in its regulations for worship, permitting evening masses under certain conditions and revising the laws of fasting in order to make evening masses feasible. These changes were the result of agitation from leaders of the liturgical movement; but until the introduction of the changes, it was the sacred duty of Roman Catholic believers to fast from midnight until they made their communion. Admittedly this was canon law, the regulation of the church, but in the piety of the people the distinction between canon law and divine law tends to be blurred.

Obedience to either divine law or canon law requires the determination of what the law is for a particular situation. Such determination is the task of moral theology, which has been developed to a high state of complexity in Roman Catholicism. Proceeding from the analysis of problems and individual cases, moral theology has sought to prescribe for and to anticipate the various circumstances in which an ethical decision must be made. The general principles and prescriptions of the church's moral teaching are relatively simple, but their application to specific cases has produced the science of casuistry. Thus the columns of the *American Ecclesiastical Review* present detailed discussions of problems in casuistry like this one:

Question 1: Is there any reason to fear that lip-stick will break the eucharistic fast?

Question 2: If the lips of a woman who is receiving Extreme Unction are coated with lip-stick, is there any danger that the anointing of the mouth will not be valid?

Answer 1: . . . . It is not conformable with theological teaching to warn women against the use of lip-stick before receiving Holy Communion on the ground that they are likely to break their fast.

Answer 2: If there is a thick coating of lip-stick on the lips, there would be grave danger that the anointing of the mouth performed on the lips would not be valid; and in that event the validity of the sacrament would be doubtful. . . . [19]

Where such minute attention to casuistic problems is accompanied by deep scruples of conscience, the result can be disastrous. The penitent can never be certain of whether he has been obedient to every detailed prescription of the law, and yet he must be certain in order to find salvation and peace. There is a noteworthy parallel between this attitude among Roman Catholics and the conscientious scruples of certain pietistic Protestants, just as there are interesting parallels between the rigorous morality of such Protestants and the legalism so easily engendered by the Roman Catholic system. Excessive scrupulosity is thus an ecumenical phenomenon, for in both

Protestantism and Roman Catholicism the virtue of obedience can take on an exaggerated importance in the scale of moral values.

The virtue of obedience is so important in Roman Catholicism at least partly because of its prominence as the third vow of monks and nuns. Together with poverty and chastity, obedience is required of all those who take up what is called "the religious life." Their obedience is not only toward the church as such but toward their superiors in the religious orders, and it applies to any act that is not sinful. Because of it, as Thomas Aquinas puts it, "a man, although perhaps he would not be willing to do the thing commanded considered in itself, nevertheless wills to obey." [20] Beginning with their childhood in the parochial school, Roman Catholics learn respect and reverence for these obedient servants of the church. The obedience of the full time religious is the foundation for at least three of the most important enterprises in which the church is engaged: education, missions, and mercy. From the sisters at the Sacred Heart school across the street to the Jesuit fathers at the Pontifical Gregorian University in Rome, the members of religious orders direct Roman Catholic education at every level—the most integrated and comprehensive educational system in the world today. It was the orders that made possible the conversion of Europe, and the absence of anything similar to them has persistently hindered Protestant missions.[21] In works of mercy, an area where even the most bigoted Protestant must concede that Rome has done wonderful things, the several congregations of Sisters of Charity and other orders have made Christian charity real to the unfortunate.

These graphic examples of the meaning of obedience are an inspiration to anyone, even to one who regards the monastic system with grave misgivings. Theoretically, the obedience of the monk or nun must be voluntary, as must the obedience of the faithful to the rules of the church. But the history of the church and the testimony of many persons both show how easily this can be distorted. If contemporary Protestantism runs the danger of becoming amorphous and of losing all structure, the peril that continues to threaten Roman Catholicism is legalistic coercion and a glorification of obedience for its own sake. Thoughtful Roman Catholics recognize this peril, and the lives of many of them are certainly free of abnormal inhibitions. Yet the system of authority remains and periodically it manifests its power. The church can still lay claim to jurisdiction over large areas of human life.

The Jurisdiction of the Church

Just how far the jurisdiction of the church extends is not always easy to determine. (We are speaking here only of the church's jurisdiction over the lives of its own members; with the question of its authority in the public realm we shall be dealing in the next chapter.) The Roman church has felt constrained to legislate in detail on many moral questions which Protestants regard as a private matter between God and the believer. Conscientious Roman Catholics are obliged to consult this legislation when deciding upon a course of action, and the moral training of the young consists in the inculcation of these rules.

Perhaps the most widely discussed legislation of the Roman church is that dealing with marriage matters, especially with divorce and with birth control.[22] The stand of the Roman church on these matters is similar in some ways to the positions which Protestantism once took.[23] Divorce is forbidden. But this general principle is subject to all sorts of qualifications: separation "from bed and board" is permitted under certain circumstances and may become permanent; a marriage may be declared null and void if upon investigation it is determined that it was not valid; a convert may, after baptism, avail himself of the "Pauline privilege" of separation from his unbaptized spouse and may obtain permission to remarry.[24] The prohibition of birth control is likewise qualified. Since the primary purpose of the sex act is procreation and since other purposes, such as pleasure and the expression of love, are secondary to that primary purpose, it is contrary to natural law to frustrate the primary purpose for the sake of a secondary purpose. Nevertheless, the couple need not have procreation as the conscious intention of the act. They may even follow certain natural methods of minimizing the possibility of conception, such as the "rhythm method," but they may not employ artificial means of contraception. While statistics are, of course, impossible to obtain, some parish priests will admit privately that this legislation sometimes succeeds more in giving their parishioners a bad conscience than in preventing the practice of birth control.

The church's stand on marriage affects not only the private lives of married people, but also the professional lives of lawyers and physicians.[25] Here, too, the church has legislated on specific issues of legal and medical ethics. Indeed, the courses on these subjects in Roman Catholic schools of law and medicine are usually in the charge of a priest whose special field is moral theology and philosophy, and practitioners are called in for consultation on special issues. The miscellaneous pamphlets on the morality of medicine which form the basis for courses in medical ethics at Roman Catholic schools of medicine are a good example of how detailed the church's prohibitions and prescriptions are in this field. Most of what the church says here it says in its function as expositor of the natural law, which is binding upon all men; but no one except a Roman Catholic will agree that all of this necessarily follows from the natural law. In effect, therefore, these regulations constitute church law and not natural law, just as the church's regulations about marriage do. Nevertheless, Protestant and Jewish graduates of Roman Catholic professional schools often testify with gratitude to the deep sense of moral responsibility which their courses in ethics have given them.

Even beyond this, the jurisdiction of the church extends into the area of ideas. In Chapter V we referred to some of the difficulties which Thomist theology has had with modern science and modern philosophy. There are certain conclusions to which a philosopher is obliged to come, and certain first principles which he is obliged to accept as the basis of those conclusions. The historian is likewise provided with premises and conclusions; if he is a priest, he is obliged to swear:

I accept sincerely the doctrine of faith transmitted from the apostles through the orthodox fathers, always in the same sense and interpretation,

90

even to us; and so I reject the heretical invention of the evolution of dogmas, passing from one meaning to another, different from that which the Church first had.[26]

The church feels that it has the right to require of him that his scholarly research into the changes and shifts in the history of Christian thought conform to this oath. The natural scientist has an easier time of it today than Galileo did; if he is careful about framing his hypotheses, he has considerable freedom. But he is forbidden by the *Humani generis* of Pope Pius XII, for example, to posit the existence of men not physically descended from Adam and Eve.[27] He must maintain that the entire human race is descended from these two individuals, because any other opinion would appear to conflict with the church's teaching on original sin.

To prevent the incursion of opinions that conflict with the church's teaching, the Sacred Congregation of the Holy Office, created in 1542, has the authority to ban books which it adjudges to be dangerous to the faith and morals of the faithful. The catalog of such books is called the "Index of Prohibited Books," and Roman Catholics are prohibited from reading any book on the Index without permission.[28] In addition, the members of the church may not read or even sell any book that is dangerous to faith and morals, even if it is not on the Index. Wherever faith and morals are involved, the church claims the right of censorship over books. No Roman Catholic may publish a book dealing with doctrinal or moral matters without having it censored. The *Imprimatur* which appears at the beginning or the end of a Roman Catholic book is the official notice that the book has been censored and that permission for its publication has been duly granted. It does not mean that the church assumes responsibility for every statement of fact and opinion in the book, but only that the book does not contain anything inimical to the faith and practice of the church. The Index prohibits, the *Imprimatur* protects. By these means the church exercises its authority over the thought of its members—or at least tries to. Prohibition of books and boycott of movies have ricocheted so often that thoughtful members of the church, both clergy and laymen, have expressed their doubts about the wisdom and effectiveness of the entire system of passing judgment upon the productions of non-Roman authors and companies. Meanwhile the system still stands.

The Church as Mother

Thus the Roman Catholic is trained to look to his church not only for guidance and inspiration, but also for direction about how to live, how to work, and how to think. Even in a complex modern society the long arm of the church's power reaches into almost every province of his life. The main course of his Friday dinner; the neckline of his wife's evening gown on Saturday night; the movie he attends on Sunday afternoon; the school to which he sends his children on Monday morning; the labor union or service club he wants to join; his attendance at the wedding or funeral of a Protestant friend —these are only some of the questions on which the church has spoken and on which the church expects its authority to be obeyed. As justification for its interference in such questions the church cites commands like "Feed my sheep"; indeed, the opening words of the encyclical against modernism, the *Pascendi dominici gregis* of 1907, are a quotation from that command. If this interference in the details of daily life and thought is combined with the notion of papal infallibility (which, technically speaking, does not apply to much of it), the result is to invest the conditioned and temporary decisions of the church with the mantle of divine authority.

When the conditioned and temporary character of the church's decisions becomes evident, therefore, the mantle is stripped off. Promulgation of papal infallibility in the nineteenth century was, of course, retroactive. All previous occupants of the see of Peter had been infallible when speaking ex cathedra—even when they did not know it. If they had known it, they might have been a little more careful about what they said and how they said it. Also the statements of the popes who have been officially infallible manifest this conditioned character, as Roman Catholic socialists in France and Germany have been at pains to explain about the condemnation of socialism by Pius IX. If one turns from the official statements of the pope to the pre-

92

scriptions of the canon law and the petty regulations of individual dioceses and parishes, the ambiguity of the church's authority is even more striking.

This ambiguity has deeply troubled sensitive catholics from Augustine and Francis to Martin Luther and Cardinal Newman. What is a faithful son of the church to do when he recognizes the human, all-too-human, elements in the church's authority and leadership? For the resolution of this ambiguity, the ancient metaphor of the church as mother is often very helpful.[29] The church is our mother because from her—or, more precisely, through her—has come our spiritual life. She is like our physical mothers in another respect as well. It is part of growing up to recognize the weaknesses and faults of our parents; anyone who regards them as perfect is still a child. Once achieved, this recognition often produces rebellion, a mark of adolescence. True maturity consists in acknowledging our parents as the frail human beings they (and we) are, and in gratefully honoring them as God's representatives and instruments. The mature Roman Catholic has similarly learned how frail even the noblest of men can be, but he has also learned how the power of God can manifest itself in the very midst of this frailty and sin. Peter denied his Lord. Yet into Peter's apostolic hands Christ put the keys of the kingdom, to him Christ gave the command to "feed my sheep," on this rock Christ has built his church. Despite the weakness of men, including Peter, the gates of hell have not prevailed against it.

VII
The Two Swords

✠ If the church is as powerful as all that and if it claims jurisdiction over marriage, education, and professional ethics, does its
authority constitute a threat to American freedom? Many thinking
people are convinced that it does.[1] They point to the assertions of
papal authority in the past, in which the pope declared both his right
to depose rulers and his refusal to be judged by anyone but God.
They cite the performance of Roman Catholicism in countries where
it is a dominant majority and can secure discriminatory legislation
against Protestants. Roman Catholics in America, on the other hand,
resent these slurs upon their loyalty. They quote official statements by
church leaders about the duty of citizens to obey the state and to
participate in civic life. They also refer to the many millions of Roman
Catholics who have been loyal citizens of their country and faithful
members of their church at the same time.[2]

Thus a part of the riddle of Roman Catholicism is its enigmatic attitude toward the modern state. As we saw in Chapter V, that attitude

has passed through many mutations since the period of the Reformation. The political history of Roman Catholicism is different in almost every country of Europe, and in the New World its relations to the state have likewise followed no single set pattern. Yet in Roman Catholic political thought there are certain underlying principles on the basis of which such shifts in policy have taken place.[3] State and church dare not be completely identified, and they must not be absolutely separated; they are two distinct elements of one divine plan. One formulation of the church's political theory is the doctrine of the two swords, summarized for his time by Pope Boniface VIII (d. 1303):

We are taught by evangelical words that in this power of his [Peter's] are two swords, namely spiritual and temporal. . . . Each is in the power of the Church, that is, a spiritual and a material sword. . . . The latter, indeed, must be exercised for the Church, the former by the Church. The former [by the hand] of the priest, the latter by the hand of kings and soldiers, but at the will and sufferance of the priest. For it is necessary that a sword be under a sword, and that temporal authority be subject to spiritual power.[4]

Twin Realms

There are two swords because there are twin realms, the spiritual and the temporal.[5] Each has its own reason for existing, each owes its existence to God. Roman Catholic political theory insists, therefore, that the state is God's creation. It insists upon this against those who treat the state as a device which the ruling class may manipulate at will; the state belongs to God, not to the king or the dictator. But it directs this also against those who would deify the state; the state is not its own god, because the state does not create itself but is created by God.[6] Although there are two realms or two kingdoms, ultimately there is only one King. To him both realms are subject, to him the rulers in both realms are accountable. Any other theory would amount to a denial that God is one. The two realms are not the same, but it is the same God who is at work through both the state and the church. He wields both swords, each within its own realm and for its own purpose.

95

Within the realm of the church God rules through the ministers of the church, its priests and bishops, among whom the bishop of Rome has primacy. Because God established this realm directly through the work of Christ, the authority of the church does not depend in principle, and should not depend in practice, upon the authority of the state. The right to choose bishops and priests and to govern the affairs of the church is vested in the church, and the state does not have the right to interfere. Similarly, the church has the right to determine the standards for its own membership, on the basis of the revealed will of God. No state may dictate those standards, because they belong exclusively to the realm of the church. In meeting the expanding control of the modern state, Roman Catholicism has been obliged to defend these rights against intrusion.[7] The challenge of totalitarianism has sharpened the issue still further. When the state has expropriated church lands or tried to depose church officials, Rome has countered with all the moral and political resistance it could summon. Sometimes this has involved defending conduct that seemed indefensible, as in the treason trial of the Nazi puppet, Monsignor Jozef Tiso in Czechoslovakia. Basically the church was not defending Father Tiso at all; in fact, many prominent Roman Catholics had denounced his political activity. What the church defends in such a case is the integrity and inviolability of the spiritual realm as the church interprets it.

Rome has not always been as vociferous in its defense of the integrity and inviolability of the secular realm. Perhaps the modern state does not need to be defended as much as it needs to be limited, but the limitation comes in better grace and looks less self-centered when it is accompanied by positive declarations concerning the inherent rights of the state. The political theory of Roman Catholicism has made many such declarations, for it does acknowledge the existence of two realms and the divine origin of each.[8] The secular realm, too, is from God. It does not depend upon the church for its right to fulfill its purpose, but is endowed by God with "the sword," that is the right and the means to do what it was appointed to do. This is what Roman Catholic political thought means when it says that

96

the state, like the church, is a "perfect society." The Roman empire before Christ, therefore, was a legitimate state so long as it remained within the limits of its ends as a state, the temporal and material welfare of its citizens. When it went on to legislate about matters of faith and morals, however, it was going beyond those limits; on such matters it is the duty of the state to support the church in its realm or, at least, not to interfere in the realm of the church. This latter duty of keeping hands off is the best that the church has been able to expect from most modern states, and in exchange the church has been willing to make explicit its endorsement of the state as a legitimate and relatively independent realm.[9]

The state is only a relatively independent realm because the church and the state have many interests in common; where these interests come into conflict, those of the church have precedence. As the soul is superior to the body, so the interests of the church are superior to those of the state. Both state and church, for example, have a direct stake in marriage: the state, because the home is the foundation of all human society; the church, because Christian matrimony is a sacrament. The marriage of unbaptized persons is exclusively the concern of the state, and the church speaks about it only in its function as the expositor of the natural law. But the church insists upon a direct right, and a prior right, when the marriage of its own members is involved. Here the standards of the state do not apply, but must defer to those of the church; it is the duty of the state not merely to defer to the church, but to support the church in such matters. The state and the church have a common interest in matters of church property, in the persons of the clergy who are also citizens of the state, and in many other areas. In any such area of organized society which is the legitimate concern of both church and state, this principle applies.

Interestingly, education does not qualify as such an area of legitimate concern to both the state and the church. Authority over education belongs to parents and to the church by divine right.[10] When the state educates, it is not doing so on the basis of any inherent right, but is merely taking the place of the parents. The residual right to determine the education of children remains with the parents. At most, the state may set the academic standards of the schools within it, and require that future citizens meet those standards. It has no right to require that all children attend its schools. As it was articulated in the course of the church's fight to save its schools, this philosophy of education vests parents with responsibility for the training of their children. It also recognizes that there is no such thing as moral and religious neutrality in a school, and it directs the church to involve itself more directly in the education of its children than one hour a week on Sunday morning will permit. Thus education certainly belongs to the realm of the church and to that of the parents; abdication by either or both is a neglect of a divinely established duty. Nevertheless, the refusal of Roman Catholicism to acknowledge that education also belongs to the realm of the state seems to be inconsistent with its political philosophy. For if the material and temporal welfare of its citizens is the end of the state, the state must have the right to establish means toward achieving that end, not merely the right to insist that others achieve that end for it.

From the way the Roman church behaves in areas like marriage and education, its critics have been able to argue that it does not mean its doctrine of the twin realms seriously.[11] It insists that there are two realms when its own interests seem to be threatened, but the only restraints it imposes upon itself are those which the state imposes. Left to its own devices, it seems willing to pre-empt much of what belongs to the realm of the state. As we have indicated, this position is partly a historical one brought on by the church's role in medieval society, partly a defensive one brought on by the almost boundless ambitions of the modern state. Now that the historical position has become impossible and the defensive position is becoming less necessary, the political theorists of the church may have time and opportunity to think through the fuller implications of their doctrine of the twin realms. That doctrine contains the necessary elements for a more balanced and defensible delinea-

98

tion of the rights and duties of both church and state than the traditional doctrine of the two swords has been.

A Twofold Law

One such element is the Roman Catholic theory of law.[12] Corresponding somewhat to the distinction between the realms is a distinction between two fundamental kinds of law, natural and revealed. Natural law is, of course, not a uniquely Roman Catholic notion, nor even a discovery of Christianity. It was the Stoic philosophers who first gave detailed attention to the idea of an eternal law within and behind the particular rules that govern human conduct. Through Paul that idea passed over into Christian thought and became the basis for most Christian theories of law, including the Roman Catholic theory.[13] According to this theory, the difference between right and wrong and the realization that one should pursue the right and shun the wrong are accessible to man's reason. He can know this of himself and does not need a special act of divine revelation to discover it. In various cultures it may indeed be possible to suppress one or another precept of natural law; even the prohibition of incest is not universal. What is universal is the awareness of a moral order that is not of our making. Reason and experience both support such an awareness, and therefore this is "natural" law, the law which is operative and which is knowable within the boundaries of man's natural knowledge.

More than natural knowledge is required for man to become aware of the full divine law. This comes only by supernatural divine revelation in both the Old Testament (especially in the Decalogue) and the New Testament (especially in the teachings of Jesus). This revealed law does not cancel the natural law, but reinforces it and completes it. Thus the Decalogue is a sort of epitome of the natural law. It is what the natural law would be if man's knowledge were perfect. Since man's knowledge is not perfect, God has had to reveal the law to him. The specifically Christian commandments have come in Christ. In Christ God has disclosed his special will for believers and for the church, the counsels of perfection for those who

99

are not content with the bare minimum of obedience to the divine law. Through Christ God has also laid down the new ceremonial law, which supersedes the Levitical regulations. By Christ God has decreed the constitution of his church, the forms of government which are to regulate its organized life. This revealed law—moral, ceremonial, and juridical—is the fundamental warrant for what the church does and for what it requires of its members. Hence the distinction between the natural law and the revealed law is one of both content and form: content, because the revealed law includes the natural law and a great deal more; form, because the natural law is knowable to man in the state of nature, while the revealed law is a supernatural thing.

The distinction between the natural law and the revealed law is matched by the distinction between civil law and canon law.[14] These two terms cover the positive legislation of the state and of the church. From the legislation of the state it can be required that it conform to the natural law, whose basic norm is justice. Charged as it is with the administration of the entire law of God, the church has the obligation to tell the state about the natural law; and the state has the obligation to listen and to heed the natural law. Although the natural law is knowable by reason, it is also possible for men and governments to ignore it or to flout it. Then the church must exercise its function as a higher order of society than the state. There is a twofold law; but because the revealed law is the reinforcement and the completion of the natural law, both natural law and revealed law are the business of the church. Many of the church's pronouncements to the state proceed from this responsibility which the church has for the natural law. For example, most of what the church says about marriage and divorce is said to flow from the natural law. It does not depend upon an acknowledgment of Jesus Christ as Lord and Savior, but upon the exercise of man's natural capacities. By making such pronouncements to the state, therefore, the church is merely urging the state truly to be the state, that is, to administer justice and to obey the natural law.[15]

As the state must truly be the state, so it must also let the church

100

truly be the church. Not only must the church tell the state to conform its positive law to the natural law, but the church must also demand that the positive law of the state refrain from interfering in the province of church law. Here the church speaks not as the custodian of the natural law, but as the divine society whose superiority the state is obliged to acknowledge. Church law or canon law must be in conformity with revealed law, just as state law must be in conformity with natural law. Since revealed law is higher and more complete than natural law, canon law is of a higher order than civil law. Where the two come into conflict—even where no precept of natural law as such is involved—there the civil law must yield to the canon law. A twofold law for the twin realms is the general principle; but as the spiritual realm judges all and is judged by none but God, so the voice of the church is entitled to speak on all questions of law, including the law of the secular realm. So well informed does the church profess to be about the details of natural law that its defense of the natural law is often a defense of its own position and prerogatives. This fact frequently invalidates that defense and makes the jurisprudence of Roman Catholicism sound like elaborate propaganda for the church organization rather than the exposition of the universal divine maxims governing all individual and social behavior.

The principle of a twofold law for the twin realms nevertheless contains the raw material for creative thought about the role of Christians and of the church in a political order where law is not the arbitrary expression of a ruler's whim, but the articulation of the will of the people under a constitution. Roman Catholic jurisprudence in the United States has recently begun to encourage such creative thought, and from it have come cautious suggestions that Roman Catholics have something to learn about law from modern developments. If the church is to speak to the citizenry about natural law, it should be able to appeal to standards of judgment which the members of the citizenry accept.[16] Not merely abstract principles, but concrete experience must also serve to verify the natural law if it is truly "natural." Too often, however, abstract speculation about jus-

101

tice, as summarized in the preceding paragraphs, is all one hears from the exponents of natural law; and whatever its validity, such speculation makes very little sense to many people. These same people might be willing to listen to a persuasive and well-reasoned discussion of moral and political issues if it were based upon experience and directed at something other than the institutional aggrandizement of the Roman communion.

Dual Citizenship

Most members of the Roman communion discover that there are tensions between the two realms, but they make this discovery more often in the concrete exercise of their duties as citizens of the twin realms than in speculations about the twofold law of God. Dual citizenship becomes most explicit in the case of the clergy, but every Roman Catholic bride and bridegroom become aware of it when they are forced to take out a marriage license from the state and at the same time to satisfy the requirements of the church. They must do both of these things because of their citizenship in twin realms, to both of which they owe obedience. As citizens of the state, they must obey its laws even when they disagree with them or regard them as unwarranted. Very few Roman Catholics urged the adoption of the Eighteenth Amendment, and those who did certainly lacked the zeal of their Protestant associates; yet once the Eighteenth Amendment had become law, Roman Catholics were expected to obey it as law. American citizenship, however, is not exhausted by obeying the law and paying taxes. The citizen has a direct and active role in the administration of the body politic. When it prescribes the civic duties of its members in such a country, the church must urge them to take that role seriously and to go into the voting booth with a conscience that is enlightened both by a desire for the common good and by the teachings of the church.

The church member who goes into the voting booth on Tuesday is the same man who went into the confessional box on the preceding Sunday. He is a citizen of both realms. Citizenship in the spiritual realm, the church, should fit him for better citizenship in the temporal realm, the state. The divine law which he learns from the church should clarify for him the natural law on the basis of which the state operates. Theoretically this is so, and practically it often works out that way. Roman Catholic citizens of America realize the tension between the two parts of their dual citizenship, but it is fair to say that they do not sense any fundamental conflict. Not in the erudite terminology of twin realms or of a twofold law or even of dual citizenship, but in the straightforward testimony of their own political careers, the Roman Catholic mayors of many of our large cities have demonstrated the meaning of dual citizenship. Their citizenship in the church has not invalidated—and sometimes has not even influenced—their citizenship in the state. Like Frank Skeffington in *The Last Hurrah*, they have learned to maneuver with skill, if not with ease, in the pluralistic world of metropolitan politics.

In his dual role as a citizen of the church and a citizen of the state, the Roman Catholic participates in each realm according to its special rules. He does indeed owe obedience to the temporal and secular realm, an obedience which the church seeks to implant in him. But he owes a higher obedience to the spiritual realm simply because it is a higher realm. The state has control over the body, which is mortal; the church has control over the soul, which is immortal. The body is God's good creature, and so is the state; but that does not make the body as important as the soul, nor the state as important as the church. Dual citizenship does not mean, therefore, equal dedication to each of the twin realms. It means a dedication to the secular realm within the limits of that realm, and a dedication to the spiritual realm that transcends citizenship in the state, membership in the family, or any other human tie.

A Divided Loyalty?

It is this transcendent dedication that brings on the charge of divided loyalty. The dedication may be transcendent, but the object of the dedication is also very real and concrete. It has bishops and priests, churches and schools, land and money; and it has a head who wears the trappings and bears the titles of a political sovereign. The higher citizenship in the spiritual realm, therefore, means subjection to his sovereignty, a subjection which millions of Americans regard as irreconcilable with loyalty to the United States. Irreconcilable in principle, that is; for these same Americans will freely admit that some of their best friends are Roman Catholics and that they would not dream of questioning their loyalty to the United States. Only— and this is as inevitable in a discussion of the Roman Catholic question as is the issue of intermarriage in a discussion of the race question—"aren't you afraid of a Roman Catholic in the White House?"

In the twentieth century that question came up repeatedly, but it was loudest during the presidential campaign of 1928. The charge that Alfred E. Smith as a devout Roman Catholic layman could not give his undivided loyalty to the Constitution came in various forms from his political opponents, and it was not absent even within his own party. Without entering into the moot question whether this charge was primarily responsible for Smith's defeat, we can point to this campaign as the high tide of suspicion and resentment against Roman Catholics in public life. Smith's insistence that his religious convictions and connections were a private matter and did not interfere with his public duties was dismissed as campaign oratory. All the prejudices and anxieties about Vatican domination of the United States received a new lease on life. Even some of those who condemned the slanders against Al Smith as bigotry sensed profound misgivings at the picture of a Roman Catholic in the White House. Granted, so they argued, that Smith was not aware of any contradiction between his religion and his public duty, and that during most of his tenure in office there would probably be no clash between them; what would he do if, under certain conceivable circumstances, it became necessary to make a choice between Americanism and Roman Catholicism?

Support for these misgivings came from both the theory and the practice of the Roman communion. There were the many extravagant statements of the late medieval popes about the superiority of the spiritual to the secular. These were reinforced by the extremism of Pope Pius IX in the nineteenth century, whose Syllabus of Errors read like an indictment of most things that most Americans held dear.[17] In reply, Roman Catholics in America insisted that any conflict of loyalties was theoretical rather than practical. Yet it was the practical area that aroused the deepest anxiety about Al Smith. Some of his Roman Catholic supporters employed tactics that only managed to alienate the Protestant public. The feebleness of the opposition which some Roman Catholics expressed against Smith on political grounds convinced many that the opposition was contrived by the hierarchy to gain support for Smith among Jews and Protestants. Even without citing the performance of the Roman communion in Europe or South America, Smith's critics could refer to the political maneuvers of the church in Quebec or to its economic manipulations in Mexico as evidence of its real intentions wherever it gained power. The pietism of many Protestants was repelled by Al Smith's stand on prohibition, the isolationism of many Midwesterners by his attitude toward Europe. All this was epitomized in the widely circulated picture of the Irishman from New York doffing his brown derby and stooping over to kiss a prelate's ring.

Embarrassed though they were by some of the arguments against Smith, his supporters did supply telling refutation of the charges. The candidate himself declared his loyalty to the Constitution in his own unequivocal and forthright way. While outstanding Protestant laymen like Franklin D. Roosevelt affirmed their confidence in Smith's loyalty and in his total fitness as a candidate, relatively few Protestant clergymen came forward to protest the insertion of the religious issue into the campaign. There was some attempt by Roman Catholic spokesmen to refute the theoretical charges against the church by reference to its teachings about the state.[18] It was on the practical level, however, that Smith's backers most effectively argued their case. They pointed to the Roman Catholics who had fought for their country ten years earlier, to the policemen and judges and magistrates who went to mass on Sunday and did their civic duty throughout the week, and to the record of Al Smith while he was governor of New York. The bogy of Vatican domination and divided loyalty certainly seemed ridiculous in the light of this evidence. The presidency was different only in degree, not in kind, from the many other positions of public trust which Roman Catholics had filled with distinction. Why should church membership disqualify a man from performing this service to his country?

It did disqualify him, at least in the eyes of many voters. As Smith said, it was too early for a man to say his beads in the White House. During the three decades after 1928 the question of electing a Roman Catholic to the presidency or the vice-presidency came up repeatedly. But even in recent years, as support for a Roman Catholic President has grown, the hesitancy has also continued. As recently as January, 1958, the group organized as "Protestants and Other Americans United for Separation of Church and State" called upon any Roman Catholic candidate for the presidency to declare himself on the school question and the American ambassadorship to the Vatican. "To challenge every catholic candidate on these issues," they declared, "is a wise and necessary precaution designed to protect our American traditions." [19]

If a Roman Catholic candidate were to be nominated, it might seem to be a bid for "the Roman Catholic vote." Yet many interpreters of national trends maintain that there is no such thing, that Roman Catholics decide their vote on the basis of the same complex of factors that is involved in anyone's political attitude. If this is so, it would also appear to provide the best possible refutation for the charge of divided loyalty. Like the Freemasons, about whose political loyalty even Pope Leo XIII raised serious suspicions, Roman Catholics have earned the chance to be evaluated on their individual merits or demerits. Membership in the Roman church does not disqualify, and it does not qualify, a man for public office. If he is qualified, I may vote for him, Roman Catholic or not; if he is not qualified, I should not vote for him even though both of us may be Roman Catholics. This is a general principle that deserves to be remembered and followed by the American electorate on both sides of the Congressional aisle and on both sides of the denominational divide.

106

A Double Standard

We have been discussing the political strategy of Roman Catholicism when it is a minority church. As long as it constitutes less than one fourth of the total population of the United States, it is unable to achieve its ultimate ideal. That ultimate ideal still remains "a catholic church in a catholic state." Around this ideal, as represented more or less adequately by the medieval political order, most Roman Catholic political theory is oriented. It does not mean merely that the missionary policy of Roman Catholicism, like that of Methodism, hopes for the conversion of as many Americans as possible to its point of view. This is the way Roman Catholic apologists seek to dismiss the issue. But the prospect of a Methodist majority in America, disturbing though it may be to many people (including not a few Methodists), is fundamentally different from the prospect of a Roman Catholic majority in America. Political theorists of the Roman communion have quite candidly admitted that the ideal of "a catholic church in a catholic state" implies recognition by the state of the church's prior rights and privileges and a refusal by the state to grant similar rights and privileges to other religious bodies. When it is in a controlling majority, the church refuses to put error on the same level as truth; it is therefore committed to intolerance.

Meanwhile, it demands a tolerance for itself which, in principle, it would refuse to others. While the ideal is still "a catholic church in a catholic state," the church recognizes that the modern state is a secular state, where the total expression of that ideal is an impossibility. Not even in Falangist Spain, where the church has almost a monopoly and enjoys the support of the dictator, has it been possible to put the medieval standard into practice. In the Western democracies it is even less possible. Despite the millions of Frenchmen who belong, at least nominally, to the Roman Catholic Church, the marriage laws of France do not conform to the church's requirements. The church's hold on Quebec is not as firm as it sometimes appears south of the border. Throughout the Western world, the rise of the welfare state has crowded the church out of many areas of service that used to be its exclusive province. Most of the church's concessions to this shift

107

have been tactical, representing the church's willingness to settle for less than the ideal. By and large, that ideal has blinded Roman Catholics to the practical advantages in the pluralistic standard of "a catholic church and many other churches in a single secular state." Abhorrent as this pluralistic standard is to the theory of Roman Catholicism, it has certainly worked very well for America.

It has also worked very well for Roman Catholicism in America, much better than Roman Catholic theory said it would. Under a pluralistic system to which the church is opposed, the church has prospered—not only materially, but in every other way as well. The message and appeal of the Roman church has not suffered from the open competition in the marketplace of ideas. Roman Catholic students at secular colleges and graduate schools have indeed passed through doubt and conflict, but the net effect for many of them was a deeper and stronger faith and a greater dedication to their church. The experience of Roman priests in the military chaplaincy brought many of them into closer contact with Protestant clergymen than had ever been possible before, but there was no mass defection to Protestantism. Laymen of the church have developed a working relationship with their Protestant or Jewish or agnostic neighbors and friends that does not undermine their fidelity to the Roman communion. Pluralism is not as inimical to the church's interests as the official standard of the church had supposed.

This suggests that the official standard of the church needs revision.[20] As the church learned to live under feudalism and even found certain advantages in the feudal system, so the church must learn to live under democracy. Under feudalism the church enjoyed the advantage of a monopoly in the religious field, and there the standard of "a catholic church in a catholic state" arose. There were also disadvantages in feudalism to offset that advantage. The church must learn from its experience in a society that is both pluralistic and democratic. To be sure, it cannot surrender its hope of converting all men to the Christian gospel and making them members of the one true church. But it can surrender its attachment to a church-state system that is dead, and look instead for a new and dynamic relationship to the modern secular state.

As we have tried to show in this chapter, such a relationship to the modern secular state should be possible on the basis of Roman Catholic teaching, some of whose implications for this problem are still waiting to be drawn. The alternation between ambition and timidity which Roman Catholics manifest in the political scene is an important element in the riddle we have been probing. The converted aesthete who grows limp at the sound of Gregorian chant ought to understand this alternation, or his affection for Roman Catholicism is purely sentimental. The intellectual who is drawn to Thomism must recognize that Thomism is the intellectual weapon of this ambition. The professional pope-baiter, who would agitate against any candidate for office on the simple grounds of his membership in the Roman church, is oversimplifying the riddle of Roman Catholicism. When the Roman church itself becomes guilty of such oversimplification and embarks upon adventures in political ambition, it constitutes a menace not only to the state, but also to itself. Then it needs to be recalled to its true genius, even if the voice that does the recalling has to come from the outside.

VIII
Mystery and Magic

✠ The heart of Roman Catholic faith and life is not the authority of the church organization, however formidable that may be, nor the relation of the church and the state, however complex that may be. Roman Catholic religious life is centered in the seven sacraments of the church. By these sacraments the faithful live and die. The church organization is there to administer the sacraments and to guarantee their proper administration, but it is the sacraments that carry the life-giving grace of God to the believers. Sociological study of authority and power in the Roman church, historical study of its evolution, even theological study of its creeds and tenets— none of these can penetrate the riddle of Roman Catholicism unless they begin to comprehend the importance of the sacramental system for the church's authority, for its historical development, and for the form and content of its theology.

The average Protestant (including the sociologist, the historian, and the theologian) will frequently dismiss Roman Catholic sacramental-

110

ism as "magic." He will accuse the sacramental system of trying to manipulate God or to encase Christ in some sacred objects or actions. There is plenty of evidence in Roman Catholic piety past and present to make such accusations plausible. The tendency of Roman Catholicism is to debase the mystery into magic, while Protestantism often shows signs that it will flatten the mystery of the sacraments into a rationalistic formula of a mere sign. Every sacramental doctrine would seem to tip the scale in the one direction or the other, either toward magic or toward rationalism; what every sacramental doctrine tries to do is to make the sacraments meaningful without dispelling the mystery.

That is just what Roman Catholic sacramental doctrine is trying to do. The definition of what constitutes a sacrament, and therefore the number of the sacraments, has varied in the history of catholic theology East and West. To qualify as a sacrament under the official definition of the Roman cathechism today, an action must meet certain conditions:

a) it must employ an external means that is perceptible to the senses;
b) it must be instituted by Christ as a permanent part of the church's life;
c) it must be intended as a means of grace, both symbolizing and conveying the grace of God.[1]

On the basis of this definition, the Roman church today affirms seven sacraments, each of which is said to meet the conditions just listed. This does not mean that God is bound only to these seven sacraments; he may and does confer grace wherever he pleases. But the church is bound to them in perpetuity, for through them God has promised to confer grace. Grace through other channels may be uncertain, but the grace of the sacraments is certain and definite.

Baptism

The sacramental system of the Roman church extends, as has been said of socialism, from the cradle to the grave. As the sacrament for those in the cradle, baptism is basic to all the others; one qualification

111

for the reception of any other sacrament is that the recipient be a baptized person.[2] The washing of baptism symbolizes the purification of the soul from the stain of sin, but it also effects such a purification. The act of washing, combined with the words "I baptize you in the name of the Father and of the Son and of the Holy Spirit," actually confers divine grace upon the recipient, forgives his sins, and makes him a member of the church. Therefore baptism is a new birth, the beginning of a new spiritual life. Once baptism has been administered, its effect cannot be obliterated; for it confers an "indelible character" upon the person baptized, a divine seal to which the person may indeed prove unfaithful but which he cannot undo. More than any of the other sacraments, except perhaps extreme unction, baptism emphasizes the passive attitude of the recipient. Its efficacy does not depend upon the attitude of the recipient at all, but upon the promise of Christ and upon obedience to the command of Christ to use water and to recite the name of the Holy Trinity.

Baptism is therefore peculiarly suited to the needs of infants, who are able to profit from it directly. Infant baptism is the rule in the Roman church, as it has been in the entire catholic church since at least the third century. All the effects of baptism just described—grace, forgiveness, regeneration, membership in the church—apply to infants, too. Hence baptism is said to work *ex opere operato*; that is, the effect of baptism is derived from the act itself, in accordance with the institution of Christ.[3] From baptism the doctrine of *ex opere operato* has been applied to the sacraments in general, even to those which are received by adults. This does not mean that the attitude of the recipient does not matter, but that the validity of a sacrament does not usually depend upon it. (One exception, as we shall see, is penance.) Since the purpose of this doctrine is to affirm that the sacraments are objective, needing only God's action and not ours to make them work, it constitutes an affirmation of the mystery of God's activity, a declaration that God moves in a sovereign and mysterious way over which we do not exercise control even by our denial. Yet this very doctrine can become the basis for the supposition that God must confer His grace automatically whenever we baptize, in

112

other words, that we do exercise control over God by our act of baptizing. That is how mystery becomes magic.

It is likewise the affirmation of a mystery when Roman Catholic teaching declares that the effect and significance of baptism are permanent and last a lifetime. On the basis of this teaching the church also says that baptism should not be repeated, but that the one baptism performed in infancy avails forever. To this one baptism the faithful are to look as evidence of God's gracious concern for them. The new liturgy for Holy Week includes an impressive recitation of the baptismal vow on Easter Eve, when members of the congregation reaffirm the relation established in their baptism. Any Christian who witnesses this reaffirmation of baptism cannot fail to be reminded of the mysterious connection between the initiative of God and our free response to that initiative. Another reminder of the same connection, the use of holy water as a so-called "sacramental," degenerates into magical and superstitious practices so quickly that it seems almost inescapable. Holy water, like baptism itself, came to the church from pre-Christian sources, both Jewish and pagan.[4] Although the church has perhaps succeeded in purging baptism of the connotations it still carries from those sources, the role of holy water in the folk piety of Roman Catholics has never been domesticated. Holy water is not primarily a reminder of baptism at all, but a means of warding off danger from the devil or from more terrestrial enemies. For the actual practice of much folk piety, the daily or weekly use of holy water is vastly more important than the sacrament of baptism.

The teaching of the Roman church about baptism takes the doctrine of *ex opere operato* so seriously that it is even willing to draw this conclusion from it: children who have been baptized by a Protestant minister in the name of the Holy Trinity are validly baptized and are therefore members of the catholic church. The personal attitude of the officiating clergyman does not invalidate baptism any more than the personal attitude of the recipient does. It is only necessary that he employ water, that he use the correct form, and that he intend his action to be the baptism of the church. After their baptism such children may sever their connection with the church by joining a Protestant denomination or by other acts of exclusion, but initially they belong to the church by virtue of their baptism. Like many another Roman teaching, this intriguing bit of logic is called upon for service whenever the church needs it, as when Pope Pius IX used it to prove his jurisdiction in Germany in the Kulturkampf. It can also disappear from view when someone infers from it that it is possible to be a Christian outside the external fellowship of the Roman communion, an inference to which we shall return in Part Three. Because the validity of baptism does not depend upon the minister, baptized Protestants who go over to Roman Catholicism are, as a rule, not rebaptized. If they have doubts about the fact of their baptism or about its validity, they may be baptized conditionally by the use of a formula like: "If you are baptized, I do not baptize you; if you are not yet baptized, I baptize you, etc." [5]

In many ways the Roman Catholic view of baptism is an epitome of its entire sacramental system, of both its positive and its negative aspects. Because the Protestant view of baptism is itself so sorely in need of restudy, neither the strengths nor the weaknesses of the Roman position have received their due attention from non-Roman theologians. Even Roman Catholics themselves have given less thought to the meaning of baptism than it requires. The theological discussions of it are so entangled in the static terminology of scholasticism that the dynamic doctrine of baptism which we see in the New Testament and in the early Greek fathers is lost. Nevertheless, it is that doctrine, not the mechanical formulas of scholasticism, that can be made meaningful for the Christian life of Roman Catholic lay people. Indeed, one is tempted to suggest that Protestants and Roman Catholics both need to look together at the biblical foundations of the doctrine of baptism and at what has happened to it in the intervening centuries. Both sides would be surprised to see what of their own position and what of the opponent's position would come into a new light as a result. Until that happens, Protestants can at least attempt to understand the Roman doctrine.

114

Confirmation

Closely related to baptism is the sacrament of confirmation. Indeed, if some historians are correct, the two rites were originally one, as they still are in the Eastern churches; even in the Western church they may be given together. If this is so, then confirmation is the part of baptism which was usually postponed when infant baptism became the rule.[6] For in the rite of confirmation a baptized person receives an anointing by which he is "sealed" in the Holy Spirit. As in baptism, this anointing confers an indelible character and is therefore unrepeatable. When confirmation was first introduced as a rite distinct from baptism, it seems to have included formal instruction of the children, at the conclusion of which they gave public testimony to their faith and thereupon were received into full membership in the church. The confession of faith required of an adult at baptism was, in the case of an infant, postponed to confirmation. With such a confession in view, the church was able to justify infant baptism as the initial step of an entire process.

As a result, confirmation as a separate sacrament has never been clearly defined within the Roman Catholic sacramental system. Theologians admit, for example, that there is no explicit warrant for the practice in the teachings of Jesus as contained in the gospels. They argue, however, that this is because confirmation confers the seal of the Spirit, something that was impossible until after Pentecost. They therefore find biblical support for the sacrament of confirmation in the practice of the apostles, who are said in the Book of Acts to have laid hands upon men and thus to have given them the Holy Spirit. Because the apostles were the only ones to do this, Rome teaches (in opposition to the Eastern churches) that only a bishop, as a direct successor of the apostles, may perform the rite of confirmation under ordinary circumstances; in the case of foreign missionaries, the pope grants a dispensation from this rule. Nor is the relation between confirmation and first communion entirely clear. From ancient practice and from the meaning of the rites themselves, it would seem that confirmation should follow some sort of catechetical instruction in the meaning of the faith and that it should be the means by which

115

children are admitted to the Lord's Supper. Thus confirmation would be important as a part of first communion.

Where there is a separation between first communion and confirmation, the people naturally ascribe greater importance to first communion; and where there is no separation, the people still put the emphasis upon first communion. It is on the occasion of their first communion, not on the occasion of their confirmation, that Roman Catholic children have their pictures taken. Both in official theology and in folk piety, then, confirmation is rather vague. Most of its meaning is borrowed from baptism, some of it from the Lord's Supper; it has little meaning of its own. Like marriage, it really does not belong in the system as a means of grace. Only by virtue of a sacramental "system," where one rite derives its meaning from the others, does it qualify as a sacrament at all. If it were restored to what seems to have been its original function, however, it could perform a valuable service as the "confirmation" of the sacrament of baptism.

The Eucharist

Although baptism is the fundamental sacrament in the sacramental system of the church, the central sacrament is undoubtedly the Lord's Supper or eucharist.[7] It is central to the worship of the church, as we shall see in Chapter XI, but it is also central to the piety of the Roman Catholic believer. Indeed, it is possible to interpret the entire genius of Roman Catholicism from the standpoint of the eucharist. As in the miracle on the altar the bread and the wine are changed into the very body and the very blood of Jesus Christ, so in the miracle of grace the external ecclesiastical organization is transformed into the very church of Jesus Christ.[8] As daily bread is a divine blessing and remains one so long as it does not seek to pre-empt the place that belongs to the bread of life in the eucharist, so the state must accept its inferiority to the church in order to be the divine blessing it was intended to be.

Thus the entire outlook of Roman Catholicism can become sacramental in the sense that the glasses through which a Roman Catholic looks at the world take their shape—and give shape to the scene,

116

in turn—from the sacramental miracle of the eucharist. Basically, that miracle consists in the transformation of bread into the body of Christ and of wine into the blood of Christ. The external qualities of bread and wine, like taste and smell and other chemical properties, all remain unchanged; they are called "accidents" in the language which theology has borrowed from Aristotle. Beneath and beyond these accidents is that by which bread is truly bread, its "substance" in that same language. What happens in the miracle of the eucharist is that this substance is changed into the substance of the body of Christ. Most changes which we experience are changes of accidents—grape juice ferments, wine turns sour. But here there is no change of accidents, only one of substance. Therefore the changing of bread and wine into body and blood is called transubstantiation. Long before it achieved the subtlety and sophistication of this formulation, the notion of a miraculous change in the eucharist had a firm place in the faith of devout catholic people. From that faith it was finally taken over by learned theology, not vice versa. The people do not need the intricacies of transubstantiation to explain the miracle of the eucharist.[9]

The miracle of the eucharist explains and justifies the sacrifice of the mass, which many Protestants regard as the most repulsive aspect of Roman sacramental teaching.[10] Because the body of Christ on the altar is his true body, the same body which he offered on Calvary as the perfect sacrifice for the sins of the world, we continue to plead the merits of that sacrifice each day as we daily offer up the same body that bore our sins. Stated as carefully as that, the sacrifice of the mass may not seem as dangerous as most Protestants make it. But many Roman Catholic theologians do not state it as carefully as that, and neither do many lay people. What was originally intended as a representation ("re-presentation") of the sacrifice on Calvary has now become an extension or even a repetition of that sacrifice. No apologist for the Roman Catholic doctrine can deny that this confusion has often appeared not only among lay people, but even among theologians. The formulations of the Council of Trent itself are subject to ambiguous interpretation. To many non-Romans all of this seems to be in direct conflict with the explicit and repeated insistence of the New Testament that what Christ has done, he has done "once and for all" in a single and unrepeatable sacrifice of perfect obedience. His sacrifice on Calvary need not and indeed cannot be extended or repeated. A sacrifice there is in the eucharist; the very word means "sacrifice of thanksgiving." But it is a sacrifice that avails because it is "in union with his most holy sacrifice," as an ancient liturgical formula has it. Roman Catholic theology and piety have not always kept this distinction clear.

What helped to obscure the distinction was the emphasis upon the sacrifice in the mass at the expense of the communion. Both Luther and Calvin criticized this distortion, declaring that the command of Christ had put the emphasis in the eucharist upon the participation of the members of the church while the practice of the church had substituted the action of the priest for that participation. The very style of architecture illustrated this; it permitted thousands to watch the sacrifice of the mass, but a mere handful to come to the altar for the communion. The sacrifice of the mass was a daily event, the communion a special occasion. In many Roman Catholic parishes this is still the case. A person is obliged to "make his communion" once a year, and for vast numbers this minimum is also a maximum; but he is obliged to attend mass and to witness the sacrifice every Sunday if possible. Although the liturgical movement has been seeking to redress the balance and to emphasize frequent communion, the weight of usage is difficult indeed to overcome. The very reverence which people feel for the eucharist causes many of them to shy away from it, just as the fear of "spilling the blood of Christ anew" was deterring people from more frequent communion until it finally constrained the medieval church to offer only the bread to the laity. Even this drastic step did not succeed in making the holy communion central in the devotional life of the people.

For many individuals and for many parishes, the center of devotional life is not the communion, nor even the sacrifice of the mass, but another by-product of the eucharist, the piety of the tabernacle. The tabernacle is the receptable on the altar into which the sacramen-

118

tal body of Christ, the bread, is set aside or reserved. So realistically is the sacramental miracle understood that the bread reserved in the tabernacle is said to be Christ himself. To this Christ prayers may be addressed and vows paid. Around the tabernacle have sprung many forms of popular devotion and "sacramentals" such as novenas, which repeatedly threaten to crowd out the mass as the genuine center of religious life in the parish. Any Protestant whose piety or good taste has been offended by sentimental ditties like "In the Garden" really should witness the closing of the tabernacle at the end of such a novena devotion in a Roman church—known to the faithful as "putting Jesus to bed"—during which the lights are dimmed and the congregation sings the lullably "Good Night, Sweet Jesus," one of the two or three most popular religious songs among Roman Catholic lay people.[11] The relatively chaste ceremonies of the mass simply cannot stand the competition of this maudlin religiosity.

The spectacle of novena competing with mass once more illustrates the ambiguity which is the theme of this chapter. Argue though we may with its formulas and rituals, the mass of the Roman church is certainly one of the greatest efforts of Christian history to give solemn expression to the mystery of the faith. Roman Catholic eucharistic devotion at its best knows the profound meaning of mystery. But this very sacrament provides the means for sentimentality and even superstition. Protestants may be overly sensitive about the worship of images, but the tabernacle piety of many Roman Catholics certainly seems to have crossed the line of idolatry. The worst part of it is that the church not only tolerates but encourages such practices. The leaders of the liturgical movement have been warned in no uncertain terms by the pope himself that they had better not disparage the popular devotions centering in the tabernacle.[12] More than one parish priest who has tried to curb the excesses of such devotions has learned how deeply rooted they are in folk piety and how dangerous they are for the cultivation of true catholic piety as well as for the sacramental life generally. Sometimes it seems that one cannot have mystery *without* magic, but that one cannot have mystery *with* magic either; for eventually the magic cheapens the mystery itself.

119

Penance

Nowhere is the ambiguity of the Roman Catholic sacramental system more evident than in the sacrament of penance.[13] At its best, it is the voice of the church announcing the gospel of God's free grace and forgiveness to its members. At its worst, it is the crucifixion of consciences. Penance is classically defined as involving three steps. The first is contrition, which means, according to the Council of Trent, "a sorrow of mind and a detestation for sin committed with the purpose of not sinning in the future." [14] One who feels this contrition is then obliged to go on to the second step, confession to a priest. In confession the penitent is to recite all his mortal sins—deliberate acts of loving the creature more than the Creator. Functioning as a judge, the priest inquires into any circumstances that might mitigate the offense. When he has heard the confession, the priest pronounces the forgiveness of sins in the formula of absolution: "I absolve you from your sins in the name of the Father and of the Son and of the Holy Spirit." Then the priest prescribes the third step of penance, the performance of certain acts of satisfaction. As a truly penitent thief will try to pay back what he has stolen, so the Christian will demonstrate his penitence and absolution by making reparation to those whom he has wronged, including God. Satisfaction usually takes the form of pious deeds like extra prayers or alms. These deeds do not buy the forgiveness of sins, as many Protestants (and not a few Roman Catholics) suppose; they merely represent a restitution for the wrong that has been committed.

Through the administration of these three steps—contrition, confession, and satisfaction—the church has a splendid opportunity to apply the healing power of the gospel to the concrete needs of the penitent. In the hands of a conscientious pastor, the sacrament of penance makes divine grace meaningful without minimizing the individual's responsibility for his sin. It is, at its best, a truly evangelical means for "the cure of souls," one whose benefits Protantism has discarded too easily, and one for which a friendly chat with the minister is not a satisfactory substitute.[15] Psychologically, too, private confession is sound, enabling a person to "come clean" about his guilty feelings and to know that he has forgiveness from God in spite of anything he may have done. The therapeutic value of this is difficult to overestimate. Members of the church will testify how useful they have found this, and former members will admit how much they miss it. Here, as nowhere else in the entire Roman Catholic system, the delicate balance between God's gifts and God's demands can be maintained and individualized.

Here, as nowhere else, that delicate balance can also be destroyed —and almost always in the direction of stressing God's demands. Christianity can easily degenerate into a religion of "Do this" and "Don't do that"; there are examples aplenty in both Protestant and Roman Catholic history to demonstrate that. At its worst, the penitential system can torture a sensitive conscience with uncertainty and guilt. In the hands of an unskilled or domineering priest, the great power and authority of the confessional can be used to pry into private lives, to arouse compunctions and scruples over petty offenses, and to impose an intolerable burden upon the penitent. All this it can do for the person who is genuinely sincere about it. The person who takes it lightly can make "short shrift" of it (a phrase that originated in the penitential system). If he does, it is his own fault; but in the case of the guilt-ridden person the fault does not lie with him, but with the system and with the way the system is administered. Like the other sacraments, penance accentuates the riddle of Roman Catholicism by bringing out the best and the worst in the church: the best, which is its concern for imparting the grace of God and its understanding of human frailty; and the worst, which is its tendency to "play God" and to tyrannize its members with the law.

Extreme Unction

"From the cradle to the grave" means literally just that. For as the believer begins life with the sacrament of baptism, so he ends life with the sacrament of extreme unction, the anointing of his body when he is in danger of death.[16] Holy oil is used here, as in confirmation and ordination, to convey the grace of God for a particular need. To receive it, the person does not have to be actually dying, but "in

121

danger of death." Most people, however, postpone the anointing until they are near death. The precise meaning of extreme unction, like that of confirmation, has usually been quite vague in Roman Catholic theology. The anointings spoken of in the New Testament, to which Roman Catholic theologians usually refer as proof that Christ instituted extreme unction, seem to have been intended principally to heal the sick and not to be a means of grace at all. (See Mark 6:13 and Jas. 5:14-15.) In the discussions of extreme unction the idea of healing has continued to play a role, but one subordinate to the sacramental. Yet the sacramental function is very difficult to define; even Thomas Aquinas has difficulty identifying the precise effect for which extreme unction was instituted, and the relation of the forgiveness supposedly conveyed by it to the forgiveness conveyed by the absolution of a sick or dying believer. More recent expositions of the church's teaching about this sacrament manifest similar difficulty with it.

In the church's piety, extreme unction does hold a definite place. This is a place it has usurped from the "viaticum," the administration of the eucharist to those in danger of death.[17] Lay people are frequently referring only to extreme unction when they speak of "the last rites of the church," or they regard the viaticum as part of the extreme unction. Actually, the preparation of a soul for death, the communication of divine grace, and the anticipation of the resurrection are all ancient functions of the eucharist in Christian thought. It is therefore eminently suited for the use of people who are *in extremis*. The problem of how to deal with the comatose, confronted also by any Protestant clergyman in his ministry to the sick and dying, led to a greater emphasis upon extreme unction, which does not depend upon the consciousness of the patient. Normally, confession (with absolution) and holy communion (viaticum) would seem to be the way for a believer to be fortified by the sacraments of the church in preparation for death.

Marriage

These five sacraments—baptism, confirmation, eucharist, penance, and extreme unction—are the constituents of the sacramental life of every Roman Catholic believer. The remaining two, marriage and holy orders, are almost (but not quite) mutually exclusive. Thus it is extremely rare for any Roman Catholic to receive all seven sacraments of the church in his lifetime. A widower who is ordained to the priesthood would receive all seven, and so would a married priest in a Uniat or Eastern rite church.

Under the qualifications of a sacrament as enumerated at the beginning of this chapter (p. 111), it is difficult to defend the definition of marriage as a sacrament.[18] It does not employ an external means in the usual sense of the word, as baptism employs water and the eucharist employs bread and wine. It cannot claim to have been instituted by Christ, for marriage belongs to the order of creation and is as old as humanity; Roman dogma is therefore obliged to maintain that Christ elevated marriage to the status of a sacrament in the case of baptized persons.[19] Nor does marriage as such function as a means of grace, for the grace that is conveyed in a Christian marriage is the grace which the word of God and the sacraments convey. Thus marriage does not meet the qualifications. Yet it is the only one of these seven sacred actions to which the New Testament applied the term *mysterion*, which is translated in the Latin version with *sacramentum*. (See Eph. 5:32.) That quirk of language and the story of Jesus at the marriage feast in Cana of Galilee are the chief scriptural grounds on which the sacramental character of marriage is based. Neither of them is very convincing, and in the nineteenth century there was an attempt to revise the church's teaching on this count as well. In reply the Syllabus of Errors condemned the teaching that "the sacrament of matrimony is nothing but an appendage to the contract and separable from it, and the sacrament itself consists merely in the nuptial blessing." [20]

At least the classification of marriage as a sacrament has acted as a curb upon the excesses of certain writers in praise of monasticism and celibacy. The official teaching of the church that virginity is a higher state than marriage has sometimes led church writers to depreciate marriage as something necessary because of the weakness of people. The church has sometimes abetted such depreciation by its

123

law that all clergy must be unmarried. Counteracting this tendency has been the church's stress upon the sacramental character of marriage. Upon this basis the defenders of marriage have been able to glorify it as a way of life blessed in the sight of God and to denounce the modern secular inclination toward ridicule and even contempt of the married estate. That is certainly a worthy intent, and one with which no Christian can quarrel, but it does not justify calling marriage a sacrament. The reformers praised marriage highly as an institution of God, but refused to call it a sacrament any more than other good and necessary things which God has instituted. In its practice and in the way its lay people actually regard marriage, the Roman church has acknowledged the validity of this criticism. The wedding ceremony is not, of course, the sacrament, but the living together of the two people is. Yet the nuptial mass which accompanies the ceremony is the most sacramental aspect of the whole thing for many Roman Catholics, and they do not look upon the actual life of their marriage as a means of divine grace in and of itself, but as an occasion within which grace can come to them.

Holy Orders

Supporting all the other sacraments as their validation is the sacrament of holy orders or ordination.[21] Baptism may indeed be administered by a lay person or even by a heretic in an emergency, but ordinarily it should be administered by a validly ordained priest. Technically speaking, the priest is not the minister in the sacrament of marriage; the two parties are. Yet they are required to execute the contract of their marriage in the presence of an ordained priest. In each sacrament, then, the grace of the sacrament is channeled through the grace of the priesthood. It is therefore appropriate that elevation to the priesthood be itself regarded as a sacrament. Like the sacrament of confirmation, the sacrament of holy orders is administered by a bishop. There is no exception to this rule. This is because the bishops are said to be the direct successors of the apostles, transmitting from them in unbroken succession "the gift of God that is within you

124

through the laying on of my hands," as the Second Letter to Timothy calls it (1:6).

From this statement and others like it in the New Testament, especially in the Book of Acts and the letters to Timothy and Titus, it seems that there is very early support for the sacrament of ordination. As we have seen in Chapter II, the concept of an ordered ministry was one of constituent elements in the rise of catholic Christianity. Its specifically sacramental character, however, has been the subject of considerable evolution. The present teaching of the church maintains that the sacrament of holy orders confers upon the priest a special measure of divine grace for the performance of the duties of his office, as well as the divine authority he needs in that office. It maintains, moreover, that even when the priest as a person is a hypocrite and therefore not in a state of grace, the sacrament of holy orders is valid and therefore validates the other sacraments which he may administer.

A nice question in the Roman Catholic doctrine of holy orders is the sacramental status of the episcopate. If the priesthood, as the validation of the other sacraments, must itself be a sacrament, then must not the episcopate, as the validation of the sacrament of holy orders, be a distinct sacrament too? Some Roman Catholic theologians have thought so, but the evolution of the church's sacramental teaching has not gone this far. Instead, most theologians maintain that the office of the bishop is the priesthood raised to its fullest power and authority. Hence the elevation of a priest to the episcopate is an extension or application of the sacrament of holy orders, rather than a separate sacrament. The right to confirm, to ordain, and to exercise the jurisdiction of the episcopal office can therefore be said to belong to the sacrament of holy orders and to be conferred upon the candidate for the episcopate as the last and highest installment of that sacrament.

Once it has been validly administered, the sacrament of holy orders is not to be repeated; for, like baptism and confirmation, it stamps an indelible character upon the recipient. Graham Greene's novel, *The Power and the Glory*, is a moving and powerful documentation of

125

what this indelible character can mean even in the case of a "whisky priest." Both the priest himself and the people who accept his ministrations know that he has been unfaithful, and yet the indelible character is there. In a Roman Catholic parish it sets the priest apart from the body of believers generally, endowing the exercise of his ministry with a divine quality. Not a little of the power borne by his office, which we discussed in Chapter VI, is derived from its sacramental character. The priesthood does not merely dispense sacraments, it is a sacrament itself.

The Sacramental System

Roman Catholicism stands or falls with the sacramental system. The sacramental system is therefore the point at which one must clarify his evaluation of Roman Catholicism. Mystery and magic—in these two terms we stated our initial evaluation; for only he has comprehended the sacramental system who recognizes the profound mystery to which it bears witness and the fearful abuse to which it is repeatedly and perhaps inescapably subject. Protestant criticism of the whole system as "magic" would be more valid if the mystery of the faith had not been so thoroughly dispelled in so many Protestant churches. Roman Catholicism, on the other hand, has not done as much as it could to avoid the criticism. In many parishes the "sacramentals" of holy water, the rosary, and the like have crowded out the historic sacraments of the church. Even in the case of the sacraments themselves, the church has not listened to the sound advice of its own children to re-examine its sacramental teaching.

From such re-examination, some of which we have echoed here, some necessary revision might come. Thus confirmation has genuine difficulty standing on its own feet as a distinct sacrament; its sacramental character is drawn from its association with baptism and with first communion. Extreme unction is likewise difficult to defend as a sacrament distinct from the absolution of the penitent and the administration of the viaticum. The sacramental character of marriage is a dubious thing in the tradition of the church itself, as well as in contemporary Roman Catholic dogmatic theology. This leaves four sacraments. Two of them, baptism and the eucharist, are accepted by all Christians who accept sacraments at all. Of the other two, penance —or really absolution—is actually the proclamation of the word of forgiveness made individual for the penitent; holy orders is a sacrament with good biblical precedent, as long as it is interpreted as the church's way of validating its ministry of both word and sacraments. Now this reduction is not intended as a handy formula on which all Christians will automatically agree, but as an illustration of the sort of examination to which the sacramental system of Roman Catholicism needs to be subjected. Such examination must also look more closely at the question of mystery and magic, to see what steps can be taken to drive away the demons of superstition from the piety and practice of the church.

Above all, Roman Catholicism needs to do something about the level and quality of its preaching. Word and sacraments belong together. Where there is word without sacraments, the result is the barren rationalism that so easily besets Protestants; where there are sacraments without word, the result is the magic that so easily besets Roman Catholics. Yet the command to preach is as explicit and as loud in the New Testament as is the command to celebrate the sacraments. If it is accompanied by a genuine proclamation of the Christian gospel, the sacramental system can be made meaningful and be rescued from its perversions. Left to stand alone, the sacramental system slips again and again into those perversions, until a reform movement arises to pull it out for a time. The tragedy of the Reformation, of which we spoke in Chapter V, is painfully evident here. Preaching and the sacraments need each other. What God has joined together, man dare not put asunder.

IX

Ave Maria

✠ "Hail, Mary, full of grace, the Lord is with thee. Blessed art thou amongst women, and blessed is the fruit of thy womb, Jesus. Holy Mary, mother of God, pray for us sinners now and at the hour of our death. Amen." These words of the Ave Maria, spoken daily by millions of Roman Catholics, summarize one of the most perplexing elements in the riddle of Roman Catholicism, the cult of prayer and veneration addressed to the Blessed Virgin Mary.

Other elements in that riddle may seem strange or even fascinating, but the cult of the Blessed Virgin is downright repugnant to many non-Roman Christians. They look upon it as a species of idolatry or a vestigial remnant of pre-Christian paganism. They smile tolerantly when they see or hear the invocation of the saints by Roman Catholics, or read notices in the "Personal" column of a metropolitan newspaper that say: "Thanks to St. Jude and the Blessed Virgin for obtaining an apartment for us." Even those Protestants who look at the mass with respect rather than suspicion are caught short by the ven-

128

eration of Mary. In the eyes of many Protestant lay people this is surely the most obnoxious feature of Roman Catholicism. Here, they say, you have to draw the line beyond which Christianity dare not go. Protestant theology, too, sees in the cult of Mary, as it has climaxed now in the dogma of the Assumption, one of the chief barriers between Roman Catholics and Protestants. Even sympathetic Protestant theologians felt constrained to warn in 1950:

> While today the majority of churches with tears of penitence confess before God that they share in the guilt of a divided Body of Christ, and in common prayer and serious scholarly effort seek to diminish the area of disagreement and increase the area of agreement . . . the Roman Church would increase the area of disagreement by a dogma of the Assumption. Creation of a dogma of the Assumption would be interpreted today in the midst of the efforts at closer relationships between the churches as a fundamental veto on the part of the Roman Church.[1]

Thus there is very little sympathy for Roman Catholic Mariology outside the borders of the Roman communion. The historical development of Mariology is not my concern here; I have sketched it briefly elsewhere.[2] What I am concerned to do is to go beyond the usual Protestant suspicions and accusations to an interpretation of the genius of Roman Catholicism as this is reflected in its picture of Mary. I also want to examine that picture critically and to point toward a biblical and evangelical view of Mary. As the text for all this I shall employ the phrases of the Ave Maria.

Holy Mary

Calling Mary "holy" was originally a way of speaking not about Mary herself at all, but about Jesus Christ. Almost every reference to her in the earliest Christian literature is, in point of fact, a reference to her son. When Paul says that Christ was "born of woman," he is saying nothing about Mary, but is asserting that our Lord was truly human. (See Gal. 4:4.) Even the narratives of Matthew and Luke, which tell of her conceiving without a man, are aimed at the glorification of Christ, not of Mary. Whatever else may be said about the idea

129

of the virgin birth, it is a declaration about Jesus Christ. It means that even in the circumstances of his humble birth Jesus manifested God's power and freedom over the created world and its laws. To that power and freedom it points as a sign. Even without the sign of the virgin birth, the gospels of Mark and John and the epistles of Paul are able to speak of the power and the freedom of God in Christ. The sign loses its power as a sign, its "significance," when it is interpreted as merely an incredible happening or when it is taken as a key to the holiness of Mary. Mary and Pontius Pilate are the only two ordinary people mentioned in the Apostles' Creed. Both are there as signs pointing to Jesus Christ—one to show his lordship even in infancy, the other to show his lordship even in death. Neither Mary nor Pilate is important as a figure in history except for the role each of them played in the career of our Lord.

Very early in the church's history, however, the Virgin Mary began to acquire importance on her own.[3] When she did, it was the virgin birth that first attracted the attention of Christian believers and thinkers, who began to surmise that Jesus was holy and sinless because in his birth he had been free of the taint of sin. Lurking just below the surface of this kind of thinking is the feeling that there is something dirty and sinful about sexual relations, and that a Jesus who was born of the normal union between a man and a woman could not have been free of sin. In Christianity that feeling took hold through the beginnings of the monastic system, which strove for purity through sexual abstinence and celibacy. It is more than chance that the same church fathers who promoted monasticism and clerical celibacy were the ones whose speculations about the virgin birth resulted in the heightening of emphasis upon the holiness of the Virgin Mary.[4] Christian people acquired the notion that there is something intrinsically holier about virginity than about marriage, and Mary the virgin has become the ideal of sexual self-denial and self-dedication. Joseph has likewise become a symbol of "the celibate husband," who vowed perfect chastity before marriage and who kept his vow unbroken throughout the years of his life with Mary.[5]

So it is that the idea of Mary's virginity before the birth of Jesus

130

has been expanded into the notion of her perpetual virginity. When the New Testament says that Joseph did not "know her" sexually "until she had borne a son," (Matt. 1:25) this must be taken to mean that he did not know her sexually afterwards either. When the gospels repeatedly mention brothers of Jesus, these must be taken to mean cousins or, possibly, children of Joseph by a previous marriage —although even this interpretation is suspect now.[6] When Jesus is called her "first-born son" (Luke 2:7) in the Christmas story, this does not imply that there were other sons after him. By such reasoning the ancient catholic church, both East and West, elevated the notion of the perpetual virginity of Mary to the status of a dogma, to be believed by all Christians. This it did in the fifth century, and on the basis of this tradition the notion was universally accepted in Christendom for more than a millennium. Luther not only repeated the tradition, but vigorously defended the perpetual virginity of Mary against its detractors.[7] Briefly stated, the catholic reasoning was: if Christ was holy, he must have been born, without the aid of a human father, of a holy virgin mother; and if the virgin mother was truly holy, she must have remained a virgin all her life.

From this reasoning it is only a step, though a fairly long step, to the supposition that if the virgin mother was truly holy, she must have been holy not only in her life but also in her very conception and birth. That supposition was advanced by many theologians and pious believers throughout the centuries, but did not achieve official recognition and dogmatic status until Pope Pius IX declared it to be the dogma of the church in 1854 that Mary "at the first instant of her conception was preserved immaculate from all stain of original sin, by the singular grace and privilege granted her by Almighty God, through the merits of Christ Jesus, Savior of mankind." [8] About the general significance of the dogma of the Immaculate Conception we have spoken earlier. It has completed the chain of reasoning begun by the surmise that the sinlessness of Jesus—asserted throughout the New Testament not on the basis of his virgin birth, but on the evidence of his life—depends upon his being free of the taint that comes from having two human parents. Now Mary may conceive immaculately

131

THE RIDDLE OF ROMAN CATHOLICISM

because she herself has been conceived immaculately. She may be addressed as "Holy Mary" because her holiness has been safeguarded throughout her life and even before. She is the unstained and holy virgin.

Mother of God

In the Ave Maria the Virgin is addressed not only as "Holy Mary," but as "mother of God." [9] Like the dogma of her perpetual virginity, this title is an inheritance from the fifth century, when its use occasioned a great theological controversy. Originally this title too was a way of speaking about Christ. Because in the one person Jesus Christ the divine nature and the human nature are inseparably joined, it is proper to say that the child to whom Mary gave birth is the Son of God, is truly God. Hence it follows that Mary may properly be spoken of as not merely the "mother of Christ" but the "mother of God." What the title means to say is that since Christ is truly God, there was no time in his earthly life when he was not God, not even the moment of his birth. The logic of this inference is impeccable. It follows necessarily from the implications of the doctrine of the incarnation as this is laid down in the New Testament and as if was developed by the church's theologians during the fourth century. If Christ is God, then his mother must be the mother of God.

Yet "mother of God" does have an almost blasphemous sound to ears that have been attuned to biblical speech. It seems to carry echoes from other places than the Bible and from other gods than the God of Abraham, Isaac, and Jacob, the Father of our Lord Jesus Christ. Historians of the ancient church have frequently pointed to the symbolic coincidence that the title "mother of God" (*Theotokos*) should have been approved in 431 by a Christian council meeting in Ephesus, the city where the temple to the mother goddess has been so important to the business of the silversmiths that they started a riot with the cry: "Great is Artemis of the Ephesians!" The worship of the divine mother, which Christian monotheism had thrown out headlong through the front door, now crept back in through the back door. The logic with which it is possible to justify the title "mother of God" in Christian usage cannot fumigate it of its previous connotations, as its role in the history of catholic piety amply demonstrates. It belongs to the riddle of Roman Catholicism that this title, which was intended to buttress the central and sole importance of Jesus Christ as the Mediator between God and man, should be used instead to foist another agency of mediation upon the church. It was a bulwark against paganism, but it has become instead a relic of paganism in the mind and soul of catholic people.

That is, of course, its actual strength in the Roman Catholic system. Mary the mother of God is the bridge between Roman Catholic Christianity and the other religions of the world. Missionaries tell of her appeal in pagan lands, of pagans who would not listen to the story of Christ but were fascinated by the figure of Mary. As we come to the Father through the Son, so they come to the Son through the mother. Recently, when a Roman Catholic graduate student had completed a study of the Babylonian goddess Ishtar, who represents many embarrassing parallels to Mary, he could say quite unabashedly: "Now I understand Our Lady better!" The longings and meanings which paganism communicates through its goddesses and its worship of the feminine principle can thus become what Paul calls the Jewish law, "our custodian until Christ came" (Gal. 3:24). They are the dim recognition of something valid and important in man's religious nature, but something that must be rescued from the debasement of pagan worship. Through the cult of Mary the church acknowledges the validity of these longings and meanings and seeks to meet them, but it also seeks to elevate them and to put them into their proper place. The worship of the feminine principle in paganism is debased and debasing because there is no historical figure in pagan religion to control and direct it. In Roman Catholicism it is not the feminine principle or female sexuality that is the object of veneration, but a specific historical figure, Mary of Nazareth, and a figure who is important only on account of her relation to Another. Thus a pagan can be transported from his mother goddess to the mother of God, and from her in turn to her divine Son; all this by easy stages—entirely too easy, in fact.

133

The mother of God is also a bridge to the entire world of nature. Christian faith has had considerable difficulty incorporating the world of natural process and of change into its view of God's activity. The battle between theology and evolution during the nineteenth century dealt not merely with the authority of Scripture, but with the problem of how to talk about God's being above the world and before the world and yet to affirm that God is involved in the processes of nature. If a theologian stresses the involvement too directly, he loses God's identity in the world of nature and makes the word "God" merely a devout way of talking about process. If he stresses the lordship and the otherness of God, he is in danger of abstracting God from the natural process. There are resources within Christian theology for dealing with this difficulty, and current Protestant theology is engaged in discovering these.[10] But for Roman Catholic theology these resources have been enriched by the addition of Mariology. She represents involvement in the processes of nature; after all, what is more directly involved in them than motherhood, even virginal motherhood? Yet she is the mother of God. By being born of her, Christ becomes truly man, involved in nature; yet he remains truly God, sovereign over nature. Like the Demiurge in Plato's *Timaeus*, Mary the mother of God is God's way of giving structure to the world of nature and yet avoiding complete identification with that world. Because of her, in Chesterton's phrase. "Man has stripped from his soul the last rag of nature-worship, and can return to nature." [11]

As the mother of God, who performs this function in the plan of God, Mary is entitled to the veneration of the church. The term "veneration" is the one which Roman Catholic writers have tried to use as a translation for dulia, the worship that may be paid to saints and angels; the Blessed Virgin is the object of the highest veneration, hyperdulia. This is to be distinguished from latria, the worship that belongs to God alone and not to any creature; for latria they have tried to establish the word "adoration." The distinction is very difficult to reproduce in English. It is even more difficult to observe in Roman Catholic religious practice. Apologists for Roman Catholicism sometimes make the charge that Protestants deliberately ignore this

134

distinction when they criticize the worship of Mary. "It is hardly needful to remark," writes one such apologist, "that catholics too, even the most unlearned, are in no peril of confounding the adoration due to God with the religious honor given to any finite creature, even when the word *worship*, owing to the poverty of our language, is applied to both." [12] To say the very least, there certainly is more than a little peril that the veneration which a devout person addresses to the mother of God might be only less than, rather than different from, the adoration addressed to God the Father.

Pray for Us!

As the mother of God, Mary is also our intercessor to whom the petition is addressed: "Holy Mary, mother of God, pray for us sinners now and at the hour of our death. Amen." Veneration belongs to all the saints and even to the angels, but she is queen of them all. The prayers addressed to her heap up titles and praises; she is queen of martyrs, queen of angels, queen of heaven.[13] As the saints hold a special place among men, so she holds a special place among the saints. Together with them, she intercedes on our behalf. Although the ultimate address of every Christian prayer is to God, a Christian prayer may nevertheless take the form of a request to a saint to intercede for us. The saints have their special provinces and areas of concern. Thus St. Apollonia has had special concern for people with a toothache, St. Vincent Martyr for winegrowers, St. Crispin for shoemakers, St. Patrick for Irishmen; medals and statues can be used to protect motorists. Historians of religion have been quick to point out analogies between this division of labor and the "departmental deities" of polytheism, where Thor was god of thunder among the Norse or Perun performed the same function among the Slavs. There are certainly instances where a Christian saint took over the patronate previously assigned to a pre-Christian secondary deity or even his name, but it is a historical mistake to explain the invocation of the saints as primarily due to this.

Originally the veneration of the saints seems to have arisen in the respect paid to the memory of the apostles and martyrs during the

135

first centuries of the church. The places where they lived and died and were buried had special meaning for the early Christians, and sometimes churches were built over their graves. The worship addressed to God in such a church naturally had overtones of the saint or martyr in whose memory the church has been erected. Augustine spoke for the entire ancient church when he clearly distinguished these churches from the temples which the pagans had erected to the glory of the Roman deities:

> They built temples to these gods of theirs, and set up altars, and ordained priests, and appointed sacrifices; but to our martyrs we build, not temples as if they were gods, but monuments as to dead men whose spirits live with God. Neither do we erect altars at these monuments that we may sacrifice to the martyrs, but to the one God of the martyrs and of ourselves.[14]

Very consciously, then, the early church sought to avoid the impression that its veneration of the memory of the saints had anything in common with the worship of the departmental deities of paganism. The distinction between them was clear.

The distinction did not remain clear, however. At the very time that Augustine was expounding his argument, the church was growing in popularity and in size as a result of the Christianization of the empire. This growth, to which we referred earlier as a factor in the rise of catholicism, also helped to transform the veneration of the saints. Because of what we have called the comprehensiveness of catholic piety, the church was able to use the veneration of the saints to attract and to satisfy its newly won converts. Having once done so, it moved very slowly in the task of exterminating the pests of paganism which it had acquired, so slowly indeed that fifteen centuries later it is still struggling against them. Although the official teaching of the church, with its separation between veneration and adoration, is a modern version of the distinction espoused by Augustine, the piety at Lourdes or at Guadalupe or at Fatima demonstrates how blurred that distinction often becomes in the common mind. "St. Jude, help!" may mean officially: "St. Jude, I ask you for your intercession to our Lord Jesus Christ, before whom you and I both stand in judgment and in prayer. As you prayed with and for your fellow-believers when you were alive, I ask you to pray with and for me now, that, if it be God's will, I may obtain divine help." But in the personal life of the person who utters the prayer, St. Jude can help directly; therefore Roman Catholics often pray to him directly.

This is pre-eminently true of the Blessed Virgin. By virtue of her elevated status among the saints, prayer to her is especially effective. There is some fear being expressed now, however, that her status may become so elevated that the people will shy away from her majesty as they have from Christ's. Then it may be necessary to invoke her mother, St. Anne—sometimes actually spoken of as "the grandmother of God"—to intercede with Mary. The history of Mariology in modern Roman Catholicism has seen the continuous elevation of her status. Its climax came in 1950 with the promulgation of the notion of her assumption into heaven as a dogma of the church: "The Immaculate Mother of God, the ever Virgin Mary, after completing her course of life upon earth, was assumed to the glory of heaven both in body and in soul." [15] This notion is a perfect complement to the idea of the Immaculate Conception, promulgated almost a century earlier. It is now the official teaching of the church that Mary is free of the taint that infects both the beginning and the end of human life. In both birth and death, therefore, she is different from other people; in both birth and death she resembles her divine Son. The dogma of the catholic church has always run the danger of glorifying Christ so much that it cut him off from the humanity he was to save. Now the dogma of the Roman Catholic Church is running a similar danger in its Mariology. More and more, the attributes ascribed to her seem closer to those of Christ than to those of common mortals. She was conceived in a special way, she performs miracles, she intercedes for us, she was assumed into heaven.

All that is needed yet is to say that she is co-mediatress and co-redemptress with Christ. That, apparently, is not very far off. These titles are already being used in church literature, with official approval. They signify the role of Mary in the redemption of mankind through

137

Christ. Her answer to the angel, "Behold I am the handmaid of the Lord; let it be to me according to your word," (Luke 1:38) is what made the incarnation possible; for if she had not given her free consent, the Son of God would not have become man. Christ is the second Adam; Mary is the second Eve. As the disobedience of Eve is the human means by which sin has come upon all men, so the obedience of Mary is the human means by which salvation has come upon all men.[16] Mary is, in the language of scholastic theology, the "secondary cause" of Christ's incarnation and our redemption. This, technically speaking, is what co-redemptress means, but like "mother of God," it is a title that aptly summarizes the function which she has assumed in the unsophisticated piety of countless millions. As in medieval painting and poetry she shows her breasts to her Son because then he cannot refuse to grant any of her requests, so in the devotion of modern Roman Catholics Mary is the mediator of all grace and the channel through which we send our prayers to heaven: "Holy Mary, mother of God, pray for us sinners now and at the hour of our death. Amen."

Blessed Among Women

What is a Protestant to make of Roman Catholic Mariology? Not merely the outspoken or unknowing critics of everything Roman Catholic, but even sympathetic and well-informed interpreters must be appalled by the direction it has taken.[17] More than one friend of the Roman communion has been constrained to say that in its Mariology it has taken into its piety and its theology a force which it cannot control. During the early centuries of its development the catholic church discovered that it could not control the speculative doctrines of Gnosticism about the origin and the fall of the world. Even though there were echoes of such doctrines within the New Testament itself, the church broke with them and has always been very reluctant to see them reintroduced. For it knows that there are some emphases which can find their proper place within Christian teaching and thus enrich it, but that there are others "too hot to handle." The promulgation of the Immaculate Conception a century ago and of the assumption at the middle of this century threatens to make Roman Catholicism a universal nature religion, and thus to disturb the delicate balance between universality and identity which has been the genius of catholicism from the outset.

This is not to deny the attractive and even profound insights which modern Mariology contains. As we have seen, it enables Roman Catholicism to incorporate a full-blown view of the world of nature into its system without sacrificing the sovereign otherness of God. Only in our own day has Protestant thought begun to realize the riches it has lost by excluding the world of nature so radically from its purview, and it remains to be seen whether its reconsideration of this area will approach the profundity evident in Roman Catholic Mariology. The cult of the Blessed Virgin Mary has likewise helped to soften the harsh picture of God which prophetic religion so frequently produces. For reasons that lie beyond the scope of this book to analyze, an over-emphasis upon the prophetic element in religion tends to exaggerate the austerity of God. Perhaps it is extreme to say, with certain psychologists and with philosophical theologians like Berdyaev, that the traditional Christian conception of God is too exclusively masculine and needs the introduction of feminine qualities. If it is right to call God "Father," then there must also be something about God that is analogous to what a mother is and does. However one may assess this criticism, it remains clear that the image of the Virgin Mother is, in Karl Adam's phrase, "as it were a gracious revelation of certain ineffable and ultimate traits in the nature of God, which are too fine and too delicate to be grasped otherwise than as reflected in the mirror of a mother." [18]

It must also be admitted that Protestant attacks upon the "idolatrous" piety of Roman Catholic believers have not always been completely realistic about the piety of Protestant believers. In a remarkably trenchant discussion of this, the Protestant theologian Walther von Loewenich has made this telling point:

The worship of God in spirit and in truth is an ideal that is only seldom attained in its entirety. Only certain individuals, as for example the great mystics, have been capable of it. Basically, all popular piety is a compro-

139

mise. Only a few people grasp the idea that we can approach God only through pictures and symbols. But it would be cruel to deprive the great mass of simple souls of such pictures and symbols, for this would cut them off from any access to the being of God itself. Why should not God hear even a prayer addressed to Mary if it rises from a simple, pious heart? To use a figure, God must smile at our more spiritual forms of devotion and our high theological skill, just as we adults kindly recognize the serious purpose manifest in the games of children. . . . Many a Protestant fanatic, who flies into a rage when he sees a votive tablet with the motto "Mary has helped me," does not realize at all how petty his own basic idea of God is. Perhaps this same fanatic regards it as his sacred duty to tie God's salvation to some particular dogmatic formula. . . . No, naïve and unconscious paganism is not the real evil in Marian piety.[19]

The real evil is in the elevation of this naïve piety to the status of a system and in the use of advertising tricks to "merchandise" the cult of Mary. The simple and unreflecting Ave Maria of a South American peon is one thing, and a multi-volume theological opus on "the prerogatives of the B.V.M." is quite another thing.[20] The theologians and bishops of the church, who ought to watch and to warn the faithful of the excesses in such piety, are actually the ones who encourage the excesses. In the autumn of 1950, in the very week when he proclaimed the dogma of the Assumption, Pope Pius XII had several visions of the Virgin, during which he also saw the sun do a dance in the sky to the honor of Our Lady of Fatima. Instead of using the picture of the Blessed Virgin as a means of emphasizing the centrality of Christ—as we have seen, this is the historic role of the Virgin in biblical and early Christian thought—the leaders of the Roman communion forbid the faithful to become so occupied with the adoration of Christ and the Father that they neglect the Virgin; for Christ and the Father will not look with favor upon anyone who is rude to the mother of God. Beyond this, there are obviously some political motives at work in the present campaign to glorify the Blessed Virgin. The apparition of the Virgin at Fatima was directly linked to the clash between the church and Portuguese anticlericalism, and it has been used as a basic weapon in the church's campaign against "Bolshevism," a term elastic enough to include all sorts and conditions of men who have opposed church policies in the Latin lands. It is all of this that the Protestant critic has in mind when he voices profound misgivings about the cult of Mary.

Misgivings are not enough, however. The Protestant criticism of Roman Catholic Mariology will not do any more than score debating points until it is accompanied by a positive discussion of the mother of our Lord as viewed from a biblical and evangelical perspective. "Behold," she said, "henceforth all generations will call me blessed." This generation should be no exception. Older Protestant theologies found a great deal of room for a discussion of the angels, about whom they were better informed than we have any right to be. Surely, if the angels are a proper subject of theological discourse though we know so little about them, the historical figure of Mary may well claim the attention of Protestant theologians. Truth is, we know very little about her either. What we do know and what we may safely say deserves to be said, if only because Roman Catholicism has said so much about her that it has done her a dishonor. In any Protestant Mariology (if one may put those two words together) there are two insights that must be included—Mary's significance for Christ and Mary's significance for the church.

Mary's significance for Christ is the one which she has had since the first century.[21] She is the warrant for the Christian declaration that our Lord was a true man, flesh of our flesh and bone of our bone. If he was not, then, as the early church discovered through its conflict with heresy, the whole of Christian faith is lost. Yet it is not only heresy that has threatened his true humanity. Devout believers in every age have tended to doubt that he was really a man in every sense, one who perspired and grew weary and wondered about things. As a counterbalance to this tendency, the church put the phrase "born of the Virgin Mary" into the creed. He must have been human, because he was born of a woman. Because this tendency to deny the true humanity of Jesus is universal among Christians, the need to counterbalance it by means of Mary is also universal. Orthodox Protestant theology certainly ran the danger of losing the true humanity of the Lord, and liberal Protestant theology was not as free of the

141

danger as it supposed. Both need to speak of Mary as the guarantee of the Incarnation.

They also need to speak of Mary as the prototype of the Christian believer in the church. The brief description of her career in the New Testament is a summary of the Christian life in its elations and in its depressions. Not only must she be a warrant for the true humanity of Christ; her own true humanity must be recaptured. There is very little resemblance between the queen of heaven and the Jewish maid whom the gospels portray. Protestant thought can speak frankly about her faith and its struggles, about her apparent misunderstanding of her Son's true mission, about the refusal of Jesus to make any physical relationship to him (even hers) a mark of true blessedness, about her doubts and her victory over those doubts. These are all themes in the biblical portrait of Mary, themes which appear in the lives of Christian believers everywhere. When the New Testament urges that Christians consider the cloud of witnesses who surround them as they run the race of faith, it certainly includes the first witness of the life and work of Jesus Christ—his mother. Not as a semi-divine being, but as an outstanding member of the communion of saints, she is blessed among women. When Protestants begin to say this out loud in their teaching and worship, and not merely to whisper it in their hearts, as most of them indeed do, then they will be better prepared to speak a word of fraternal warning to their Roman Catholic brethren. Then they will be able to say that their regard for Mary is so deep that they must protest against the cult of the Blessed Virgin.

X

The Angelic Doctor

✠ Roman Catholicism is a house with many mansions. For the man who cannot stand alone, its organization provides a fellowship that supports and directs. For the man whom the appetites of the body cannot satisfy, its sacraments provide the food and drink of the soul. For the man whose mind refuses to be content with scraps of knowledge, its theology and philosophy provide a world-view so comprehensive and so profound that he can truly bring his intellect with all its powers into the service of Christ the King. Although many Protestants criticize Roman Catholicism for its ignorance and superstition, they must also acknowledge that in Roman Catholic Thomism they confront a system of thought for which there is no equivalent in Protestantism. That system of thought takes its inspiration and insight from the theological and philosophical work of St. Thomas Aquinas (d. 1274), nicknamed "the Angelic Doctor." [1]

143

The Origins of Thomism

The Thomistic system came into existence as a response to a two-fold need of the medieval church, an internal need and an external need. As we have seen, the church calls upon theologians to perform a dual responsibility in its name. Theologians have a responsibility for the definition of the church's teaching in relation to its sources in divine revelation. At the same time, theologians also have a responsibility for the clarification of the church's teaching in its relation to the situation of general human thought and culture. There have been many men and movements in the history of theology who have concentrated upon one or the other of these responsibilities as the need of the hour seemed to require. There have been very few who have been able to ignore either responsibility completely, even fewer who have managed to do equal justice to both. It is the greatness of Thomas Aquinas that in recognizing the theological need of his hour he did do justice to both responsibilities, writing a system that was churchly theology as well as what Paul Tillich has called "answering theology." [2]

By the thirteenth century the church needed a theological system that would bring together the principal elements of its tradition into a unity. Responding as it had to the challenges of heretics and to the immediate needs of its life, the theology of the church contained many emphases and viewpoints that were in need of clarification and harmonization. Indeed, so varied were many of these emphases and viewpoints that it was possible for a theologian like Peter Abelard (for reasons that are still the subject of debate) to line up traditional answers on both sides of many important theological questions.[3] The time had come for someone to look at these traditional answers and to show the connections between them. In a way, the situation of the church resembled that of a political candidate who has been asked to summarize his philosophy of government. Although he has been obliged to speak out on many specific issues as they arose, he is now required to synthesize the central position from which he has spoken out. So, too, the church of the thirteenth century needed a theologian to act as its spokesman and interpreter in expounding the central position expressed through the creeds, dogmas, and doctrinal declarations of its history. There is an inner dynamic within the Christian faith itself which demands such a systematic exposition. It is the need to include the arc of the intellect in the circle of faith.

Thomas Aquinas recognized that need and he met it. He undertook the composition of his great theological work at the behest of a divine vision which commanded him to write. He prepared himself for the task by studying the church fathers, especially Augustine, and by commenting in detail upon most of the books of the Bible. When he came to compose his great *Summa* of theology, therefore, he possessed the necessary equipment for a grand synthesis of the church's faith and teaching. Drawing upon this equipment and upon the learning of predecessors like Peter Lombard (d. 1160 or 1164 [4]), Thomas was able to line up the alternative Christian answers to theological issues ranging from the Persons in the Trinity to the nature of baptismal grace. There are three parts to the *Summa Theologica*. The first deals with the nature of God and the origin of all things in God; the second describes the nature of man and the renewal of that nature by the Holy Spirit; the third takes up the doctrine of Christ and the meaning of the sacraments.

Thomas did not finish the third part of the *Summa Theologica*, but from the way he proceeded in the main body of the work it is possible to gauge the method of his entire synthesis. Where the contradictions within the tradition were based upon semantic differences, Thomas was quick to note that the same word was being used in different ways. Where a church father had erred, Thomas corrected him gently, preferably by citing a passage from the father's own writings. Most often, however, Thomas was able to show that each of the positions he had cited was part of a larger whole, and thus to affirm the entire tradition by going beyond its apparent contradictions to the unity of the faith. What seemed to be a conflict between one father and another was thus resolved, and the harmony between them was manifested.

In order to deal this way with the contradictions in the tradition of the church, Thomas made use of the newly discovered works of Aristotle. Aristotle taught him, for example, how to distinguish the several "causes" that come together to produce an action or event. What is the cause of man's predestination? Over this question Augustine and Pelagius had clashed during the fifth century. By a deft manipulation of the Aristotelian distinction of causes, Aquinas could show that the predestinating action of God was indeed the sole "primary cause" of man's salvation, but that the co-operation of man's free will with God was nevertheless the "secondary cause." [5] Other distinctions and definitions from Aristotle were likewise helpful in the task of clarifying the meaning of the church's decrees or the fathers' dicta. What Abelard and Peter Lombard had lacked in their considerations of traditional teachings Thomas got from Aristotle— an apparatus of thought comprehensive enough to include the whole tradition and yet particular enough to clarify and define the terms employed by this or that doctor of the church. It is difficult to imagine how any other apparatus of thought could have managed to do both. If this was his assignment, it seems that Thomas Aquinas almost had to be an Aristotelian.

Being an Aristotelian also enabled Thomas to perform the second task that needed to be undertaken, that of showing the relation between faith and reason. It is interesting that the theology of the church did not get around to a thoroughgoing treatment of this question until the primacy of faith had been universally acknowledged. When the church was in the minority, as we have seen, its spokesmen had to deal with the despisers of Christianity among the cultural classes, showing the harmony between the church's message and the best in classical culture. A systematic statement of that harmony had to wait until the church was no longer on the defensive. Then—as though to make sure that it had not won its victory too cheaply— the theology of the church looked with serious attention at the claims of the unaided human reason to know the way to God. Anselm of Canterbury (d. 1109) is the most famous of the thinkers who raised again the question of how much the human mind can know about God. He looked within the mind itself for the answer to this question, coming to the conclusion that the structure of the mind and the nature of thought demonstrated the existence of God. Even though one may repudiate this conclusion, as Thomas Aquinas did, Anselm did lay upon subsequent theologians the responsibility of inquiring into the capacities and limitations of human reason in matters of religion. After Anslem, this was a responsibility which no theologian could evade.

Thomas certainly cannot be accused of evading this responsibility. His other great work, the *Summa contra Gentiles*, is addressed specifically to it. Before undertaking the theological synthesis of which we have just been speaking, his great theological *Summa* also made extensive inquiry into the ways of knowing that were identified with philosophy. These could only deal with the realm of nature, to be sure, while the revelation of grace in Christ belonged to a realm above nature; but as Thomas says in the theme of this entire discussion, "grace does not abolish nature, but sustains and perfects it." [6] This theme he directs against anyone who would so completely identify grace and nature, or theology and philosophy, that there is no need of the former. He is also attacking those extremists who would deny the validity of what reason and nature can discover on their own. Ultimately, then, faith and reason are directed toward the same objects, but are different ways of reaching them. There are some things which reason cannot discover, not because they are contrary to reason but because they are above reason; the two best known examples in Thomas are creation out of nothing and the doctrine of the Trinity. What reason does know, it knows for sure. Thomas wants nothing to do, therefore, with any attempt to glorify God and his grace by disparaging the powers of human reason. Because he is a theologian of the church, he wants to take philosophy seriously.

Theologian and philosopher at the same time, and neither one without the other—this is the Angelic Doctor. He combined his great learning and astuteness with a genuine appreciation for the non-intellectual aspects of man's life in God, for liturgy and the sacraments and mysticism. Even those who have criticized his theology and philosophy most seriously have found his life and character wholly admirable. But it is on his theology and philosophy that he must finally be judged. Seldom before and seldom since have these two

147

ways of knowing been as carefully balanced, integrated without being identified, distinguished without being divorced. The problems with which Thomas deals are in many ways peculiar to the thirteenth century, and his solutions also betray their historical setting. Yet the issues behind the problems are universal in Christian thought; and therefore, as we shall see in the rest of this chapter, Christians have repeatedly been forced to a consideration of those issues, with or without the help of Thomas Aquinas.

The Enthronement of Thomism

For anyone accustomed to the dominant position of Thomistic philosophy and theology in modern Roman Catholicism, it may be a surprise to learn that the initial response to Thomism was cool. In the decades following Thomas' death in 1274, his system of thought was condemned not only by the Franciscan monks, who were the rivals of his Dominican order, but by theological faculties and by bishops.[7] So deep-rooted had the church's suspicion of philosophy been, especially of the philosophy of Aristotle, that the Thomistic synthesis looked like a sellout of the Christian faith. Nor did it help matters that Thomas had corrected Augustine on both philosophical and theological grounds.[8] Because earlier efforts to harmonize the faith with the philosophy of Aristotle had seriously undermined fundamental tenets of the faith, Thomas' critics took these corrections of Augustine to be a subjection of Augustine's theological orthodoxy to the judgment of an alien philosophical system. Actually, as Thomas' defenders maintained, it was an effort to rescue Augustine from some of the philosophical consequences of his own thought, and to do so in the name of the theological orthodoxy which Augustine had so nobly advanced. Far from being a repudiation of Augustinianism, Thomism was Augustianism purged of some of its concessions to Neoplatonic philosophy. Or, to put it in Thomistic language, Thomas does not abolish Augustine, but sustains and perfects him.

It did not take very long for the church to recognize this. In 1323 Thomas was made a saint, and by the time of the Reformation his star was clearly in the ascendancy. The polemics of the reformers testified to this by the severity of their attacks upon Thomism, attacks that were frequently based upon very poor knowledge of Thomas' writings. Other philosophical and theological movements continued in the church; the best known of these is the Franciscan school of theologians represented by Duns Scotus (d. 1308) and William of Ockham (d. ca. 1349). The dependence of the reformers upon this school only helped to fortify the authority of Thomas. The doctrinal decisions of the Council of Trent, consequently, have often been read as the official acceptance of the Thomistic system. In many individual doctrines this is clearly not the case, and current scholarship is drastically revising both the Protestant and the Roman Catholic stereotypes about Trent. Nevertheless, the method which Trent employed in dealing with the controversial doctrines was closely akin to the theological method of Thomism: a study of the alternative positions bequeathed to it by the tradition, followed by an effort to find a formula that would include the valid insights from each of them. Although its doctrine of justification differed from that of Thomas, the Council of Trent did advance the cause of Thomism by sanctioning the Thomistic method.[9]

Since the Council of Trent, the Thomistic system has steadily increased its hold upon the intellectual life of the Roman communion. In part this has been due to the attacks of modern secularism upon the gospel and the church. As these attacks from the outside have become more overt, the prestige of Thomism inside the church has grown. During the eighteenth century those attacks came primarily from a rationalism which rejected Thomas as too traditional and authoritarian. During the nineteenth century the attacks began to come from the other pole, as Kantian, Darwinian, and Freudian thought (each in its own way) accused Thomism of being too rationalistic and intellectual. Against the first the church defended Thomas' theology, against the second it defended Thomas' philosophy; against both it defended his synthesis of theology and philosophy. A series of brilliant defenders and expositors of Thomism, beginning with Cajetan (d. 1534) in the period of the Reformation, helped to prove that the Thomistic system could speak to an intellectual milieu quite

149

different from the one in which it originally arose. No other theological or philosophical tradition has fared as well. Augustinianism has always had an honored place, but it has a bad habit of spawning heretics—Gottschalk, Luther, Pascal, von Hügel, to name only a few. But even under the fire of the secularists Thomism has stood up well.

Thomism has also stood up as a bulwark against modern theology. Already at the Vatican Council of 1870 it was noised about that the study of Thomism was a road to ecclesiastical advancement, for there were "red hats lying between the pages of the *Summa*." During the decades after the Vatican Council the modernists launched their program of theological revision, in which both the philosophy and the theology of Thomas came in for fundamental criticism. The church's reply to this attack upon Thomism from within was the same as its reply to the attacks upon Thomism from without—to assign an even more secure place to Thomas on the throne of the thought. Pope Leo XIII underscored this in repeated pronouncements about Thomism as *the* Christian philosophy. Societies and academies were established for the study of Thomism. An endless stream of monographs, dissertations, and journals began to appear, dealing with the significance of Thomism for everything from angels to witchcraft.[10] After the excesses of Protestant and secular books about the "Dark Ages" (which sometimes seem to have lasted until Luther), came the excesses of modern Roman Catholic historians, who have canonized the thirteenth century as "the age of faith," "the greatest of centuries," and "the springtime of Europe." The Thomistic revival has wiped out much of the resistance to Thomas within the church, though by no means all of it, as we shall see a little later. It has enthroned Thomas Aquinas as the one thinker who is indispensable to any Roman Catholic thought in any field of human knowledge.

The Appeal of Thomism

The rise of Thomism to a dominant place in the life and thought of the Roman communion is due in part to the espousal of its cause by the leadership of the church. That there are more Thomists in

150

the world today than there are adherents of any other philosophical position is not only because Thomism is so convincing as a philosophical position. Like Marxism, it has the advantage of being an official ideology, which one may examine but which one may not fundamentally question. A Roman Catholic thinker once said to me that he was "a Thomist, of course." But a philosophical and theological viewpoint is not something to which one comes "of course." It depends for its acceptance upon more than its official endorsement as the party line of an authoritarian group, whether this group be a church or a political party. Its appeal, therefore, must be based upon its intrinsic correctness, upon the way it makes sense out of human knowledge and experience.

Entirely apart from the Roman Catholic party line, Thomism is capable of making such an appeal, and of making it very effectively. It has, indeed, been instrumental in drawing to Roman Catholicism people who regarded other features in the life of the church with suspicion or even hostility. As the program of Thomism represents both an interpretation of the Christian tradition and a dialogue with philosophy, so its appeal is based upon both tradition and philosophy. It holds an appeal for any theologian who has outgrown the naïve notion that all he needs to do his job as a theologian is a Bible and a prayer. As soon as a theologian recognizes his debt to the history of Christian doctrine, he must listen seriously to those theologians who have consciously endeavored to use history in the construction of their theological systems. The Protestant theologian who has gone through the reformers to the ancient church, upon which the reformers depended, must feel himself drawn to this theology; for it tries to codify and to consolidate the dogmas of the ancient church, without accepting wholesale all the philosophical and scientific notions attached to those dogmas in the formulations of the ancient church.[11] Critical though he must be of the way Thomism handles the tradition of the church, a Protestant theologian must also see in Thomism a responsible alternative to his own interpretation of the tradition, if any, and an alternative whose power he must acknowledge before he rejects it. The recovery of tradition by Protestant theology, of which we shall speak in Chapter XIII, makes it necessary that Protestant theologians recognize the appeal of Thomism as a synthesis of the Christian tradition.

Protestant theologians must also recognize the appeal of Thomism as a theology with intellectual respectability. Although the minority status of the Roman Catholic intelligentsia in America has made even theology suspect in the eyes of many, the Thomist theologian can ply his craft without the apologies that so often form the preface of Protestant theology. There are times when Protestant theology seems forced to choose between capitulation to philosophy and hostility to philosophy, with no alternative in-between, while Roman Catholic theology not only speaks to the philosophers but even listens to the philosophers—at least to certain philosophers. Thomist theology recognizes what a large sector of conservative Protestant theology refuses to recognize—that the tradition of the church, the inner urgency of the faith, and the nature of the intellectual enterprise all compel the theologian to pay attention to philosophy. A theologian who, for one or another of these reasons, discovers the necessity of philosophical inquiry cannot evade the claims of the most widely held philosophical theology in all Christendom. Both the need for a sympathetic-critical use of the tradition and the necessity of a dialogue between philosophy and theology endow the Thomist scheme with an appeal for any Christian theologian.

The theologian is not the only intellectual for whom Thomism holds an appeal. It has managed to speak persuasively to the problems of thoughtful men in many fields of inquiry. When a probing mind sounds the depth of any field, it finds itself faced with questions about God, man, and the world. Nothing seemed further from these questions a generation ago than modern physics; yet in its own study of the universe as well as in the moral problems raised by the atom and hydrogen bombs, physics has begun to sound its own depths and to come up with these very questions. What such a mind needs is an interpretation of the relation between God and the world that will provide ultimate meaning without endangering the freedom of research and inquiry. Thomism is such an interpretation, or at least it

152

is the starting point from which such an interpretation becomes possible. As it stands historically, the Thomistic system is deeply involved in the scientific notions of the thirteenth century. Therefore it cannot be transplanted directly into the thought world of a nuclear physicist. Yet the openness toward non-Christian scientific thought which Thomas manifests in using Aristotle's *Physics* should enable modern Thomists to be equally open toward the scientific thought of a new age.[12] The transfer is, to be sure, not as simple as all that, as the struggle between Thomism and modern science during the eighteenth and nineteenth century makes painfully evident. Nevertheless, the "middle way" of Thomism does enable its adherents to be both modern and devout.

It is amusing, therefore, that the conversion of an intellectual to Roman Catholicism is usually interpreted as an abject surrender to an authoritarian system, and often interpreted by means of categories from Freud. Actually, there is no orthodox Christian tradition in the modern world that demands less of an intellectual surrender than Rome! Roman Catholicism is not the last stop on the line, but a halfway house between the church and the world, where the secular mind may get just enough religion to satisfy its needs but not enough to question its natural propensities. In spite of its violent opposition to Roman Catholicism, the liberal Protestant theology of the past century has actually been an attempt to construct a similar halfway house under Protestant auspices. Protestantism lacked the overarching and undergirding of the church and the tradition, within which Roman Catholicism is gradually learning to be quite relaxed about modern thought. Hence the appeal of Thomism to the intellectual is not merely the attractiveness of an ultimate authority that has all the answers, but the allure of an ultimate authority that lets me have my own answers to any questions except the ultimate questions. For, after all, grace does not abolish nature, but sustains and perfects it. All that is required of nature is that it know its own limitations and remain within them, leaving to grace what properly belongs to grace but meanwhile doing its own distinctive task as well as it can.

153

The Revolt against Thomism

Yet all is not so tidy among Roman Catholic thinkers either. In many sections of the church today there is a growing restlessness with the domination of Thomism over the intellectual life, and an increasingly vocal demand that other points of view be allowed to assume a legitimate place among Roman Catholic intellectuals. This demand is coming, for example, from natural scientists. Despite the friendly attitude toward nontheological thought which is a basic part of Thomism, some Roman Catholic scientists are critical of the predominantly deductive bent of Thomistic thought and its lack of emphasis upon empirical study, experimentation, and the assembling of data as means of arriving at truth. This is, they maintain, a blind spot in Thomism, which prevents it from developing a sound method for either the natural sciences or the social sciences. Thomistic thought prefers to move from axioms and premises to conclusions, reasoning about what is "fitting" in view of what we know about the world. Until comparatively recent times, by contrast, modern science has espoused a method that moves from particular data to hypotheses; historians have sometimes made similar claims for their method. Even when scientists and historians are becoming more self-conscious about the role of hidden axioms in their work, they have seriously questioned the ability of Thomism to make room for either experimental science or history in its theory of knowledge, and have therefore asked Thomism to learn from modern science and historiography as it once learned from Aristotle.

Spokesmen for contemporary literature and contemporary philosophy have likewise questioned the adequacy of Thomism as a philosophical framework for what they have to say.[13] The most provocative such criticism is coming, interestingly enough, from a small group of philosophers. In an earlier chapter we noted the estrangement between Roman Catholic philosophers and their philosophical colleagues outside the church. Partly as a means of overcoming that estrangement and partly as a reflection of the philosophical mood of our time, several Roman Catholic philosophers have become engaged in the philosophical movement known as existentialism.[14] Whereas

154

scholastic philosophy has concerned itself almost exclusively with "essence," these men have made a plea for a philosophy of "existence," a philosophy of life rather than a philosophy of being. Although there have been several efforts to show that Thomism contains the resources for a Christian existentialism, some Roman Catholic existentialists have frankly admitted that they are actually going far beyond the comparatively static "essentialistic" categories of the Thomist system.

Still the principal source of the revolt against Thomism has not been among scientists or philosophers, but among theologians. They are the ones who have been chipping away at the authority of Thomas on the grounds that an undue concentration upon Thomism may rob the church of the blessings and insights that are available in the rest of its tradition. Thus Martin Grabmann (d. 1949), an outstanding authority on Thomas, complains that too many Thomists have neglected his relation to the church fathers, and that the Thomism which emerges from such neglect is thereby improverished.[15] Even beyond recognizing that Thomas Aquinas stands on the shoulders of the fathers, especially of Augustine, many Roman Catholic theologians have begun to discover that the fathers are giants in their own right and do not need an Aquinas to give them stature. Students of medieval thought have begun to remind us that there is a tradition of medieval philosophy quite apart from the Thomistic, and that this tradition deserves to be studied.[16] Augustine continues to find exponents and defenders, who point to the resources which his thought provides for a more profound theology than that of Thomas. In recent years several Roman Catholic scholars have paid new attention to the Greek fathers, who speak about the mysteries of the faith in a way that is more dynamic and more relevant than the static language of scholasticism. Thomas spoke as an expositor of the catholic tradition; therefore it is by the catholic tradition that his work must be measured, and from the catholic tradition that his work must be corrected and enriched.

More even than the catholic tradition, the Scriptures are decisive in the thought of Thomas. Both from what he says about them and

155

from the way he uses them it is evident that he wants his theology measured against this criterion. More perhaps than any theologians since the days of Thomas, the Roman Catholic theologians of the twentieth century have taken him up on that. For in the first half of the twentieth century there has been a revival of biblical study within Roman Catholicism more profound and far-reaching than any since the Reformation. Instead of using biblical texts as mere props for official dogma, many a Roman Catholic theologian today asks first what the text means and only then how this meaning squares with official dogma. Sometimes it does not seem to square very well, and this puts the theologian into a difficult spot. The rationalizations employed here are fearfully and wondrously made, and the personal convictions of the theologian clearly incline him toward a position different from the official dogma. In addition to the warnings which one might expect, the Holy See has given definite encouragement to the resurgence of biblical theology and has allowed it considerable freedom in discussing conclusions that appear to diverge from the church's teachings. The biblical theologians, in turn, have allowed themselves to become more explicit about their divergence from the majority opinion and from Thomas. For instance, they lament the inability of Thomas to grasp the Old Testament background of New Testament ideas and his resulting tendency to interpret New Testament theology more according to Greek than according to Hebrew concepts.

Such a general criticism is fundamental, for it strikes at the very ability of Thomism to present itself as an interpretation of biblical religion. Its authors make this criticism stick when they deal with specific biblical passages or particular biblical teachings. The Sermon on the Mount, which at the hands of Thomism sounds like a combination of Aristotle's ethics and the rules of the monastic life, now becomes an exposition of life in the kingdom of God as that life is rooted in the history of God's people in the Old Testament and as it is embodied in the career of Jesus Christ.[17] Only the most inflexible Thomist will refuse to admit that this new insight into the Bible has enriched Roman Catholic theology and given it a quality and a depth which it lacks in its Thomistic interpreters. From the increasing attention to biblical theology among Roman Catholics in France, in Germany, and even in the United States it is clear that the Roman church is in for an exciting period of theological research and debate.

The Future of Thomism

What will be the outcome of this theological research and debate? Will it be in a position to pose a serious threat to the authority and prestige of Thomas? It seems unlikely that it will, at the level of the church's official teaching. To hope otherwise requires more optimism than most observers of the Roman church are able to summon. So deeply did Pius IX and Leo XIII commit the official theology of the church to the Angelic Doctor that a dethronement of Thomas Aquinas is extremely difficult to imagine. Rome is, of course, capable of amazing shifts. She has changed her mind before on issues where she had seemed adamant. Hence it is just possible, but not at all probable, that the Holy See will trim Thomism down to size and assign to it a place in the theology of the church that corresponds more closely to its intrinsic worth.

What seems somewhat more likely is that the teaching of the church will add the new insights of biblical and historical theology to the theology it already has. It will not abolish Thomism, but will sustain and perfect it. The power of the biblical message, once unchained in any church, has a way of compelling the church to revise its actual teaching even when it does not revise its official position. Thus one should hope not that Rome will convoke a council to "de-Thomasize" its theology, but that the theologians of Rome will continue to study the Bible and the tradition of the church without the blinders of Thomism. How they square the results of such study with the official Thomism of the church is ultimately less important than the honesty and open-mindedness with which they go at the interpretation of the Scriptures. As we shall see in Chapter XIII, the new emphasis of Roman Catholicism upon the Bible requires that Protestant theology do two things: renew its own willingness to hear

157

the message of the Holy Scriptures even when that message contradicts cherished prejudices and traditions, and pay attention to the word of God as it is spoken even and especially by the biblical theology of the Roman communion.

There is one more thing that Protestant theologians may be able to do—to rescue Thomas from the Thomists. As we have pointed out several times, a contrast between Thomas and his expositors usually comes out in favor of Thomas. His thought relied on the fathers much more than modern Thomism has. In his theological work the Scriptures bulked larger than they do in the tomes of the Thomistic theologians. He was a philosopher in order to be an honest theologian and did not make his philosophy an end in itself. Beyond these formal differences, the content of Thomas' theology is itself a surprise to any Protestant who expects a medieval version of present-day Roman Catholic teaching. As we have seen, Thomas went very far in his view of the superiority of Scripture to other sources of doctrine. He followed Augustine in glorifying divine grace rather than human merit as the ground of the relation between God and man. In these and other ways Thomas discloses an approach to Christian doctrine with which Protestant theology can come to terms more easily than it does with the papal encyclicals. Since this is so, Protestant theology needs to recover its contact with Thomas. It will discover that he is not as bad as his critics and his pupils make him out to be. In the process it will strengthen and deepen its own catholicity. Thus the future of Thomism would help to shape the future of theology throughout the church catholic, and that would be highly appropriate; for the Angelic Doctor died as he was traveling to a meeting in Lyons aimed at the reunion of a divided Christendom.

XI

Cultus and Culture

✠ These chapters have taken upon themselves the ambitious task of discovering and interpreting "the genius of Roman Catholicism." As they have shown, perhaps too well, this is a subtle thing, elusive of any simple definition or formula. For the genius of Roman Catholicism involves nothing less than an entire world view, an interpretation of nature and culture from a special perspective. The Blessed Virgin is a symbol and a bearer of that world view; so are the sacraments. In the way it handles the problem of church and state, Roman Catholicism is carrying out the implications of its distinctive view of the world. These implications also appear in its very definition of church and authority, as well as in its philosophical theology. Thus each of the main themes of Roman Catholic life and thought with which Part Two of this book has been dealing is illustrative of a whole attitude toward the world, and to each main theme the others are organically related through what we are calling the genius of Roman Catholicism.

Perhaps the most characteristic expression of that genius is the worship of the church. Here the church shows in action as well as in words and music how it regards the world around it, and how it interprets its own faith and inner life. The liturgy has often preserved Christian insights that have disappeared from the church's theology. Its intuitions have often been sounder than those of the clergy who used the liturgy. Its forms, archaic and ornate though they often are, have been the source of renewal and of reformation in the church throughout its history.[1] To study the worship of the Roman communion as merely the proliferation of these forms is to miss the deepest meaning both of the Roman communion and of its worship. This is true regardless of whether the study is bent upon wholesale criticism, as it is in the hands of many aggressive pamphleteers, or upon wholesale imitation, as it is in the hands of many precious specialists in liturgics. Liturgy is more than forms. The cultus is the church's commentary on culture.

The World Community

The attitude of Roman Catholicism toward culture is an interesting combination of the impulse to deny the world and the impulse to conquer the world. Both these impulses represent explicit imperatives in the New Testament, both are part of the church's historic strategy. Sometimes the one, sometimes the other has dominated that strategy, as the church's role in the culture has shifted. Werner Elert has spoken of "synthesis," the attempt to conquer culture by merging with it, and of "diastasis," the attempt to save the church's soul by a separation from culture.[2] Diastasis is clearly the major emphasis in the first two centuries of the church, synthesis is clearly the dominant emphasis in the Middle Ages. No church has ever pursued a strategy of only diastasis or only synthesis, and the strategy of Roman Catholicism uniquely brings the two together.

Denial of the world is an integral part of Roman Catholicism. Just as the monastic orders are a continuing reminder of the virtue of obedience, so they also serve to warn the church against following the example of Martha and neglecting the example of Mary. The famous interview between Pope Innocent III and Francis of Assisi, immortalized in the frescoes of Giotto, stresses the extent to which even this pontiff, hailed by church and state as "the lord of the world," had to submit to the ascetic ideal of poverty and world-denial, incarnate in *il Poverello*. To understand Rome, the tourist must visit not only the Vatican and St. Peter's, but the catacombs. The church has never forgotten them, and periodically in its history it has learned to go back to them. Sometimes Roman Catholicism seems so wrapped up in the world and its affairs that denial of the world sounds almost heretical. But those sociologists who have permitted this to delude them have failed to grasp the genius of Roman Catholicism, which has continually cherished and encouraged the denial of the world for Christ's sake.

Denial of the world there is in the Roman system, but the denial is often overshadowed by the conquest of the world. The use of secular culture by the church is more prominent than is the repudiation of culture. Some of this prominence is due to the glorification of the Middle Ages about which we have spoken here several times. Because the church maintained a control over culture that looks to modern eyes as though it were undisputed, the vision of "Christ above culture" provides the goal in the church's effort to conquer the world for Christ's sake.[3] The world community is the proper target for this effort because Christ is the Lord of all, and that through the church. Although the church in modern culture has had to content itself with much less than the conquest of the world, it has never surrendered the conviction that both for the church and for the culture the best arrangement is a Christian culture, where the faith of the church is the soul of the entire cultural life. These two themes of denial and conquest act and interact throughout the program of the Roman church.

The liturgy of the Roman church is the place where these two themes come together with the least distortion of either. Denial of the world expresses itself in more than the cloistered atmosphere of

161

the usual Roman chancel or the absence of a tonic in Gregorian chant. The liturgy of the church is peculiarly its own, separated from the world by the nature of the event it commemorates. Here the church celebrates an action of God to which it owes its existence, an action beyond that act of creation through which God created the world and made culture possible. Thus liturgy stresses the particular in the church's faith and life. What stands at the center of the liturgy is not culture but Christ, who is the distinguishing element between the church and culture. Therefore liturgy throws a highlight upon that feature of catholicity which Chapter II of this book calls "identity." At the same time it betokens the "universality" of the church and the conquest of the world by the church. The garb of the clergy, sacred now through centuries of association with the cultus, is the adaptation of secular clothing from other centuries. The language and the music of the liturgy are a mirror of the culture out of which they came. Indeed, the worship of the Roman church is one of the best available places to study late Roman and medieval culture. It is, in a way, a living fossil; so completely did the church conquer culture, and so completely was it conquered by culture. Identity plus universality is the ideal of catholicity, and the liturgy of the church is catholicity in action.

The Worshiping Community

Because liturgy is so important in the life of the Roman church and in its relation to culture, it can also serve as a basis for religious revival within the Roman church. During the past fifty years that is exactly what liturgy has done, producing in the modern liturgical movement a most profound and hopeful sign of change. Very few Protestants have paid any attention to the movement, and there is only one satisfactory Protestant treatment of it in English.[4] Yet it deserves the careful attention of any Protestant who wants to understand Roman Catholicism as it actually is, not as its defenders or its slanderers portray it. Originating in Europe, the liturgical movement has now taken hold in the American church as well. Although it is sometimes interpreted as merely a program for the revision of liturgical forms, the liturgical movement has set out to purify the church's worship as such, and thus to renew the church itself. Not merely the forms, but the substance of the church's worship is in need of reformation. To accomplish such a reformation, the liturgical movement has had to tread on many toes; for the attachment of clergy and laity to the types of worship which the movement seeks to eliminate, or at least to minimize, is so deep that there has been stout resistance to innovations, even when these innovations originated in Rome itself. Thus certain leaders of the American hierarchy did their best to prevent or to slow down the introduction of the new liturgy for Holy Week, which has now been adopted throughout the Roman church in America.

On a local scale, just such resistance is what a priest meets when he tries to wean the members of his parish away from the secondary forms of piety (like novenas, rosaries, and the "benediction of the blessed sacrament") and to draw them around the table of the eucharist. There is a revealing analogy between these secondary forms of piety and the devotion of many Protestant Christians, especially those in the "evangelical" tradition. In both groups the emphasis is upon the worshiping individual rather than upon the worshiping community and upon subjective feelings rather than upon the objective events of salvation. There is also an interesting analogy between the efforts of the liturgical movement to do something about the piety of the tabernacle and the efforts of Protestant leaders to find a more adequate expression of the faith of the church than the sentimentality that so often characterizes Protestant worship. The difference between the two is also important as an indication of the genius of Roman Catholicism and the genius of Protestantism. For while Protestant leaders have usually sought to do this by greater emphasis upon the word of God, the liturgical movement in Roman Catholicism has emphasized lay participation in the liturgy of the mass and communion as means by which the church may grow beyond the subjective attitudes associated with what we have called the secondary forms of piety.

Obviously this involves more than a question of forms. The nature

163

of the church itself is the real issue at stake here. If the church is primarily or exclusively the external organization of pope, bishops, priests, buildings, then it is permissible for the faithful to seek and to employ whatever forms of devotion this organization may permit them to have. Churchly worship is any worship that is sanctioned by the church. If the liturgical movement is correct in its recovery of the traditional Christian emphasis upon lay participation, upon communion, and upon an understanding of the liturgy, then the church must be something more than the external organization. Then the church must be something organic, not merely something organizational. The mystical body of Christ is what gathers together as a family around the table of the mercies of God. Here all the members of the body are priests, exercising their priestly office with and through the priest at the altar. Despite its high antiquity and its noble ancestry in the New Testament and the fathers, such a view of the church and the priesthood has often been suspect within Roman Catholicism because of its association with the reformers. By resuscitating it, the liturgical movement has restored the spiritual and mystical dimension to the doctrine of the church, which otherwise runs the danger of being simply a theological rationale for the existing structure of church organization.

If the church is indeed a worshiping community, its members must learn what is going on in their worship. To help them learn, the liturgical movement has emphasized the role of the sermon and of instruction about the liturgical year. The changing of the seasons in the church year corresponds to the main events in the life of Christ, and thus living the liturgical year can mean reviewing the life and work of Christ each year. The sermon is intended to explain this for the daily life of the people, who can follow the mass through the use of special missals prepared for them. As a result, a Roman Catholic layman of average intelligence and education can gain an excellent grasp of the liturgy and, through the liturgy, of the faith of the church. He can know himself to be part of a community of faith and worship, extended across both space and time. The ancient forms of that worship can acquire new relevance in his life as they are ex-

164

pounded to him. At its best therefore the liturgical movement can have a profound effect upon the Christian life and convictions of lay people. Any Protestant who has never attended mass in a liturgical parish is missing a highly meaningful experience.

Worship and the World

Liturgy belongs to "diastasis," the church's declaration of its identity. But it also belongs to "synthesis," the church's declaration of its universality and of its concern for the world. Paul Tillich is summarizing the best in both catholicism and Protestantism when he says:

The cultus is supposed to give an ultimate meaning to the daily life. It is not so important to produce new liturgies as it is to penetrate into the depths of what happens day by day, in labor and industry, in marriage and friendship, in social relations and recreation, in meditation and tranquility, in the unconscious and the conscious life. To elevate all this into the light of the eternal is the great task of cultus, and not to reshape a tradition traditionally.[5]

This is why cultus and culture belong together not only in their etymology, but in the life and strategy of the church.

To elevate the world of nature into the light of the eternal, the liturgy of the church employs the language and the symbols of nature worship, but seeks to exorcise them of their earlier meaning. In a culture where most Roman Catholics live in cities and where many of them have little daily contact with the processes of the created universe, liturgy is one remaining point of contact. As we shall see later in this chapter, this continually threatens liturgy with irrelevance to the problems that really bother people. But it can also serve to make urban worshipers conscious of what Peter Brunner calls "the cosmological setting" of Christian worship.[6] The palms and the lilies, the water and the salt, the fire and the ashes, above all the bread and the wine—all these are symbols of man's affinity with the rest of creation, and at the same time they are symbols of the church's worship. By these means the church can train the children of an in-

165

dustrial society to celebrate the tenderness and the fierceness of the world into which the Creator has put them, and to see in the Christ of the liturgy the assurance that the God who creates is the same as the God who redeems. There seems to be little danger in America that this will degenerate into nature mysticism, but a great deal of danger that without this element in the liturgy people may lose their membership in the world of nature or find the symbols of that membership completely outside the church.

A similar danger hangs over the arts, with which the liturgy of the church once had an exciting and fruitful interchange. For that reason, after centuries of mutual hostility between Roman Catholicism and some of the most creative forces in modern art, the liturgical movement has made an effort to enlist those forces in the service of Christian art and architecture once more. It has done this at the same time that it has agitated for the revival of ancient forms of worship. This conflict between ancient and modern is more apparent than real, because there are striking affinities between, let us say, the windows at Chartres and the work of a modern artist like Rouault. In keeping with their principle that the truly fine in Christian art has a timeless quality about it, the spokesmen for the liturgical movement find nothing inappropriate about chanting the sonorities of Gregorian amid the angularities of a modern church.[7] Here, too, the liturgical movement has stepped on many toes. The same piety that prefers sacramentals to sacraments and novenas to the mass will also prefer plaster saints and effeminate pictures of Jesus to the art forms advocated by the liturgical movement. While the liturgical movement in many Protestant communions has contented itself with an antiquarian interest in archaic forms for their own sake, the liturgical movement in Roman Catholicism has joined with the avant-garde of Protestant theology and culture to sponsor the use of contemporary art in the service of the church. Such Protestants and such Roman Catholics are both intent upon establishing some communication again between the worship of the church and current trends in the arts.

Communication with the arts is as difficult as it is because the liturgy of the church has lost touch with the daily life of the people. Restoring this will take some bold and imaginative planning. So many of the bridges between liturgy and life that were part of Roman Catholicism in Europe cannot do the job in America. The feast of the local patron saint is almost unknown this side of Quebec. A church which was so skillful in producing rituals for seedtime and harvest has no comparable ceremonies for steam fitters or insurance salesmen. One charming effort at a bridge between liturgy and life is a little cookbook published by the Catholic Rural Life Conference. Entitled *Cooking for Christ*, it is a collection of recipes for the entire liturgical year. In America it can draw upon the traditions of a dozen nationalities, each of which had invented special foods for certain days and seasons of the church calendar. Besides being interesting and delicious, the foods suggested in *Cooking for Christ* have a symbolic association with the liturgy, an association explained with cleverness and theological sophistication in the text of the cookbook.[8] But this is one of the few creative attempts to bring the rhythm of the liturgy into the tempo of everyday life, and much more remains to be done.

No single step would do more toward that end than the adoption of a liturgy in the language of the people. There are undoubtedly great advantages in the Latin liturgy, and anyone who knows Latin will find a stateliness in the Latin psalter not duplicated in any other translation, not even in the psalter of the King James Version. But there are more important qualities in the church's worship than stateliness. One of these is its adequacy as an expression of the church's life under the authority of God. Yet the very qualities that make the Latin liturgy most attractive may be an obstacle to its use as such an expression. The best arrangement that is possible under present regulations is the dialogue mass, in which the congregation speaks the responses usually chanted by the server. But this is still a makeshift. Happy though one must be over the introduction of this and other devices, lay people still find it disconcerting to hear Latin being chanted and English being spoken simultaneously, or to follow in their missals the English translation of the Latin being chanted at the altar. The mass of the church takes on some of the features of a foreign language movie with English subtitles, which, for all its attractiveness, remains the product of a foreign culture. Yet even this is an improvement and a step toward a vernacular liturgy. Someday it may become possible to introduce such a liturgy in Roman Catholicism.

Whether it does become possible or not depends upon whether Rome ever applies to Western cultures some of the principles which it has announced, if not always applied, with respect to Eastern cultures. The encyclical *Orientalium dignitas ecclesiarum*, issued by Pope Leo XIII on November 30, 1894, severely condemned the tendency of some Roman Catholics to insist that Eastern Orthodox churches Latinize their liturgies when they re-establish communion with Rome. On the contrary, this encyclical declares, they dare not do so, but must retain the rites of their own cultural traditions. Those Eastern groups who have come over to Rome, however, have not always received this courtesy. Some of them decided—and some of them were forced by the zeal of certain Roman orders—to alter their liturgies and to include elements of Western rites. But the principle stands as a demonstration of Rome's expressed desire for variety in unity rather than uniformity in the liturgical articulation of the church's faith. When it comes to the West, uniformity is the rule. Ruthenians in Gary, Indiana, or Scranton, Pennsylvania, may have the mass in their liturgical language, which is still not the spoken language of the people. But their Irish or German neighbors dare not have the mass in English. All this is, of course, a matter of church law and not of divine law; it may therefore be changed at any time. Hence the possibility continues to exist that the church may one day build a bridge of language between worship and the world. But all such possibilities lie in the future.

Worship and Community

Students of Roman Catholic liturgy like to speculate about the possible course of its further development. What, for example, will be the forms which Roman Catholic liturgy will acquire as it enters into a creative interchange with the cultures of Africa? The missionary enterprise of the Roman communion on the Dark Continent is already successful enough to arouse misgivings not only in Protestant churchmen but in French politicians, who see in it a further threat to their domain across the Mediterranean. The church's policy of encouraging the development of an indigenous clergy in the new areas of its work will certainly have a profound influence upon its liturgy. The Roman liturgy a century or two from now will bear traces of African, Chinese, Indian, and Japanese cultures, just as its present forms contain vestigial remnants of Greek, Roman, and Germanic cultures.

The lesson of liturgical history is the infinite adaptability of the liturgy to new needs and new cultural conditions. For most Protestants and for many Roman Catholics, the liturgy seems to be a stable, almost a stale thing. It is one of the things that remain the same amid the changes and chances of this present life. Such a static conception of liturgy is, as Roman Catholic observers have pointed out, part of the image which Roman Catholics in America have of Europe as "the old country," where all things are as they were when grandfather crossed the ocean.[9] Actually, the Christian liturgy has displayed astonishing plasticity—more, it must be admitted, in its Eastern than in its Western branch—and every indication points to even greater changes in the next centuries. In an intriguing book called *The Mass of the Future*, the Jesuit scholar Gerald Ellard has set down his speculations about the liturgical import of the changes awaiting the Roman church.[10] As Father Ellard makes clear, there is always a noticeable lag between the life of the church and the forms of its liturgy. Hence those forms often look toward the past rather than toward the present or the future. In an era of pervasive social and cultural changes the lag becomes so prominent that the liturgy may represent needs that no longer exist or use symbols that no longer speak for the common life. In several areas of the church's life within the American community, such a lag is manifesting itself; and thoughtful leaders of the Roman church are trying to interpret the meaning of this lag for the liturgy and the strategy of the church.

169

Perhaps the most obvious lag between liturgy and life is this: the major symbols of the liturgy are still drawn from the world of nature and from agricultural life, while the framework of reference for most Roman Catholics in America is urban and technological.[11] It is difficult to participate in the liturgy if its language is strange and its symbolism alien. One way to narrow this gap is to reclaim the land for Roman Catholicism, and the National Catholic Rural Life Conference has undertaken a program of such reclamation.[12] Believing that the Roman church has suffered in America through its close identification with the cities, the able leaders of the Conference seek to create Roman Catholic communities of farmers in the midst of the Protestant agricultural areas of the United States, transplanting groups of families from the steel mills to the cornfields and helping them to get a start in farming. There are many advantages to be gained from such a program, not the least of them the restoration to the church of an entire dimension of life without which large parts of the liturgy are unintelligible. But if liturgy and life are to come closer together, changes are necessary in the liturgy too. It must begin to draw upon the components of contemporary life—of streets and corners, shops and offices, parks and plazas—for its symbols.[13] The road to Walden, even to a Walden with shrines, is not the way out of the liturgical and cultural impasse of Roman Catholicism in America. Since it serves the culture of the city, it must draw upon the life of the city for the symbols of its cultus.

Cultus is important for the culture of the city in other ways as well. Increasingly, the institutions that work in the city are being forced by law and by necessity to face up to the changing racial complexion of the city. Even the churches have begun to reconsider their programs in the light of the constituency around them. The difference between Roman Catholic and Protestant churches on this score has been noted by a leading Protestant theologian, Reinhold Niebuhr:

Catholicism has been much more rigorous and successful than the Protestant churches on the racial issue. Partly this success is due to the hierarchi-

170

cal structure of the Church, and the consequent ability of bishops and priests to set standards even in defiance of lay opinion. . . .

The Catholic Church brings to issue the inclusive community of a sacramental rather than a chummy fellowship. The fellowship of the Protestant Church is always degenerating into a sanctified sense of kind, whether of race or class or neighborhood. The sacramental dimensions of the Catholic communion enlarge the communion of saints and conform it more nearly to the universal dimension intended in the gospel.[14]

Upon the insistence of their bishops, Roman Catholic parishes have stayed put in changing neighborhoods and have changed with their neighborhoods.[15] As Professor Niebuhr comments, a liturgical and sacramental orientation is a genuine asset in meeting this cultural and social challenge.

Yet the church cannot legislate for its members where they ought to live. Even though the church presses for racial integration in a changing neighborhood, therefore, many of the members prefer to join the great postwar emigration to the suburbs. These emigrants, like the earlier immigrants from Europe, take their Roman Catholicism with them; but they are also assiduous in learning the ways of their new culture. Sociological studies of Roman Catholic parishes in the suburban culture of America reveal that the suburban woman, for example, is the family chauffeur and an inveterate joiner, irrespective of the church she attends.[16] Further study of Roman Catholic sodalities in the suburbs would disclose how remarkable are the parallels between Roman Catholic and Protestant forms of social organization in this new culture, and how closely they both resemble the secular groups in these areas. Statistical success therefore is no criterion of how the Roman church is faring in suburbia. As one priest said to me, "St. Transfer is gaining more parishioners for me than all the saints in heaven!" It remains to be seen whether Roman Catholicism will avoid the dangers and capitalize on the opportunities in this setting. Recognition in the suburbs can mean the end of the ghetto for the church and acceptance as a legitimate and permanent part of a pluralistic America. The church can gain a position of intellectual and cultural leadership which it has never had in the United States. But

171

it faces the threat of a Babbittry with which it has rarely had to cope before. The churches, Protestant and Roman Catholic, can be the life of the suburbs; but the suburbs may also be the death of the churches.

The suburbs are, significantly, the location of some of the most creative liturgical experiments in the United States. Utilizing the desire of their members for closer social ties with their neighbors, the liturgical parishes in such a setting cultivate togetherness at the mass as a divinely appointed expression of the corporate life. Many of them have used the Cana conferences on Christian marriage as a means of applying the power of gospel and liturgy to the personal and social problems of their parishioners. Here again cultus is the church's commentary on culture and the church's bridge to culture. The more boldly the American church adopts the suggestions of the liturgical movement for making the cultus meaningful, the better will it be equipped to handle the spectrum of problems it faces as it operates in the rural, the urban, and the suburban climates. The genius of Roman Catholicism is the unique way it has found in the modern world of combining universality and identity. That genius enables it to meet people where they stand and to bring them the message of the church. It also equips the church to invite Christians of all denominations to make their faith complete by joining its membership. The Protestant who drives by a church and says to himself, "I wonder what it's like to be a Roman Catholic," has a better opportunity to find out today than he ever had before. What all of this means for our Protestant churches and for their relations with Roman Catholicism will concern us in Part Three of this book.

PART THREE

A THEOLOGICAL APPROACH
TO ROMAN CATHOLICISM

✠

Roman Catholicism is here to stay. Our brief survey of its evolution has revealed to us its staying power, our brief survey of its genius has given us a glimpse of its adaptability. Men have been predicting its downfall since the Reformation. Science, nationalism, democracy, historical criticism, universal literacy—these and other forces have all been hailed as the *coup de grace* that would crush the Roman church. But it has survived them all, though not without serious losses, and it is with us yet. Despite what its foes had hoped and its friends had feared, it survived the onslaught of Luther, Marx, and Darwin. It seems reasonable, therefore, to conclude that Protestants had better give up the hope of ever converting all Roman Catholics to a Protestant point of view. To some outside observers, indeed, the future of Protestantism is more problematical than that of Roman Catholicism. But even to an observer like this one, who believes that both Protestantism and Roman Catholicism have a function in Christendom and that they should be permitted to exercise it, the continued existence of the Roman communion has a greater significance for the life and faith of Protestant churches than most of their members and leaders are willing to face.

If the demise of Rome does not represent a genuine alternative in the years to come, Protestantism needs to develop an approach to Roman Catholicism that transcends the vacillation between aggressiveness and defensiveness which is the usual Protestant posture. Such an approach ought to be unabashedly theological in the sense that it proposes to deal with the questions of Christian faith that are at issue between the two parties. But in its insistence upon theology, the

175

Protestant approach must remember that Rome regards as matters of faith many issues in which Protestantism has traditionally allowed a difference of opinion. An approach to Rome must therefore include what might be called "a theological interpretation of nontheological factors."

How important it is for Protestants to develop this approach to Roman Catholicism has become evident from Protestant reactions to the announcement of January 25, 1959, that Pope John XXIII was issuing "an invitation to the separated [Christian] communities to seek unity, which so many desire in all parts of the world." Vatican sources have made it known that the primary purpose of the invitation was to re-establish theological discussions with the separated East rather than to enter into negotiations with Protestantism. The ecumenical council being summoned, presumably for 1961, will take up the points of difference between Orthodoxy and Rome. Yet Protestants cannot be indifferent to the outcome of such a council, even if it should turn out that they are not directly involved. The role of the Eastern Orthodox in the ecumenical movement would itself be enough to make the council a vital matter to Protestants. But Protestantism has a stake—and a much larger one—also in the question of the future course of Rome's relations and attitudes to "separated communities," be these communities Orthodox (and therefore schismatic or "dissident") or Protestant (and therefore not only schismatic, but also heretical). These relations and attitudes will largely determine the future course of any Protestant approach to Roman Catholicism.

Above all, any approach to Roman Catholicism must be simultaneously realistic and faithful—realistic in its assessment of the actual situation and its appraisal of what is possible short of unconditional surrender; faithful in its realization of the responsibility we all have as members of the church catholic not to "shrink from declaring . . . the whole counsel of God" (Acts 20:27) even when it hurts. The development of such an approach—not in five short chapters, but in the ongoing strategy of our churches—may well be the greatest single assignment to which the coming generations of American Protestants are summoned.

XII

The Unity We Have

✠ To meet the assignment of developing an approach to Roman Catholicism that is both realistic and faithful, Protestantism must begin with a survey of the common ground between the two. This is a task which the Protestant denominations will have to undertake separately as well as together, for they need to measure both their own distance from Rome and their relative distance from all the stations this side of Rome. Measuring both those distances becomes necessary for each new generation because the points are not fixed; as we have seen, even Rome has sometimes shifted. Repetition of old measurements can be disastrous if it overlooks the shifts in position on all sides. We begin with the common ground, with the unity we have, because this may revive in us a sense of urgency about the unity we seek. As Archbishop Temple said twenty years ago, "We could not seek union if we did not already possess unity. Those who have nothing in common do not deplore their estrangement." [1]

What we have in common is, in Albert Outler's happy phrase, "our common history as Christians," our participation, however varied and fragmented, in those saving events of Jesus Christ by which our Christian community was constituted.[2] We do not look for some least common denominator (or interdenominator) which means different things to different people but unites them on the basis of a formula. Rather, we look for the areas of agreement precisely because they are also the areas of our most basic disagreement. The unity we have is, when studied in its depth, also a revelation of our disunity. A study of this unity is therefore a guarantee against the fuzzy-minded idea that all our differences are matters of semantics or of sentiment or of "mere doctrine." But it is also an antidote against the type of Protestant chauvinism which refuses to think of Rome as anything except our ancient foe and the harlot of Babylon. In four fundamental affirmations—that the church is one, that the church is holy, that the church is catholic, that the church is apostolic—we shall examine the unity we have and with it the disunity we have.

The Church Is One

The church is one because Christ is one. "One body and one Spirit, . . . one Lord, one faith, one baptism" (Eph. 4:4-5) appears in both Protestant and Roman Catholic Bibles. We agree that the final ground for the unity of the church is not in anything men have done or ever can do for themselves, but in what God has done for men in Christ. The extent of this agreement dare not be overemphasized, for there is much debate over just what it is that God has done for men in Christ. But it dare not be underemphasized either. It represents the court of appeal beyond the usual claims on both sides. That Christ is, as the apostles and catholic fathers unanimously insist, the Head of the church; and that Christ is, in Luther's phrase, "the King and Lord of Scripture"—these admissions by both parties make the unity of the church in Christ something more than a slogan. They make it possible for us to submit our separation and our unity to the judgment of something given, something that has happened once and for all. Even though Roman Catholics may say that the only Christ we have is the Christ whose will is continually being expressed

178

by his vicar on earth, and even though Protestants may say that the Christ of Christian authority is the Christ interpreted by the Bible (interpreted, in turn, by these Protestants), we do have in our common allegiance to the name of Christ a common loyalty that is greater than our dedication to our churches or to their interpretation of the Bible. On this allegiance we all agree.

Where we disagree is on how this allegiance to Christ and this unity in Christ affect our unity as churches. As we saw in Chapter VI, Roman Catholicism is predicated on the conviction that it was Christ's intention to establish an external visible institution, built upon the rock of Peter the apostle and his successors at Rome. The unity of that institution is not subject to question, for the church simply cannot be divided. In repudiating the validity of Anglican ordination, Rome has expressly ruled out any "branch theory" of the church, according to which the Roman, the Eastern, and the Anglican (plus perhaps the Swedish) are all branches of the one catholic church.[3] Even more alien to Roman thinking would be the suggestion that oneness in Christ does not necessarily imply an agreement about the organization of the church at all, and that it is possible for Christians under various forms of church organization to acknowledge one another as brethren in the unity we have in Christ. Because of the equation of Roman Catholicism with the church, such a suggestion about the unity of the church begs the question, according to Rome; it assumes that there is a church membership which does not logically issue in submission to Roman authority. Discussion of the forthcoming ecumenical council makes clear that eager as many Roman Catholics are for reunion with Protestantism, they are unable to consider such reunion in the same way that Protestants have learned to view it as a result of the ecumenical movement.[4]

Instead, Rome's eagerness for reunion comes in the form of an invitation—"Return to Mother Church!" Whatever unity we have in Christ presses us toward a restoration of unity in the church, which we have lost. Since, by the Roman Catholic reading of history, Protestantism forsook the fellowship of the true church, reunion comes when Protestantism, like the prodigal son, comes back from the far country to be forgiven and accepted. The unity in Christ takes the form of a unity in church organization and in church doctrine. Traditionally, Protestants denounce such a view of unity as arrogant and stubborn, and it often is. But as one speaker reminded the Amsterdam assembly of the World Council of Churches, the basis of the difference is not arrogance or stubbornness, but a different interpretation of what the church is.[5] External and visible as the nature of the church is, the unity of the church must likewise consist in the acceptance of a uniform authority on earth. The only conclusion which even an irenic Roman Catholic can draw from this is the invitation to return. The corollary of "returning" is repudiating the Protestant heritage as a fundamental aberration from Christian truth and Christian love. The price of reunion with Rome seems indeed to be unconditional surrender.

In trying to achieve reunion with Eastern Orthodoxy, Rome maintains that it is not bent upon unconditional surrender at all, but wants the churches of the East to retain their own rites and their own patriarchs. All they need to do is to acknowledge that among the patriarchs of Christendom the patriarch of Rome has a primacy both of honor and of jurisdiction and that he is infallible in matters of faith and morals when he speaks ex cathedra.[6] That is certainly a great deal to have to acknowledge. Yet it is something less than a total repudiation of the Orthodox heritage. In the congress on Orthodox-Roman relations held at St. Procopius Abbey, Lisle, Illinois, on September 28, 1956, Western leaders sought to make clear that Rome accords to Orthodoxy a certain status as an equal in the ecumenical conversation; the same tone is evident in Pope John's invitation to an ecumenical council. Meanwhile Rome will not grant a similar status to Anglicanism or to any of the branches of Protestantism. Because Orthodoxy has remained orthodox in its faith and catholic in its polity, it must be fundamentally different in Roman eyes from any other separated part of Christendom. Two questions arise in this connection. First, does Roman Catholicism really mean what it says about respecting the integrity of the Orthodox tradition? The present voice of the church says yes, but the past record says no; therefore very few

Orthodox churchmen are willing to trust the seriousness of these protestations. Second, can Roman Catholicism ever apply a similar criterion to Protestantism? The present voice of the church and its past record both say no, and that seems to be the only possible answer; for a different approach to this heretical and schismatic group within the Western church would require a redefinition of the church, and that would mean a repudiation of the Roman Catholic heritage.

Nevertheless, the unity we have in Christ does give us a base of operations. The future of Protestantism, as Karl Adam says, is God's business; so, we might add, is the future of Roman Catholicism.[7] Because our unity is in Christ and will be in Christ, we know that it can come only as a gift from God. Gathered together by our common loyalty to him, we speak to one another as the Holy Spirit enlightens us through our several traditions; and we listen to one another as the Holy Spirit enlightens us through alien traditions. If the outcome of such speaking and listening is a new and deeper unity, so be it. If it is not, then we go on speaking and listening. The basis of our agreement is not a prayer that our opponents may be convinced of the rightness of our position, but a willingness to have the rightness of all our positions examined in the light of the allegiance we have to Christ and the unity we have in Christ. Whatever may come from such examination, God's will be done.

The Church Is Holy

As the church is one, so the church is holy. Indeed, the attribute of holiness seems to have been the earliest term applied to the church, for a very early version of the creed reads: "I believe in the Holy Ghost, the holy church." All Christians, Roman and non-Roman, would agree that the church is holy, but they would disagree about the specific meaning and content of its holiness. Most of them would probably agree that when we say that the church is holy, we do not mean that the individual members of the church have attained a state of moral perfection. Time was when many Protestants sought to contrast Protestantism and Roman Catholicism on this basis, contending that Roman Catholicism tolerated all sorts of deviations from the

181

standards of sound morality while Protestantism had tightened ethical lines by excluding manifest sinners from the company of the church. Thus the church in Protestantism could be holy in a sense in which the church in Roman Catholicism was not. But the attrition of the centuries has brought thinking Protestants to the recognition that their churches have no discernible moral superiority to other churches. If the church is holy, therefore, we must look beyond sexual standards or the statistics on consumption of alcoholic beverages or the relative honesty of Methodist and Roman Catholic public officials. The holiness of the church does not depend upon such issues as these.

In fact, the holiness of the church does not depend upon anything human. Like the unity of the church—like the church itself—the holiness of the church is a gift and creation of God. As we agree on this, so we disagree on the ways God uses to give and to create the holiness of the church. Roman Catholicism follows the position of Augustine in defining God's way of making the church holy.[8] When the Donatists were insisting that the holiness of the church was jeopardized by the ministry of hypocrites, Augustine came out for the objective validity and holiness of the church's sacraments, irrespective of the holiness or unholiness of those who administered the sacraments. In the words of Augustine's predecessor, St. Optatus, "the holiness of the church depends upon the sacraments, not upon the pride of people." [9] Such is still the teaching of the Roman church, a teaching which (as we have seen in Chapter VIII) many Protestants are inclined to dismiss as magical. Magical or not, the teaching is subject to the same criticism that can be directed at the entire sacramental system: that the word of God, spoken and written, does not receive enough attention as God's way of announcing and conferring the forgiveness of sins and of making the church holy through forgiveness. Instead, the grace of the sacraments becomes what scholasticism calls a "habit," something within a man that confers a character upon him and makes him acceptable to God. Protestants cannot accept therefore the definition of the holiness of the church in primarily sacramental terms.

Nor can they accept the implication which Roman Catholics draw from this definition: that because the church is holy and because the pope is the visible head of the church, the pope must be infallible in his pronouncements ex cathedra. At the same time, the church's holiness actually seems to depend upon the pope's infallibility. Then the church remains holy so long as it remains faithful to the infallible magisterium which God has entrusted to the Roman pontiff. Apostasy from that magisterium necessarily entails loss of holiness, because it entails loss of membership in the church. Protestants object that the papacy has repeatedly manifested its fallibility and that therefore the holiness of the church dare not be made to depend upon an infallible papacy. They also point out that the Holy Spirit sometimes confers grace and truth and holiness upon persons and churches with whom the papacy would refuse to have any fellowship. It is a fallacy to tie the holiness of the church to one institutional form of the church. From this it would appear that Protestants and Roman Catholics can agree in the abstract that the church is holy, but must disagree fundamentally as to what this means in the concrete.

Yet there is one point of agreement beyond the abstract statement, "The church is holy." It is the concrete statement, "The church is unholy." Both Protestantism and Roman Catholicism have room somewhere in their interpretations of the church for the idea that the complete holiness of the church is not the present possession of the church, but its ultimate hope. On the basis of this idea both are able to speak in rather vivid language about the unholiness of Christendom as it exists in the world. From the local priest lamenting the conditions in his own parish to the prophet or mystic denouncing the worldliness of the church and even of the papacy, Roman Catholicism produces critics of the empirical church who refuse to equate its spotted actuality with the holiness of that church "without spot or wrinkle" (Eph. 5:27). Protestantism is less handicapped than is Roman Catholicism in admitting the cleavage between profession and performance and therefore pointing beyond the empirical church to the holy church. So easy is this for Protestantism that its doctrine of the church invisible may sometimes deprive it of all incentive for achieving in this life and in the church visible some image

183

of the holiness which the church has in hope. Although they err on opposite sides, however, both Protestantism and Roman Catholicism are in a position to begin discussing the holiness of the church—by admitting that Christendom is not holy.

The unity we have is, at least in part, a unity of weakness. When we consider it together therefore we begin by recognizing that weakness. As we shall see again in Chapter XV, mutual repentance is a precondition of any improvement in relations between Protestants and Roman Catholics. Such repentance must begin within the limits prescribed by the two traditions. Thus Roman Catholics cannot be expected to admit that the church erred in promulgating the dogmas of the Immaculate Conception and the Assumption, and Protestants cannot be expected to do penance for the Reformation. Nevertheless, both can be asked to judge the empirical life of their churches not by comparison with each other, but by the criterion of that holiness which all the churches claim to have in Christ. Out of such judgment no church can hope to come unscathed. "If thou, O Lord, shouldst mark iniquities, Lord, who could stand?" (Ps. 130:3.) Then it may be possible to consider the divinely appointed means for restoring the divided church to the unity and the holiness which it has, but does not yet possess.

The Church Is Catholic

The church is one, and yet it is not one. The church is holy, and yet it is not holy. So also the church is catholic, and yet it is not catholic. Catholicity, as we have defined it in Chapter II, means identity plus universality. The ancient church became the catholic church when it achieved this combination. To confess that the church is catholic means to declare that this combination, or some such combination of identity and universality, is a necessary aspect of the church's life. We are at one in affirming the need for identity and in acknowledging the urge toward universality. In this sense it is correct to say that Protestantism and Roman Catholicism both believe that the church is catholic.

Both Protestantism and Roman Catholicism believe that if the

184

church is to be the church, it must establish and maintain its identity. The church is the ecclesia, the group which has been called out and set apart from the rest of humanity by what God has spoken and done in Jesus Christ. When we define the church, we must speak of that which identifies the church and sets it apart. Within classical Protestantism the emphasis has traditionally fallen upon identity even at the expense of universality, while Protestant liberalism sometimes seemed to be in danger of surrendering the specific identity of the church. The main body of Protestant belief and thought would, however, agree with Roman Catholic teaching in asserting that the church must preserve its identity. It would disagree with Roman Catholicism as to how the church is to do this. When a Roman Catholic is asked about the identity of the church, he can point to a discrete social institution. It is one institution among others and can therefore be located in human life and history, but it is a special institution whose organized life and history have taken special forms. Hence it is to these forms or organization that we are to look when we seek to define the church and its identity. A Protestant is much less confident about his ability to locate the church. It is, he declares, where the word of God is preached and the sacraments are administered; he knows that it can appear in the strangest places and under the most unpredictable circumstances, and that it appears, among other places, in Roman Catholicism. When he comes to speak of its identity, therefore, a Protestant speaks of Christ and of the word of God, but he also declares his faith that the true church is often hidden to the eyes of men and known but to God.

A related similarity and difference manifest themselves when Roman Catholics and Protestants speak of the universality of the church. Both in their statements about the church and in the conduct of their missionary work, they give voice to the universal ideal of the Christian faith. As Christ died for the whole world, so the body of Christ contains within itself the drive to incorporate all men into him. All Christians share the vision of the seer of Revelation, who saw "a great multitude which no man could number, from every nation, from all tribes and peoples and tongues" (7:9). They do not all share a common conviction about how the church is to make its universal vision a reality. If only because of its sheer size, the Roman church finds its catholicity verified by the almost half a billion human beings whom it embraces, who have nothing in common—neither language nor color nor culture nor politics—except their humanity and their membership in the Roman Catholic Church. Protestantism has no panorama of such proportions to illustrate its universality, not even after "the great century" of Protestant missions. Neither horizontally across the cultures of the world nor vertically across the classes of Western culture does Protestantism manifest the inclusive and universal capacity of Rome. For that very reason, however, Protestant thought has been obliged to show its universality by looking for the church beyond the borders of Protestantism. Only the most extreme sectarian Protestant would maintain that the church is confined to his own sect. Most Protestant thinkers manifest their catholicity by freely acknowledging that the church is more universal than Protestant Christendom.

Identity plus universality—this is the ideal of both Roman Catholicism and Protestantism. The harsh actuality is that the two can neither define nor achieve true catholicity so long as they are separated. As they cannot agree about the identity of the church, so they cannot establish that identity in isolation from each other. As they do not speak about the universality of the church in the same way, so they both make universality less than universal by going their separate ways. Protestants are in a position to acknowledge that this is so, for they need Roman Catholicism to prove their own catholicity. Protestants are catholic if they realize that Roman Catholicism is Christian. Roman Catholics have a more difficult time keeping in mind that their Western church is not coextensive with Catholic Christendom, and they often speak as though it were. Yet the stubborn fact of the Eastern churches (whose catholicity even Rome cannot successfully dispute) and the repeated appearance of catholic phenomena in the non-Roman Western churches (for which Rome cannot always take credit) combine to show that it is still a mistake to equate "catholic" and "Roman Catholic." Perhaps this, too, can form a basis for dis-

186

cussion. One part of the unity we have is our common fidelity to the ideal of catholicity and the mutual impoverishment of our catholicity by the reality of our divisions. Because we both believe that the church is catholic, we both have the obligation to work for its catholicity.

The Church Is Apostolic

When we assert that the church is one, that it is holy, and that it is catholic, we must make clear in each case what are the criteria and the sources to which we look in making such an assertion. That raises the question of what makes the church apostolic, for this question is in many ways the key to the other three. Concerned as we are in this chapter with the nature of the unity we have, we must ask the question of apostolicity in relation to the unity and the disunity between Protestantism and Roman Catholicism. Whatever it is that makes the church apostolic will also make the church one. To the Roman Catholic, this means that the unity of the church lies in its allegiance to the apostolic foundation, the rock upon which Christ has promised to build the church. Peter is the prince of the apostles, and the church is apostolic because and insofar as its obeys his apostolic authority, which has been vested in the bishop of Rome. The advantage of this view is that it points to a precise locus of apostolic authority in the present. Protestants, meanwhile, tend to say that the criterion of apostolic authority is loyalty to the apostolic scriptures of the New Testament. The church is apostolic because and insofar as it obeys the apostolic message in the Scriptures. The apostolic unity of the church, consequently, comes through the common acceptance of the apostolic Scriptures, which are taken to be both clear and uniform.

Actually, as John Knox has pointed out, "in respect to [the] matter of organization and government, as in every other respect, the early churches reflected the diversities of their several backgrounds, their several origins, and their several histories." [10] Saying that the church is apostolic cannot mean the same as saying that the church is uniform, for the spectrum represented by the New Testament is wider than any one of its individual colors. No individual color, neither Paul nor Apollos nor Cephas, makes the church apostolic, but the presence in the church of all that all of them represent as apostles. More than previous generations of students, we are in a position to appreciate, and not to be shocked by, the variety of the apostolic witness. At the same time, we can still affirm the unity of the apostolic witness and of the apostolic church, as that unity makes itself evident in the variety. The implications of this insight for the unity of the church are compelling. The church will be apostolic when it finds its unity in the one Lord and one faith confessed by the apostles at the same time that it cultivates the unity-in-diversity manifested by the apostles. If this is the criterion of apostolicity, then neither Roman Catholicism nor the several branches of Protestantsm may legitimately call themselves apostolic in the full sense of the word.

For the very same reason, however, the several churches have more of a hold upon apostolicity than their opponents in the other churches are willing to concede to them. The conflicting claims of the churches to be apostolic are the battle of beggars over a treasure which all of them want but none can have until everyone shares what he has and accepts what the others have. This does not mean that everything in all the churches is apostolic, or that the church becomes apostolic by simply dumping everything from all the churches into a single pot. It means that the churches in quest of apostolicity, and the bits of apostolicity in quest of a church, need the kind of exchange and interchange that was so prominent a characteristic of the apostolic church. We have referred before to the clash between Peter and Paul in the early church. The importance of that clash lies not only in its outcome, which helped to make Christianity catholic, but in its setting. It was a clash within one church, not a clash between opposing churches. The church is truly apostolic not when it avoids such clashes, but when it keeps them from creating schism. Every indication in the New Testament points to many more such clashes than its pages describe, and they continued into later centuries. But the main body of the church remained together and remained apostolic despite all the conflict and all the variety in its life and doctrine.

Such is the picture of the early church drawn for us by the past several generations of historical research, Protestant and Roman Cath-

188

olic. To an extent that neither the reformers nor their Roman opponents could grasp, modern study of the New Testament by their successors on both sides has made clear that it is idle to look for uniformity in the apostolic church and that it is also idle to strive for uniformity in the contemporary church. Yet the unity of the apostolic church remains the ideal in whose name both Protestants and Roman Catholics shout slogans across the great divide. Although they understand that apostolic unity differently, they do have in their formal loyalty to it a starting point for further discussion. In the recognition of apostolic variety within apostolic unity they have implications for true catholicity which neither side has been willing to face. We share both poverty and a vision. We have, and yet we seek, a church that is one, holy, catholic, and apostolic. For deep within, when the battle cries are stilled, all of us know that the church we now have is less than the church we want, and that the church we want will be, in ways that are known only to God, the fulfillment of the church we have. Thus, when we measure the unity we have, we also begin to discern the dimensions of the unity we seek.

189

XIII
The Unity We Seek

✠ A theological approach to Roman Catholicism should begin with our areas of agreement, and then it should consider the resources we have for deepening and extending these areas of agreement. Perhaps the time is coming soon when Protestants and Roman Catholics in America can sit down for earnest and open discussions about the unity they have and the unity they seek. Privately such discussions have been going on for years, but they have seldom achieved a formal status; perhaps they should not. Yet anyone who has participated in more than one or two exploratory conversations between Protestant and Roman Catholic theologians knows the sense of frustration which comes after we have exchanged expressions of friendship and have stated our official positions. Where do we go from here? This chapter is based upon my own experiences in Protestant-Roman conversations and upon an analysis of current theological trends on both sides.

Those experiences suggest that these conversations work best and accomplish most in clarifying both agreement and disagreement when they are based upon a significant text or a crucial book or personality, rather than upon statements from either side or from both sides of their respective party lines on one or another issue. Discussion of a text does not eliminate the party lines, but it sets up a polarity between them and the text, and it sometimes provokes the participants to assume positions that do not belong to the party line at all. The current status of thought within both Protestantism and Roman Catholicism confirms this suggestion, for in both groups certain books and movements have assumed such prominence during the past generation that a new consideration of the issues seems possible. Such consideration could clarify the hidden assumptions on both sides. It could uncover meanings in the text which have been hidden by these assumptions. Thus it could open up the possibility of achieving greater understanding and perhaps greater agreement than might seem likely at the outset.

The Testimony of the Scriptures

Certainly the most important basis for any renewed discussion between Protestants and Roman Catholics is the Bible. The role of the Bible in past controversies between them does not provide much reassurance about its possible value as a means of cultivating unity today. For although they used the same Bible and sometimes the same passages, Roman Catholic and Protestant theologians came to exactly opposite conclusions. The Bible functioned as a device to support the confessional position of the disputants, and so neither side was really listening either to its opponents or to the Scriptures. From such study of the Bible we can expect very little of positive value. Although many theologians on both sides would still be inclined to use the Bible this way, several significant shifts have come on both sides which justify the hope that the testimony of the Scriptures will not be without effect in Protestant-Roman conversations.

A truly amazing shift has taken place in the study of the Old Testament. During the nineteenth century, the heyday of biblical criticism, Roman Catholic interpreters of the Old Testament resisted many of

191

the theories of historical study of the Old Testament because they seemed to be treating the Old Testament merely as a piece of Near Eastern literature, with little or no reference to its significance as a book of the church. Today most Protestant interpreters take this significance very seriously, but without sacrificing their attention to historical questions; and Roman Catholic interpreters have come to realize that there is no incompatibility between the historical-critical study of Old Testament literature and its use in the theology and devotion of the church. As a result, such Protestant interpreters sense a greater affinity with such Roman Catholics than they do with other Protestants who still reject the historical-critical study of the Old Testament. At the congress of Old Testament scholars held in Strasbourg in late August and early September of 1956, Protestants and Roman Catholics mingled freely, exchanging viewpoints and interpretations; often the viewpoints and interpretations did not betray the confessional position of the scholar espousing them. The Roman Catholic view of the history of religions, to which we referred in an earlier chapter, makes it easy for a Roman interpreter to come to terms with the historical interpretation of the religion of Israel—so long as there is room for the church's use of the Old Testament as a Christian book. This is a use which increasing numbers of Protestants recognize as legitimate.

Underlying this shift in the theological interpretation of the Old Testament is an important shift in literary interpretation which affects both Old Testament study and New Testament study. While previous generations of scholars went at the literary analysis of the Bible in order to discern the hands of various individual writers, the emphasis in current biblical study is upon the function of the community, both Christian and Jewish, not only in assembling but in actually shaping the documents of the Scriptures. Translated from literary to theological terms, this means that biblical scholarship today acknowledges the role of tradition in the interpretation, but also in the very composition of both the Old and the New Testament.[1] Books on tradition have begun to come from biblical scholars in both the Protestant and the Roman camp, and the Commission on Faith and Order of the World

192

Council of Churches has even created a theological commission to deal especially with the issue of tradition.[2] Tradition, which was a term of opprobrium for the reformers, is now becoming an acceptable concept among Protestant theologians and biblical interpreters.[3] If, as Protestant interpreters like Dibelius and even Bultmann concede, the Christian community, through its tradition, shaped the forms of the New Testament, then it might well follow that the Christian community, again through its tradition, ought to have some voice in the interpretation of the New Testament.

It is for this authoritative voice of tradition that Roman Catholic theology and Orthodox theology have been contending against Protestantism for four hundred years. Suddenly now, Protestant theology has begun to listen to tradition as it has not since the Reformation. At the very same time Roman Catholic theology has begun to listen to the Scriptures as it has not for many centuries. We have referred earlier to the resurgence of interest in the Bible at every level of thought in the Roman communion. Roman Catholic scholars have managed to accept many critical theories about the New Testament which were condemned by the leaders of the church. Instead of fitting biblical teaching to the Procrustean bed of scholastic categories, these scholars stress the Semitic and unspeculative character of biblical language. The picture of Paul which emerges from their studies is not as different from Protestant pictures as one might expect. Even when they interpret the life and teachings of Jesus in the gospels, Roman Catholic scholars find it possible to make astonishing concessions about the genuine limitations of his humanity. Although the gap between Protestants and Roman Catholics is much wider in New Testament study than it is in Old Testament study, it is also much narrower than it used to be. In areas like textual study the gap has been virtually closed, and in other areas it is becoming narrower all the time.

Yet it would be a mistake to exaggerate the agreement here or to expect that biblical study alone will close the gap between the churches. Despite the explicit encouragement of the Holy See to pursue their studies unhampered by a priori dogmatic considerations, the biblical scholars of the Roman church are constantly aware of the danger that they will go too far and be stopped short. They remember the fate of modernism at the turn of the century, and they are much more judicious about relating their exegesis to the official teaching of the church. On the Protestant side, the systematic theologians and the churchmen are only beginning to grasp the implications of what their biblical colleagues have been saying about tradition. It therefore remains to be seen what concrete contribution the study of the Scriptures will make to the unity we seek. Even after the literary and historical issues have been clarified and we have a measure of agreement, the differences between us remain differences of a fundamental nature; and these cannot but affect our interpretation of the Scriptures. Nevertheless, when we have said all of this, we must still express the hope that an obedient hearkening to the testimony of the Scriptures may make a difference in the way Protestants and Roman Catholics bear witness to each other.

The Heritage of the Fathers

When Protestant theologians acknowledge the place of tradition in the composition of the New Testament, they mean by this not the continuing tradition of the church, but the apostolic tradition to which Paul refers in passages like I Corinthians 15:3. The crucial question is whether the New Testament exhausts that apostolic tradition or whether the development of the church's life and teaching after the New Testament is also an exhibit of the primitive tradition, supplementing the witness of the New Testament. If the latter is the case, then the authority of the apostles in the church extends beyond the first century and comprehends the continuing apostolic tradition of all the centuries. Hence the teachings of the church fathers are an indispensable part of Roman Catholic theology, which often assumes a proprietary attitude in speaking about them.

Protestant theology has usually disputed this attitude. In asserting their catholicity, the reformers drew upon the church fathers as proof that it was possible to be catholic without being Roman. Study of the fathers thus became an important part of the Protestant panoply as well. In fact, the very word "patrology" as a title for a manual on the church fathers and their works is a Protestant invention, first used by Johann Gerhard (d. 1637). When Protestant liberalism developed during the nineteenth century, one of its principal contributions to theological literature was its work on the fathers. The *Patrology* of the Roman Catholic scholar Johannes Quasten and an essay by the Jesuit scholar J. de Ghellinck both reveal the dependence even of Roman theologians upon the scholarly achievements of Protestant historians, the outstanding of whom was Adolf Harnack (d. 1930).[4] Although the generation of theologians after Harnack has not been as interested in the field of patristic study, Protestants have not completely forgotten the heritage of the fathers.

Meanwhile, Roman Catholics have begun to put an assessment upon the fathers that differs significantly from the traditional one. Instead of measuring the fathers against the standards of a later orthodoxy, Roman Catholic historians now interpret them in the context of their own time. This means, for example, that a church father like Origen is no longer interpreted on the basis of his later (and politically motivated) condemnation for heresy, but on the basis of his own writings and career.[5] It means, too, that Roman Catholic theologians have enriched their thought by fresh insights from the fathers of the Greek-speaking East. So enthusiastic has the adoption of such insights become in both theology and liturgy that the liturgical movement has been warned against an overemphasis upon the Eastern at the expense of the Western tradition. The historical scholarship accompanying this new attention to the fathers is truly impressive. Editions, translations, commentaries, and scholarly studies of the highest quality have been coming from Roman Catholic presses here and abroad in impressive number. The study of the church fathers is now a predominantly Roman Catholic building, even though many of the foundations for it were laid by Protestant hands.

Both Protestantism and Roman Catholicism, then, have acquired a new perspective on the heritage of the fathers. Both have been influenced in this perspective by the rise of modern historical study, which has made the purely polemical use of the fathers obsolete. If the implications of this joint participation in the reassessment of the fathers were ever to reach the level of the church politicians, this could make a contribution to mutual understanding and thus to the unity we seek. It would become clear that the heritage of the fathers does not belong exclusively to either side. Roman Catholics must acknowledge the presence of evangelical or "Protestant" ideas in Irenaeus, and Protestants must come to terms with the catholic elements in the same father. When they have done this, they may begin to ask why it is that emphases joined together in Irenaeus—and in Ignatius before him, as in Augustine after him—have to be put asunder today. Once that question has been asked by both sides in honesty and in humility, we may be ready to speak of the unity we seek.

The Witness of the Reformation

Separating us from the heritage of the fathers is the Reformation of the sixteenth century, and no attempt at *rapprochement* is honest if it ignores the witness of the Reformation. Like the testimony of the Scriptures and the heritage of the fathers, the witness of the Reformation has been the victim of party spirit on both sides. Protestants have often refused to see the slightest shortcomings in the Reformation and have exalted only that in the Reformation which was congruent with their own particular brand of Protestantism. Roman Catholics, on the other hand, have been so blinded by their hostility to what they regard as the greatest apostasy in Christian history that they cannot see the positive meaning of the Reformation for them. Protestant historians have painted the Middle Ages in the darkest colors on the palette. Roman Catholic historians have described Luther as a man with a mind like a cesspool and a mouth to match. Thus the mutual accusations and slanders have been passed back and forth, until they have muffled the witness of the Reformation to both sides.

There is some indication that this may be changing. The same historical scholarship which has revised our picture of the New Testament and of the early church has also been at work on the reformers. Their writings have been edited and are being translated, their lives and their thought are receiving the attention of historians and theologians; and out of this work a new picture of the Reformation is emerging which will not satisfy the extreme partisans on either side. The interpretation presented in Chapter IV of this book is a reflection of that new picture. As Protestants have begun to scrutinize their traditional view of the Reformation, some Roman Catholics have also inquired into the historical honesty of their traditional interpretation. A remarkable book has appeared, tracing the caricatures of Luther that have marked the history of Roman Catholic literature since the Reformation.[6] The author of the book is a Roman Catholic church historian, who laments the slanders against Luther and the Reformation that have figured so prominently in that literature. Other theologians and historians have begun to raise the question of what Rome has lost in richness and comprehensiveness by its precipitate action against the Reformation.[7] Despite these signs of improvement, however, the conventional picture of Luther and the Reformation among Roman Catholics continues to be that of Jacques Maritain's *Three Reformers*.[8]

If the Reformation is ever to do what it once set out to do—to establish the life and the unity of the church on the foundation of the gospel of God, rather than on a human organization—both Protestants and Roman Catholics will have to pay new attention to its total witness. Protestants will have to realize that the Reformation is meaningless apart from the context of the catholic tradition within which it took place. As we have seen, Luther was able to expound the Scriptures as mightily as he did because he was sustained by the dogma and the piety of the church, and Calvin drew upon many sources in the catholic tradition for his insights into the Christian faith. Apart from the tradition the Reformation looks like a struggle for individualism or a conflict over power. But when we see it within the framework of the church, the stature of the reformers grows and their work takes on new depth. Such a Luther or such a Calvin, however, can no longer be the exclusive property of Lutherans or Presbyterians. As it was the total church that produced them, so it is to the total church that they speak. What we have called "the catholicity of the reformers" implies that the witness of the Reformation is truncated if it remains within

197

the confines of any Protestant church—or even of all the Protestant churches put together.

For Rome, too, must hear the witness of the Reformation. In the sixteenth century it spurned that witness, cutting itself off from what it needed most. The reasons for its action were both good and bad. Some were political, some religious, some personal. Four centuries later, it seems time to take a second look. Rome is currently taking a second look at Origen, even though it was party to the condemnation of Origen in the fifth and sixth centuries. Father Danièlou's book on Origen elevates Origen the churchman and the expositor of Scripture over Origen the heretic and the speculator. In the same way it would be possible for a Roman scholar to maintain that the reformers were fundamentally churchmen and expositors of Scripture, and that as such they deserve a hearing in the very church which condemned and excommunicated them. The amusing fantasy of Johannes Rüber, called *Bach and the Heavenly Choir*,[9] tells the story of a pope who wanted to make a saint of the stoutly Lutheran composer, Johann Sebastian Bach (d. 1750). Behind the humor of the book is the recognition that through the Reformation a piece of catholicity has been passed to its heirs, and that Rome is impoverished by the loss of it. A facetious way of putting the same insight is to say that the canonization of Martin Luther would be the first step toward the unity we seek. Short of actual canonization, Rome must begin to ask itself more seriously than it ever has about the implications of the Reformation witness for its life and teaching.

The Tradition of the Liturgy

Perhaps the most neglected resource for the unity we seek, neglected at least among Protestants, is the liturgy. The so-called free churches have been so afraid of formalism that elimination of the liturgy, rather than study of the liturgy, might seem to be the precondition for unity. Rome has been so reluctant to undertake liturgical reform that many Protestants are convinced of the uselessness of talking about liturgy with Roman Catholics. It is most instructive to sit with a group of Protestants watching a televised mass and to listen to their comments

198

about the "chancel-prancers." From such comments it would seem most unlikely that liturgy will ever become a unitive factor.

Here, too, conditions are changing. Within the free churches there has arisen a new appreciation of the values in the tradition of the liturgy. Every major Protestant denomination has experienced a liturgical renaissance during the past generation. Although the varieties of Protestant worship still make the picture kaleidoscopic, there are more catholic elements in it than there have been for centuries. Often the adoption of these elements has been unreflective imitation, sometimes with amusing consequences. Yet the more profound implications of this change have not been lost on the churches. A new sense of what Moffatt calls "the thrill of tradition" has enriched their worship and has begun to change their own interpretation of what makes them churches.[10] Through ecumenical contact with traditions outside their own borders, these churches have learned something of the meaning of catholicity in the church's life and confession, and also in her worship. The critics of the liturgical movements within Protestantism, who have denounced every such revision as "Romanizing," are wrong in their assumption that it is Roman to adopt the forms and rites of the catholic tradition for the enrichment of Protestant worship. But they are right in their intuitive realization that the adoption of these forms may facilitate contact and conversation with Roman Catholicism.

The liturgical movement within Roman Catholicism, which we have discussed in Chapter XI, makes such contact and conversation easier than it has ever been before. Stressing as it does the participation of the congregation in the mass and putting a new value upon such Protestant emphases as preaching and hymn singing, the movement has been the rallying point for evangelical forces within the Roman communion. Thus critics of the liturgical movements on both sides accuse liturgical reformers of making too many concessions to an opposing tradition. These criticisms from both Protestants and Romans show that both sides might well examine the potentialities of liturgy for the unity we seek. As the liturgical movements on both sides gain in strength and influence, those potentialities will also increase. In its study of "ways of worship," the ecumenical movement has discovered that through liturgy one may gain insights into a communion that are not available to other methods of inquiry. Perhaps Roman Catholics and Protestants may also begin to use this method of inquiry for a deeper grasp of what separates them and of what unites them.

The Ministry of Reconciliation

If there is any point at all in attempting to inaugurate conversations between Protestantism and Roman Catholicism about the Bible, the fathers, the Reformation, and the liturgy, it will be most important to select the proper auspices for such conversations. Both sides have done so much proselyting that any initiating from either side immediately arouses suspicion in the other, even when the initiative is a well-intentioned desire to do no more than understand and communicate. Summit talks at high official levels can do very little to clear the air. The great interdenominational agencies like the World Council of Churches and the National Council have been so identified with the Protestant cause that even some Orthodox have been wary of them; Roman Catholics would look upon any invitation from them, however sincere, as a partisan gesture. Conversely, the centers of learning within Roman Catholicism have been so closely linked with the apostolate to Protestants that they are disqualified as meeting-places for free and serious discussion.

Responsibility for providing such meeting places must therefore fall upon men of good will who are not directly identified with either Roman Catholicism or Protestantism. Joint groups of laymen from both groups could take the lead here. The ministry of reconciliation between Roman Catholic and Protestant is a service which the great private universities of America could well consider, particularly those which do not have an interdenominational (Protestant) divinity school attached to them. Institutes for joint study and mutual confrontation under friendly but neutral auspices could help us realize the true nature of our separation. The scholarship of the university could do much to point up the nontheological factors in our separa-

200

tion, lest we assume that it is all a matter of doctrines and books. There is, of course, a risk involved in proposing or establishing such institutes. Creation of formal agencies for Roman-Protestant discussions could have the effect of wrecking the informal discussions we now have, from which so many of us on both sides have profited so much. Then the net effect would be a loss. But the informal discussions we have are so sporadic, and the temptations to irresponsibility in them are so great, that we really need something more substantial than what we have now.

What we have now is, on both sides, a picture of the other side that is part photograph, part old daguerreotype, and part caricature. Correction of the picture is virtually impossible today unless one is willing to hear invitations from the other side and accusations from his own side; for as things stand now, such correction can be done only on "enemy territory." Yet if the ecumenical cause is as important to the church as most of us believe it is, we must discover and create the agencies we need to carry on this phase of the ecumenical task. What we need above all is the opportunity for the churches to meet one another as churches (even though Rome would withhold the designation "church" from Protestant groups), instead of continuing to lose and to gain individual members in both directions—members who have grown weary of waiting and have decided instead to take the quick and easy way of conversion.

XIV
The Way of Conversion

✠ Although theological discussion may be the road to an ultimate solution of the divisions in the church, there are many who cannot wait. After all, there have been sporadic discussions going on since
the Reformation, and nothing is much better on account of them. The
old lines remain drawn, the old issues are still being argued, the old
positions are stubbornly unchanged. One can understand the im-
patience of those who expect very little good to come out of further
negotiations between Protestantism and Roman Catholicism. They
may very well be right! This book takes the position that even if they
are, the discussions must go on. For the only other alternatives are
admitting that the division into two armed camps is the only permanent arrangement we can accept, or resolving the division prema-
turely through conversion and capitulation. The first alternative is a
denial of the fundamental imperative in the Christian doctrine of the
church, the primary responsibility of Christians to and for one another regardless of denominational or confessional allegiance. The

202

second alternative, the way of conversion, is the one with which the present chapter is concerned.

In the opinion of many serious-minded people, it is time to travel the way of conversion. The road may be hard, but the waiting is harder. It is a road on which others have traveled, a rather distinguished company of pilgrims in fact.[1] Perhaps the only way to meet the crisis of our separation is to take that road. This much at least is certain: only that Protestant who has considered taking the way of conversion and, having considered it, has decided that he can best obey the will of God for him by remaining where he is can conscientiously remain a Protestant. The converse of this also applies. Only that Roman Catholic who has listened to the challenge of Protestantism is truly entitled to his Roman Catholicism. The case for conversion can be made attractive, as is evident from the vast literature produced by the converts to Roman Catholicism during the century since the conversion of John Henry Newman in 1845. [2] We shall be quoting from that literature in this chapter, not because these converts are the most typical, but because they have most articulately stated the case for conversion. We are not interested in judging the sincerity or the rightness of the step they have taken; that is for Another to do. Nor are we interested in psychoanalyzing these converts in order to find out "what their real problem was." We are only interested in considering the case for conversion as a way of eliminating the scandal of our separation.

A Two-Way Street

Ordinarily the case for conversion comes from Protestants who have become Roman Catholic, but despite their intentions such spokesmen are also stating the case for conversion in the opposite direction. More basic than the question of where to go is the question of whether to go elsewhere at all, and in answering this prior question the converts on both sides are agreed. As will become evident later, there is much to be said against conversion in either direction as an answer to the problem of Protestant-Roman Catholic relations. First we must make it clear that the conversions have been going on in both directions, and that the traffic is also quite heavy from Rome.[3] Statistics are notoriously unreliable in this area. Many of those who cross over live in a no man's land after they leave the one church and before they join the other. Are they converts from the other church or from the "unchurched"? Thus it is impossible to arrive at any figures regarding conversion that are at all meaningful, and the usual boasts from both sides are usually just that—boasts.

One source of defections from Roman Catholicism in America is the generation born in this country from immigrant parents. There is no study of this generation that corresponds in scope and scholarship to Gerald Shaughnessy's *Has the Immigrant Kept the Faith?* of 1925, which has become a classic document of sociological church history.[4] From Shaughnessy's materials and from the few studies that have appeared it is clear that the first generation born in America has raised special problems for the strategy of the Roman communion.[5] The rebellion of this generation against the ways of the Old World and the painful lag between the mores of the immigrant parents and those of their English-speaking children have threatened the influence and authority of the church in the cities of America. Now that the colonies of East-European and South-European descent are moving from this stage to the stage where the grandchildren of the old settlers begin to cherish Old World values, it is possible to gain some perspective upon the process. For these rebels, considerable numbers of whom have found their way into Protestant churches, Roman Catholicism symbolized the old ways of their parents—authoritarian, reactionary, outmoded. To forsake these ways, as the novels of James T. Farrell make clear, is to tear up one's roots and then to let them down in an alien soil. More than once, the attitudes of priests and bishops helped to confirm the impression that the church was permanently on the side of reaction, and only in our own time has the hierarchy made a serious effort to revise that impression and thus to make a new appeal to the grandchildren of the immigrants. Meanwhile, countless thousands have packed their bags and left the church.[6]

Their departure has been easier because of the stand of the church on marriage, divorce, and related subjects. Here again statistics are

204

unobtainable; but when the Roman church insists that the non-Roman partner to a forthcoming marriage sign a premarital agreement to respect the religion of his spouse, this is an indication that many Roman Catholics have left the faith as a result of mixed marriages. Others have found the absolute prohibition of divorce more than they could bear in their own lives, and they have taken the road from Rome on that account. It is common among Roman Catholics to dismiss such defections as rebellion against the authority of God (which is, of course, identified with the authority of the church). More than once, this is exactly what the defections are. Yet they may also be a serious indictment of the legalism with which the Roman communion approaches moral matters. In principle, everyone is in favor of marriage, in favor of children, and opposed to divorce. Rome, however, has put itself into the position of saying that in every specific case marriage is preferable to divorce and unlimited childbirth is preferable to contraception. Defection from the church on account of this position is not automatically rebellion against the authority of God, but may well be a defense of the freedom of God against an ecclesiastical system that has sought to usurp the authority of God by legislating on all the details of private life.

In other words, neither Protestants nor Roman Catholics are entitled to act as though conversions in their direction always proceeded from sincerely Christian motives, while conversions in the other direction always proceeded from selfish or ignoble motives. Motivation is a complex and subtle thing, especially in matters of religion and most especially in a decision for or against conversion. Rome will be able to deal with the problem of conversion only when it recognizes that the way of conversion is indeed a two-way street, and that the pilgrims in both directions are motivated by a mixture of desires and convictions. Under the Roman Catholic view of the church that recognition is difficult, but it is not impossible. Thus Roman Catholics may believe that conversion to Protestantism is apostasy and still discern the Christian reasons for such conversion. Some scholars have done just this in the case of Luther, and some priests have said as much about the drift of parishioners across the borders in both direc-

205

tions. The usual attitude, however, is regret if not recrimination, without much sign of a serious self-examination. This, unfortunately, is the usual attitude not only of Roman Catholics when one of their number walks down the two-way street to Protestantism, but also of Protestants when one of their number takes one of the many roads that lead to Rome.

The Roads to Rome

As it is possible to leave Rome for any of several reasons, so it is possible to go to Rome for a variety of reasons. Roman Catholic apologists contend that the logic of any Christian position, if thought through to its conclusions, will lead to Rome. Even if this is not true, it is quite revealing to consider not only the destination of the roads to Rome, but also their origins and their course. These tell us something about Roman Catholicism and something about Protestantism. One way to get at the riddle of Roman Catholicism is through the personal testaments of those who have found in this riddle the solution for the riddles of their own existence. Perhaps these testaments can also help Protestantism to reassess its own strengths and weaknesses and thus to understand better its position vis-a-vis Roman Catholicism.

For many of those who have taken it, the road to Rome is the path to certainty. The late Monsignor Knox describes his journey over that path:

I did come to wonder whether I had a right to believe in anything—to believe, that is, without being in visible communion with that one visible body of faithful people of whom the prophet foretold, "All thy people shall be taught of God." For authority played a large part in my belief, and I could not now find that any certain source of authority was available to me outside the pale of the Roman Catholic Church. Once inside, I should not care how the authority came to me; I did not crave for infallible decrees; I wanted to be certain I belonged to that church of which Saint Paul said proudly, "We have the mind of Christ." [7]

Belonging to that church was for Knox the logical outcome of the quest for certainty which began with Anglicanism. The quest for certainty likewise led Louis Bouyer through Karl Barth to Rome, for in Barth's emphasis upon the authority of the word of God Bouyer found the first step toward the authority of the church as the spokesman for the word of God.[8] Probably the classic road map for this journey is the one provided by Cardinal Newman's *Apologia*, which has been called "the story of the effort of the intellect to assume its proper place and function in the soul of a man—the effort to reach a position where it actually did settle the matter." [9] Intellectual or emotional, the path to certainty led these men to the Eternal City.

At the same time, the road to Rome may be the road to catholicity. Since catholicity is identity plus universality, one may come to it *via* identity or *via* universality. Thus the Protestant emphasis upon identity may arouse a feeling of need for greater precision in this identity than Protestantism is able to supply. Others have gone to Rome because they felt the need for a universality which the Protestant emphasis upon identity seemed to make impossible. As an interpreter of the New Testament from the school of Rudolf Bultmann, Dr. Heinrich Schlier had studied the influence of Gnosticism upon the Ephesian letter and upon the writings of Ignatius.[10] Although he was inclined to treat this universalism as a foreign body in early Christianity, he found in it an element which he missed in the Protestant churches. Eventually he became a Roman Catholic, out of the conviction, born of his studies in the New Testament, that the church is:

> . . . the body of Christ or the dimension of God . . . a concrete temple, a concrete city, a concrete house of God, in its most universal aspect a concrete aeon of God. God has made up his mind in favor of one new world, his new world in the church; and therefore all the forms and structures of the world serve the purpose of carrying out his decision.[11]

Because Protestantism seemed to him incapable of incorporating this universal and catholic dimension into its life, Schlier found the combination of universality and identity elsewhere.

Certainty and catholicity are theological goals which men have sought by going to Rome. It is also possible to look there for other religious goals. Although Roman Catholicism in this country has frequently taken a role that ignored or even opposed the life of the intellect, the road to Rome has often been the road to a synthesis of faith and intellect which appeared impossible anywhere else. Americans (including American Roman Catholics) are surprised to see the number of intellectuals in Britain and in Europe who take the road to Rome in order to find freedom for their intellectual and cultural pursuits. Graham Greene, Evelyn Waugh, Edith Sitwell, Sigrid Undset, Gilbert K. Chesterton—these and many more transferred their allegiance to Rome because Protestantism did not seem to them capable of co-ordinating Christianity and culture without sacrificing one or the other or both. Some of them were appalled by the separation between faith and modern culture and by the compromises involved in Protestant efforts to bridge the separation. To all of them Rome represented a liberating force within whose walls they could do their creative work. Although it is sometimes said that a convert never writes a good book again—and the case of men like Tolstoy suggests that conversion to "religion" may be a literary soporific—there are certainly many instances where conversion to Roman Catholicism did not destroy, but rather heightened the creativity of a writer or artist.

The way of conversion has been a path toward the synthesis between Christianity and culture for another type of pilgrim too, of whom the Russian philosopher Vladimir Soloviëv (d. 1900) is the best example. His *Russia and the Universal Church* expounds this thesis:

> The fundamental and distinctive idea of Christianity is the perfect union of the divine and the human individually achieved in Christ, and finding its social realisation in Christian humanity, in which the divine is represented by the church, centered in the supreme pontiff, and the human by the state.[12]

Soloviëv came to believe that this perfect union could be achieved only by a synthesis between Russia and Rome, since the Western nations had lost the spiritual power to act as the arm of the church and Orthodoxy was not capable of reviving Russia. He therefore led the way toward such a synthesis by embracing Roman Catholicism.

Because he had been Russian Orthodox, Soloviëv's conversion was an extreme form of the more general supposition that union with Rome is the only way to meet the threat of a secularized culture. Roman invitations to Protestants frequently contain echoes of this supposition, suggesting that only a return to Roman Catholicism will cure the cultural maladies of the Western world.

A Short Cut to Reunion?

"All roads lead to Rome," the ancient proverb said. No modern Christian in the West can ignore the possibility that they do. The pilgrims whose careers we have been describing in this chapter have taken the road to Rome because they were convinced that only such a journey could get them from where they were to where they wanted to go. Where they wanted to go, varied from one individual to the next; but a prominent feature for most of them was the re-establishment of Christian unity. The case for conversion to Roman Catholicism is thus the case for a reunion of Western Christendom here and now, or at least for a reunion of as much of Western Christendom as I carry in my own person.

Anyone who takes a short cut has to reckon with the peculiar dangers and difficulties of such a trip, and therefore with the possibility that the trip may spoil the joy of arriving at his destination. The case for conversion must begin with the admission that the convert to Rome will have to accept compromises that he does not like. But then, membership in any church body involves the necessity of compromise and of settling for a great deal less than one would like. As one Protestant theologian has been heard to observe, the church may be likened to the ark of Noah because the only reason one can stand the stench inside is on account of the deluge outside. Only the most extreme organization man will seriously try to give the impression that everything is satisfactory in his own communion, and even he will do it only when he is defending his communion against outsiders. A certain amount of compromise belongs to membership in an organized church, but the question is how much compromise one must be prepared to stomach for the sake of peace and unity. The case for conversion declares that the compromise of obedience to Rome is no different in kind, and not much different in degree, from the compromise involved in any church membership. What the Protestant who accepts Roman Catholicism is being asked to put up with is no worse than what he must put up with in his own Protestant church—or in all the Protestant churches put together.

The rejoinder to this may be that it is precisely in its variety that the strength of Protestantism lies, in contrast to the monolithic character of Roman Catholicism. The case for conversion is thus a case for uniformity, but this uniformity is what the experience of modern Protestantism has taught us not to expect or desire. According to the apologists for Roman Catholicism, this is a straw man. Within Roman Catholicism there is room for an incredible number of variations, they say, and Rome is as broad and inclusive as the history of the catholic tradition itself. Not Rome, but Protestantism aims at uniformity with its special denomination for every emphasis and every whim. As such emphases and whims arise within the catholic tradition, Rome gives them their freedom, receives from them what is good for the common body, and then lets them wither away when their usefulness has passed. They are not obliged to perpetuate themselves beyond the period of their usefulness, because they have not constituted themselves as churches but have remained as movements or religious orders within the one church. Where the reformers and "other" heretics made their mistake was in refusing to work within the church. Rushing headlong out of the church, they deprived the church of their witness and deprived themselves of the church's correction and fellowship. Even for Reformation emphases there is room, provided that they form part of the total life and teaching of the one church.

Conversion is thus a short cut to reunion, because within the church the convert may retain the sort of emphases he has been supporting outside the church. Instead of a voice crying in the wilderness, he becomes a member of the cathedral choir, singing to the church and for the church. Although this path to the cathedral is difficult, it is faster than the long road over which the Protestant churches have been traveling. If one is convinced that the low road and the high road both lead to the cathedral, he may well decide not to wait any longer for all the slowpokes with whom he has been trudging along all these years. I do have my own soul to save; and if all roads eventually lead to Rome, I may as well leave the company and take the short cut directly home.

A Blind Alley

The road that looks like a short cut is sometimes a blind alley, as any traveler has discovered to his chagrin. After taking a wrong turn, the traveler may continue on his way in order to keep from admitting that he has made a mistake in his calculations. But he is lost, even though he may have a detailed map and a lot of natives telling him how to get back on the main road. A confusion very much like that of the straying traveler may affect the person who switches churches; for despite the valid personal reasons that a particular individual may have for making the switch, the way of conversion is really a blind alley. Persuasive as the case for conversion may be, there is also a convincing case against conversion.

The case against conversion to Roman Catholicism begins with the grim reality that despite the coaxing of apologists for Rome, conversion implies the unconditional surrender of the Protestant heritage. The apologists may speak about enriching Roman Catholicism by including the neglected wealth of Protestant piety and hymnody, and they mean this quite sincerely. Yet the very act of conversion speaks a no to the fundamental convictions that make up our Protestant legacy. That the church is continuously in need of reformation, that the church has no right to interfere with the sanctity of personal judgment and conviction, that the word of God in the Bible is sovereign over any tradition and over any contemporary voice in the church—these and many other principles of Protestantism must give way when a Protestant crosses the line and becomes a Roman Catholic. He may indeed be willing to give them up, but he should know what he is doing. He is saying that the tragic necessity of the Reformation has passed, and that only the tragedy remains. Whatever the Reformation can do for Rome, it has already done; whatever it has not

211

yet done, we may well relinquish. Thus the compromise of conversion is finally a compromise in only one direction: the Protestant must surrender everything that makes him a Protestant and must accept everything that will make him a Roman Catholic.

Regardless of what this may mean for Protestantism itself, such a conversion actually cheats Rome of what it deserves to hear from Protestant thought. As we said in the preceding chapter, Rome has never really listened to the witness of the Reformation. Most of the leaders of Roman Catholicism still feel under no constraint to listen to it now. The way of conversion is a blind alley because it bypasses the witness of the Reformation to the Roman communion. Prospective converts should have no illusions about carrying that witness into the inner life of Rome. What Rome refused to take from her obedient son, Martin Luther, she will not take from a returning and penitent prodigal. Even those prodigals who have tried to reinterpret the Reformation to their new found brethren have discovered how deaf Rome is to the true accents of the Reformation. Nevertheless, it is precisely the witness of the Reformation that Rome continues to need, lest the reformatory movements which it has called forth lose themselves once more as they have so often in the past. It is a disservice to the church of Rome when individual Protestants, by finding "the grace of conversion," beguile her into believing that she need not pay attention to the witness of a moribund Protestantism. Rome needs Protestantism as much as Protestantism needs Rome; and that, as this book has sought to show, is very much indeed.

For the convert himself, the search for an unambiguous church often ends in disillusionment. While the psychology of conversion is not our business here, we cannot avoid the impression that many a convert in either direction is like Don Juan, who was so entranced with the vision of the perfect woman that he refused to be satisfied with any of the imperfect women he seduced and yet continued to be fascinated by all of them. This danger affects converts from either side, but at least the convert to Protestantism has (or should have) the opportunity to be told that the church he is entering is no more perfect than the one he is leaving. The convert to Roman Catholicism may also hear this warning from his mentor, but it can easily be drowned out by the sonority of the magic words, "the true church of Jesus Christ on earth." Only after his conversion will he discover that many of the features that had repelled him in Protestantism are present in Rome too, and others besides, so that the net result is not the total gain he had expected. If he remains a Roman Catholic, he will learn to live with the ambiguities of his new situation. If he returns to Protestantism, he will become the most pathetic of all figures, the ecclesiastical vagabond who shuttles from altar to altar without ever assuming the responsibility of serious church membership anywhere.

Such an ecclesiastical vagabond is an incarnation of the basic flaw in the case for conversion, namely, that conversion is an individualistic solution to a church problem. Put somewhat sharply, the logic of conversion to Roman Catholicism is this: Protestantism has over-emphasized the individual at the expense of the corporate aspects in the Christian life; as a sovereign individual, I shall correct this over-emphasis for myself by renouncing the individual in favor of the corporate. The alternative to this is not to minimize the problem, but to realize that it is a church problem. The individual who rashly seeks to hasten its solution by a precipitate action of his own may well be postponing the day of eventual solution. The road to solution, as we have been saying in this book, is through mutual understanding, study, and witness. That road is longer and slower than the way of conversion, but it is the only road on which we have a right to travel. As we travel along this road, we must shoulder our responsibilities and bear together the burden of our separation.

XV

The Burden

of Our Separation

✠ If we measure the unity we have and the unity we seek, and if we find that we cannot go the way of conversion, then we must find a way to bear the burden of our separation. The time has come to speak a candid word about this burden, and a book like this would seem to be the right place to speak it. Because so many of the battle slogans on both sides have become clichés and so much of the defiance from both camps has become shrill, there are many people in both groups and outside them who really do not care any more. As we have seen, Roman Catholics maintain that by definition the church cannot be divided, and that therefore it has never been divided, even by the Reformation. Protestants maintain that the church was corrupted, and that the Reformation cleansed it. Thus they may forget about each other most of the time, and they can go on about their

214

own ecclesiastical business as though the other half of the divided church did not exist or at least did not matter.

But in moments of sober reflection personally, and in times of severe crisis corporately, we remember our brethren in other parts of the church and we become aware of the separation, as the Protestants of Germany and their Roman Catholic brethren discovered one another during the Third Reich and became deeply conscious of their separation.[1] We may wish that the separation were not there. We may even hope that a day will come when Christendom will be reunited, with Orthodox, Protestant, and Roman Catholic in renewed fellowship with one another. But for our own lifetime at least, we must face the certainty that the separation is permanent. That indicates that we must learn to live in a divided church, to live in it, as the *Book of Common Prayer* says about marriage, "reverently, discreetly, advisedly, soberly, and in the fear of God." In the fear of God, then, of a God who is not mocked by our illusions, our pride, and our pretense, we must learn to bear the burden of our separation for ourselves as Protestants, and also to bear it for those many, whether Protestants or Roman Catholics, who do not see the burden or who refuse to bear it.

Mutual Responsibility

The burden of our separation means that Protestants and Roman Catholics have a mutual responsibility to and for each other.[2] Following as it does from our common membership in Christendom, this mutual responsibility requires that we extend our ecumenical perspective to include Roman Catholicism. The double standard of many Protestants is truly amazing on this score. While their ecumenicity has performed a service in enabling them to reach out to Protestants on the distant fringes of the Christian tradition, they still balk at the suggestion of some responsibility to Roman Catholicism. An interdenominational discussion may include spokesmen for Unitarianism and even for the Jewish faith, but the inclusion of a spokesman for Rome puts everyone on edge—including the spokesman for Rome. Although interdenominational schools and faculties of theology take

215

pride in their inclusiveness and sometimes have Jewish theologians as professors, they usually do not include any Roman Catholics. These concrete instances illustrate how little responsibility most of us feel for our separated brethren, even though we do admit that despite their separation from us they remain our brethren.

It is really no answer to point out that our separated brethren do not regard us as brethren at all and that the only responsibility they sense for us is the responsibility to bring us back to Mother Church. As we have seen repeatedly in the preceding chapters, the Roman understanding of the church makes any other attitude difficult or impossible. According to that understanding of the church, Protestantism has left the true faith and the true church, and it must now be brought back. Acknowledging Protestantism as an equal in the ecumenical conversation is, from the Roman Catholic point of view, a denial of the truth and a disservice to Protestantism. Within the limits of this point of view, however, Roman Catholics are in some position to acknowledge a responsibility to and for Protestants. Although the prescriptions of *Humani generis* carefully circumscribe the expression of that responsibility, Roman Catholics do not regard Protestants as pagans to be evangelized but as erring Christians to be restored to the truth. [3] Rome thus recognizes a bond with Protestantism that is more intimate than the mere bond of a common humanity. There is something that binds together all those who name the name of Christ, even though Rome cannot admit that they are all members of the church.[4] To this extent Rome, too, senses a responsibility for other Christians.

Despite this shortcoming in the sense of responsibility among Roman Catholics (or even because of it), Protestants who bear the burden of our separation must be even more deeply aware of their responsibility. If the church is to call itself "the body of Christ," it assumes the task of carrying on what Christ did—teaching and healing and praying and bearing burdens. The church does this when it becomes a place for Christians to strengthen and support one another in its worship and instruction and fellowship. The church does this, too, when the churches bear one another's burdens. In ecumenical

216

contacts across denominational lines, this generation of Protestants has begun to learn this. Our common faith in a common Lord has helped us to examine the strengths and the weaknesses of our denominational differences, to learn from one another, and to bear the burden which this imposes upon us. But the common faith in a common Lord which we share with Roman Catholics has not succeeded in piercing the iron curtains erected by both sides. Even if the wall erected by one side were to fall, no one would notice, because the wall erected by the other side is as high and as thick as ever. Good fences do not always make good neighbors, and we do not bear one another's burdens. Yet the nature of our separation from Roman Catholicism requires us to do so, as does the constantly recurring need to discover our own identity as Protestants. Thus there is a burden on both sides, some motes and a few beams. Therefore both sides have the duty of assuming responsibility to and for each other. Only in this way can the churches be, in Augustine's phrase, "the servants of all the servants of Christ."

Gentle and Firm Testimony

Bearing the burden of our separation means that we must bear gentle and firm testimony against each other's faults. The history of four centuries of mutual accusation and recrimination has given both of us ample opportunity to find such faults in the others and to reveal them in ourselves. During the first century and a half after the Reformation, discovering these faults was the way a young theologian on either side won his spurs; and a favorite exercise for the mature theologian was the composition of a new treatise on the errors of Luther or of Trent, as the case may be. In many such treatises, needless to say, the arguments of the two sides passed each other without even touching. Not very many readers were convinced by them, and political allegiance influenced church membership far more than did confessional rhetoric. The theological polemics of the sixteenth and seventeenth centuries undoubtedly offended against the virtue of charity more than once, though it must be added that Protestant theologians were as hard on other Protestant theologians as they were

217

on Roman Catholics. With the rigidity of men who knew before they started just where their analysis would lead them, the defenders of the faith demolished their opponents without ever meeting them or their arguments. But as it was carried on by men like Martin Chemnitz and Johann Gerhard on the Protestant side or Robert Bellarmine on the Roman side, the polemical theology of these centuries did voice a testimony that was always firm and sometimes even gentle.

The modern world, including the modern church, finds polemical theology impolite, rather like eating peas with a knife. The usual civilized alternative to it is a tolerance which disposes of the burden of our separation by dropping it on the side of the road—a road on which, after all, "we are all traveling together to the same place." Useful though this attitude of "live and let live" may be as a means of preserving domestic tranquility, it is really no solution. For the separation remains, and neither side can afford to be indifferent to the separation if it is to be faithful to its own position and history. By the very fact of its continued existence, each side is convinced that the other side has distorted the full meaning of the Christian gospel. If this is so, then there is no alternative to gentle and firm testimony. As we have seen in this book, Protestantism is obliged to define itself with specific reference to Roman Catholicism. When Protestantism asserts and defends its right to exist, it must deal with the fact of our separation and with the question of its continuance. That means looking at the present state of Protestantism and examining current conditions in Roman Catholicism. To conclude from this that the day of Protestantism is over, as the converts have concluded, is to deal frivolously with the seriousness of our separation; and to conclude that mutual testimony is useless, as much of the leadership on both sides has concluded, is to negate the very grounds of our separation.

Gentle and firm testimony, then, is what we as Protestants owe to Roman Catholics, and also what Roman Catholics owe to us Protestants. If we refuse to read each other's books or attend each other's schools or meet for genuine discussion of the issues that separate us, how can there be any testimony, gentle or firm or any other kind? As Chapter XIII suggests, we need to consider the creation of arenas

218

where such testimony could be the regular order of the day. There are hindrances on both sides that would have to be overcome, but we must try to overcome them. The fear and the defensiveness that have characterized the attitudes on both sides often transform testimony into aggression, or they drive both sides back into their ghettos. Some of this is due to what we know about each other, some of it is due to what we do not know. Both Protestants and Roman Catholics need to be better informed about what is actually going on in the thought and the life of the other party. In some ways this may be better, and in other ways it may be worse, than we had imagined. The sermons delivered at Reformation festivals suggest that many Protestants are still battling the Inquisition and the Renaissance papacy, while the "Letters to the Editor" during the fight over the banning of the film *Martin Luther* on a television station in Chicago made it clear that many Roman Catholics still interpret the Reformation as the spawn of the devil. Perhaps books such as this one can help to clear the air—not in order to obscure our differences, but in order to clarify our real differences.

So long has it been since there was genuine testimony in either direction that representatives of both sides become tongue-tied when they do have the opportunity. It is far easier for groups of Roman Catholic bishops or of Protestant churchmen to pass resolutions in the safety of their own councils and thus to voice their testimony through the press rather than directly. Only by the intervention of some third party can the two sides really be brought face to face for the kind of testimony they both need to give and to receive. The theological alienation has been going on for so long that it would probably be necessary for a philosopher to stand between two theologians and translate the one to the other—if we could find a philosopher who understands both theologians. Historians and social scientists need to point out to both sides how many of their differences are related to trends in society as well as to issues in the interpretation of the faith. Providing the setting for such conversation and confrontation is a primary need in the life of the churches today, and all the more so when the churches do not recognize the need. For in no other way can we live up to the moral obligations imposed upon us by our separation.

Honest Self-Examination

The obverse side of such gentle and firm testimony is a program of honest self-examination. The only way to rescue the churches of the Reformation from the very thing against which the Reformation protested is for each generation to regard the Reformation as an unfinished task and a new opportunity. Over and over again the dynamic of what Paul Tillich calls "the Protestant principle" must be applied to the forms of theology and church life that have come out of Protestantism. In Tillich's own words:

> The central principle of Protestantism is the doctrine of justification by grace alone, which means that no individual and no human group can claim a divine dignity for its moral achievements, for its sacramental power, for its sanctity, or for its doctrine. If, consciously or unconsciously, they make such a claim, Protestantism requires that they be challenged by the prophetic protest, which gives God alone absoluteness and sanctity and denies every claim of human pride. This protest against itself on the basis of an experience of God's majesty constitutes the Protestant principle.[5]

Protestantism stops being Protestant when it forgets to address to itself the same prophetic criticism which it is so willing to address to Roman Catholicism. Throughout the career of Luther we can hear this call to self-examination and self-criticism. He was almost ruthless in the honesty of his self-examination. His personal piety, his theological formulas, the quality of Protestant preaching, the church life and devotion of the evangelical churches, the increasing political involvement of his Reformation—these and other central questions never ceased to trouble him, and he never stopped wondering whether the Reformation had not been a mistake. Out of such wondering came his certainty that despite all its weaknesses the Reformation had indeed been God's work. This did not make him smug about its achievements or blind to its failures. When the reformers speak about justification by faith, they

220

are applying this to the church as well as to the individual. The church, too, is "righteous and sinful at the same time." This Reformation insight, upon which we drew in Chapter XII, makes honesty and candor in self-examination a necessary corollary of the church's proclamation; and the sermons of Calvin in Geneva are sufficient evidence that such honesty and candor can be altogether compatible with the conviction that one's theological position is the correct one.

Nevertheless, the conviction that one's theological position is the correct one can become so overwhelming in the life of a Protestant church that it no longer examines itself but examines only its members to see whether they conform to the standards of its arbitrary orthodoxy. Hence honest self-examination cannot be taken for granted in a church simply because it teaches justification by faith or traces its lineage to the Reformation. Repeatedly in Protestant history the churches have forgotten the meaning of justification and have become self-satisfied in their wealth or their political power or their orthodoxy or their moralism. So it has been necessary again and again for the Protestant principle of self-criticism to assert itself against this self-satisfaction and to issue a call to repentance. Just how much of this self-criticism there has been in Protestant history is only now becoming evident. Studies by Arnold Schleiff and other scholars are unearthing the continuing barrage of criticism directed at the church by the church during the period of Protestant orthodoxy and since.[6] The power of the Protestant principle refuses to be submerged in the life of the Protestant churches.

In the Roman church, the situation is different and more difficult, partly because anyone who issues a call to self-examination runs the danger of sounding like a Protestant. Yet the liturgical movement, discussed in Chapter XI, and the current preoccupation of many Roman Catholic scholars with the Bible, discussed in Chapter XII, are both instances of such self-examination. There are also many among both theologians and parish priests who are intensely critical of the *status quo*. Books like Father Ong's *Frontiers in American Catholicism* or Monsignor Ellis' *American Catholics and the Intellectual Life* speak with a ringing candor about the shortcomings of the church's perform-

221

ance in the United States.[7] In *Commonweal* and in other publications the articulate laity of the church adds its note of critical self-examination. Although all of these men, clerical and lay, must be extremely cautious about the form of their criticism and although they may run a certain risk in voicing it, I think it is fair to say that there is no valid criticism of Roman Catholicism from Protestant ranks that has not found an echo somewhere within Rome. Much of the criticism is ignored or even stifled, but it goes on. A Protestant churchman can only pray, "May their tribe increase!" and meanwhile see to it that our own church life and our own theology are ever open both to the critique that comes from Roman Catholicism and to the self-examination which is the peculiar vocation of the Protestant theologian.

Assessment of Needs and Debts

When honest self-examination goes beyond a summary of the contemporary condition of the church to a thorough audit of its accounts, it comes to an assessment of our mutual needs and of our mutual debts. Implied in an honest self-examination is the obligation that we honestly face up to what we have all lost through the division of the church and to what we have received from the other half of the divided church. This is not easy for anyone to do, and initially at least we might have to do it in private. For such an assessment asks that the church institute a system of bookkeeping to which neither Protestantism nor Roman Catholicism is accustomed. Not only must the liabilities be listed in detail, but the assets must also be labeled "accounts payable."

We have lost something through our separation, all of us have. Neither Protestantism nor Roman Catholicism has as direct an access to the fullness of the Christian tradition as it should have, and neither is as free to possess the completeness of Christ. The prophetic and priestly belong together, and either is truncated without the other. Yet they have been in proper balance only seldom. The extremes represented by Jeremiah and by the priestly code in the Old Testament have had their counterpart in Christian history, and since the Reformation it has been possible for these two extremes to claim that they are represented by the two divisions of Western Christendom. Bear-

222

ing the burden of our separation means admitting that this is so. As Jeremiah needed the very system of priests and cult against which he protested, so Protestantism has needed the catholic substance against whose idolatry it warns. As the cultic system of the Old Testament needed the prophets to save it from itself, so Roman Catholicism needs to hear the prophetic voice of its separated brethren. This means that on both sides we must seek to incorporate into our own church life as much of the total Christian tradition as we can. It means that Protestants must look for ways to strengthen and to articulate their catholicity, as we shall point out in Chapter XVI, and that Roman Catholics must discover means of becoming more evangelical. This has become infinitely more difficult for both sides because of our separation, and we do not bear the burden of our separation unless we face our mutual needs.

Matching our mutual needs are our mutual debts. We are what we are as Protestants partly because of what we have inherited from our catholic past. Modern Roman Catholicism owes a greater debt of gratitude to the reformers than it has ever been willing to acknowledge. To summarize what we have said in Chapters IV and XIII, we Protestants must discover what made the Reformation possible, while Roman Catholics must discover what made the Reformation necessary. For too long Protestant theologians and historians have treated Luther and Calvin as creations out of nothing or as a "sports" in the Darwinian sense of the word, who had no real continuity with preceding generations. What is more, they have often gloried in this. At a congress of Reformation scholars in Denmark I heard an eminent European authority on Reformation theology declare that "only that is genuine in Luther which is different from the tradition that produced him." Yet the research of that very scholar and of many others substantiates what a mature doctrine of the church would also oblige us to say: that in their reformatory work Luther and Calvin were administering the heritage of the church and acting in the name of the church— not merely the church of the first century, but the church of all the centuries. That is why Chapter IV could speak of "the catholicity of the reformers."

223

Rome, on the other hand, needs to measure the extent of its debt to the Reformation and to Protestantism since the Reformation. Indeed, Roman Catholicism is at its positive best when it is confronted by Protestantism. Without making invidious comparisons, it is possible to say that Roman Catholicism has succeeded in finding such maturity within German and French culture at least partly because of the theological vigor in the Protestantism it has confronted there. The intellectual leaders of the American church look wistfully at the church in France, and they have a chance to achieve some of the same power here because of the presence of a Protestantism that is acquiring an ever deeper theological consciousness. The Roman church thus owes more to Protestantism than either might be able to see. That debt goes all the way back to the Reformation. As children of the church, the reformers spoke out against what threatened the church. Its initial reaction was to excommunicate them, but in subsequent decades it went on to correct many of the abuses to which they had pointed. The program did not go far enough; and many of the revisions were not improvements at all, as the decrees of the Council of Trent make painfully evident. But revisions there were, and these have strengthened and purified the Roman church. For these and for some of its continued health it is indebted to Protestantism; and some day it will have to acknowledge this more openly than it has, and open itself to the witness of the Reformation. Thus both Roman Catholicism and Protestantism have several needs to recognize and several debts to pay if they are truly to bear the burden of our separation.

Concern for the Total Church

If Protestants and Roman Catholics ever recognized their mutual needs and their mutual debts, they might develop a concern for the total church and an awareness of the consequences of their actions for the total church of Christ. When Protestant churchmen and spokesmen persist in making Protestantism merely the negation of Roman Catholicism, they are threatening the foundations of Protestantism. It is often easier for a Protestant to take the voice of secularism seriously than it is for him to hear the witness of his Roman neighbor. Protestants and secularists band together in an opposition to Rome that is sometimes hypersensitive to the point of condemning a crèche on the high school lawn as "sectarian." In the days following the Communist coup in Czechoslovakia, some leaders of the Protestant churches were beguiled into believing that Communism opposed the Roman church merely because of its wealth and power, and that therefore the Marxist state was actually supporting the Protestant cause by its attacks upon the hierarchy. There was just enough justice in these attacks to make the case plausible. Since then it has become clear that an attack upon Roman Catholicism may be an attack upon Christianity itself. When Protestants join in the chase merely because someone is beating the antipapal drum, they may discover that the mob will turn on them next.

On the other hand, when the myopia of some Roman Catholics causes them to act as though the Christian cause and the Roman cause were always identical, the whole cause of Christ suffers, including the Roman cause. The political maneuvers of Roman Catholic leaders here and abroad harm not only them and their church, but Protestants and their churches and the church of Jesus Christ as a whole. Writers in *Commonweal* and other periodicals may disown the tactics of the late Cardinal Segura, for whom even Franco was not restrictive enough in his measures against Protestantism. But the voices that are raised against such maneuvers are usually thinner than the voices of the prelates who engage in the maneuvers. Although some Protestants take a certain pleasure in observing the embarrassment of Roman Catholics in America at these maneuvers, the real calamity lies in their evil consequences for Christians everywhere. As the New Testament says, "The name of God is blasphemed among the Gentiles" (Rom. 2:24) because of what some members of the church do. Each side has managed to do a great deal of damage to the other side as well as to itself by these tactics, and Christendom is poorer as a result. When Protestants surrender the gospel to some modern idea; or when Roman Catholics, supposedly in the name of the gospel, oppose some modern idea merely because it is modern—

225

then the whole body of Christ suffers. To bear the burden of our separation, both Roman Catholicism and Protestantism will have to have a greater concern for the total church.

Although they were not written to a divided church, but to a confused church, the words of Paul's letter to the Galatians have a peculiar relevance to both parts of our divided church as we carry the burden of our separation:

Brethren, if a man is overtaken in any trespass, you who are spiritual should restore him in a spirit of gentleness. Look to yourself, lest you too be tempted. Bear one another's burdens, and so fulfill the law of Christ. For if any one thinks he is something, when he is nothing, he deceives himself. But let each one test his own work, and then his reason to boast will be in himself alone and not in his neighbor. For each man will have to bear his own load. Let him who is taught the word share all good things with him who teaches. Do not be deceived; God is not mocked, for whatever a man sows, that he will also reap. (6:1-7.)

XVI
The Challenge
of Roman Catholicism

✠ This book is a Protestant discussion of Roman Catholicism. But the discussion moves in both directions, and Roman Catholicism also has something to say to Protestantism. Just as Protestantism cannot afford to overlook Rome when it weighs its own plans for the future, so it cannot overlook the fundamental questions which Rome addresses to it about that future. The purpose of this final chapter is to raise several of the questions which come from Roman Catholicism to Protestantism, for these questions constitute its continuing challenge to Protestant Christianity.

A Comprehensive World View

Can Protestantism provide its adherents with a world view which is as comprehensive and yet as Christian as the Thomistic? Or must Protestant thought choose between comprehensiveness and evangelical loyalty?

As we have seen in Chapter X, the Thomistic world view has man aged to be both comprehensive and Christian. Thus it enables Roman Catholic thinkers, whether laymen or theologians, to locate the field of their special concern within the range of truth and to pursue their study under the generous auspices of a total system. Taking his start from the Thomistic understanding of justice, the lawyer can discover the implications of the system for his work and the implications of his work for the system—so can the physician, the soldier, the philologist, and the housewife. Each has his place in the grand design, and to each the power of the faith can be applied in some special way. For it would be a mistake to suppose that only the philosophers can make use of Thomistic thought. While its more rarefied discussions belong only to the philosophers and the theologians, its basic implications can reach into the life and work of anyone who reflects on his own area of interest and its connection with the rest of reality. By relating nature to grace in the way we have described in Chapter X, Thomism maintains a balance between faith and reason that gives each its due without doing violence to the other.

This balance between faith and reason addresses a basic challenge to Protestant thought. The history of Protestant thought demonstrates how difficult it has been for thinkers in the evangelical tradition to achieve the comprehensiveness which a world view demands, and how difficult it has been for the philosophical thinkers of non-Roman traditions to keep the Christian faith central in their world views. During the conflict between liberalism and fundamentalism this was one of the issues at stake; and now that the conflict has died down, it may be appropriate to point out that the issue has not been settled. Current discussions of Christian higher education have made clear that Protestant thought is still looking for a way of thinking about science and the humanities that will do justice to them without surrendering the gospel.[1] The literature coming out of these discussions also manifests a greater difference of opinion among Protestants than there is between some Protestants and some Roman Catholics on this entire question. Meanwhile, the Protestant churches continue to maintain hundreds of colleges, all of them involved (whether they like it or not) in this very issue. The answers offered by these colleges range from the claim that religion offers certain moral values, and nothing more, all the way to the claim that the doctrinal system of the denomination supporting the college is the final truth, to which the sciences and the humanities must conform or perish. Between these two extremes are various other answers, but it is difficult to formulate the Protestant alternative to Thomism in such a way as to include all of them.

Yet Protestant theology has proved that it can supply alternatives to Thomism that are just as comprehensive and yet just as Christian. An outstanding instance of such an alternative is the thought of Friedrich Schleiermacher (d. 1834). Taking as his explicit assignment the exposition of the Christian faith in a form that could be mediated to the culture of his time, Schleiermacher was so successful in this task of mediation that his orthodox critics have been able to accuse him of treason to the gospel.[2] More recently, however, this criticism has undergone some revision, as Protestant theologians have come to realize that they need more than the recitation of traditional formulas to make their theology meaningful to contemporary thought.[3] Now it is becoming evident that in the thought of Schleiermacher Protestantism possesses a resource for a world view that is simultaneously comprehensive and Christian—comprehensive in the sense that it takes seriously what the sciences and the humanities have learned about reality, Christian in the sense that it relates all of this to the revelation of God in Jesus Christ. Since "comprehensive" in this context refers to "universality" and "Christian" in this context refers to "identity," what this really means is that the theology of Schleiermacher is catholic in the best sense of the word. Though his contemporaries even accused him of undue sympathy for Roman Catholicism, he certainly is a catholic thinker and therefore one to whom Protestant thought today needs to listen again.

If Protestant thought today recognizes the challenge of Roman Catholicism to its traditions and prejudices, it will take another look at those thinkers who, like Schleiermacher, displayed the marks of the catholicity that belongs to the Protestant heritage. In this way

229

the challenge of Roman Catholicism may help Protestantism to recover its own true catholicity and to recover the monuments from
its theological past by which such catholicity is both sustained and
judged. Then Protestant thought will prove that it does not have
to choose between comprehensiveness and evangelical loyalty, but
that it can develop world views—and by the very nature of Protestantism, there will always be more than one—which are as comprehensive
and yet as Christian as the Thomistic. However one may evaluate the
thought of Paul Tillich, upon whom this book has drawn for many
of its insights, he does represent a continuation of the work of
Schleiermacher in formulating an interpretation of reality that is
truly catholic.

An Inclusive Appeal

Can Protestantism be truly inclusive, meeting men on every level
right where they are and bringing them the meaning of the Christian
faith? Or must it restrict itself to certain social classes?

One of the steps by which Christianity became catholic was its
adoption of an inclusive appeal and its willingness to accept men
just as they were. This meant that the standards of church membership were revised to permit the inclusion of the Roman citizens and
barbarian invaders who became Christians more by decree than by
conviction. Ever since, it has been a mark of catholic Christianity
that it seeks to give everyone as much Christianity as his present
situation permits him to bear. As Harnack put it shortly before his
death:

The raison d'etre of the [Roman] catholic church is quite incontestable.
Anyone who takes men as they are, and as they will remain for many generations to come, cannot doubt the justifiability of this world-wide institution. This church goes right on nourishing saints, and at the same time it
teaches the rest of its children "to hurl their spears and honor the gods,"
that is, to take religion as the masses have always taken it and as the masses
require it. What more do you want? . . . One must concede the necessity
and the usefulness of an institution which disciplines the common man and
still gives delicate consciences what they want. . . .[4]

As a rule, Protestants can dismiss this challenge by showing the compromises it has necessitated in the program of the church. After four centuries of work in Latin America, the church has managed to bring its people all the way from A to B. Such an answer still has a point, but the point is dulled by the hard facts of Protestant church life. Rome has no monopoly on casual church membership, nor on a laity that is ignorant of what the church teaches, nor on compromise with sub-Christian principles and practices. Many Protestant churches now pride themselves on their policy of "open membership." I know of one congregation where the only requirement for membership is that one must be Caucasian. This is, of course, an extreme example of the plight of Protestantism in America, which has concentrated upon one segment of society even while it has been engaged in revising its own standards for membership. The revision has been horizontal, reaching out to the less committed members of the same social stratum, rather than vertical, reaching to other social strata. To the non-Christian observer, the contrast between Protestantism and Roman Catholicism on this score is quite obvious. As an official of the Urban League, no church member himself, once asked me, "If you were a Negro, which white man's church would you join—or could you join?" The same embarrassment attends the efforts of Protestant congregations to reach the intellectual and the artist or any other social group with which, in that particular locality, Protestantism has not been identified before.

Any unbiased observer must admit, however, that contemporary Protestantism in America is more concerned about this exclusiveness than it has ever been before. An entire generation of Protestant ministers has developed an acute conscience over the snobbishness and the segregation that have risen to haunt Protestant church life in various parts of America. Although some of their people have occasionally accused them of being radical because of this, these ministers have succeeded in injecting this acute conscience into their laity too. It would be interesting, for example, to study the impact of the East Harlem Protestant Parish upon the thought and the plans of Protestants throughout the United States. Begun in comparative obscurity by a group of seminarians, this project has drawn the attention and the approval of church leaders in many Protestant denominations. Unfortunately, the newspapers often are quick to report on the actions of a minister who fights the integration of the races, but slow to describe the steady progress toward integration that is going on in many Protestant congregations on both sides of the Mason-Dixon line. In these ways Protestantism is showing that the inclusiveness of the gospel has not been lost in its message and strategy, and that it can meet men on every level right where they are. It is difficult to imagine how, having set out in the direction of greater inclusiveness and catholicity, American Protestantism can ever turn back again.

An Urban Ministry

Can Protestantism in America develop an urban ministry that recognizes the values of urban life and relates these to the obedience of the gospel?

Ever since the great migrations of the late nineteenth century Protestantism has been engaged in a losing battle for control of the American city. Waves of immigrants from the predominantly Roman Catholic countries of Southern and Eastern Europe and from Ireland rolled into the cities, until they became a majority in many of them and a plurality in many others. So much was this so, as we saw in Chapter XI, that Roman Catholicism in America became almost exclusively urban in its makeup and in its outlook, with a consequent impoverishment of its liturgical and spiritual life. In ministering to its urban membership, the Roman church has adapted its program and its strategy to the needs of people who live and work and play close together. At its best, this strategy takes the measure of the loneliness that so often marks urban life. Originally a part of the immigrant's struggle to keep his identity in a Protestant culture, this strategy has managed to make membership in the church the characteristic mark of identity in place of the vanishing ethnic differences. So it is, as Will Herberg has shown, that the Roman Catholic in the American city now uses his church as a means of defining what he

232

is, while his father or grandfather used the country of his origin.[5] The Roman church is now a dominant element in the urban life of America.

Meanwhile, the great migration has become a Protestant movement—the migration from the city to the suburbs. We have touched upon the implications of the migration for the churches in an earlier chapter. It belongs here because of what it means for the challenge of Roman Catholicism to Protestantism in the cities. The growth of the suburbs in postwar America has decreased the chances of Protestantism to recover a position of influence in the urban life of our land. Of course, Roman Catholics are moving to the suburbs too, and Roman Catholic churches are going up there. But the old church back in the city does not close down operations when this happens. All too often, as thoughtful leaders of Protestant denominations have been pointing out recently, the entire scale of values which is preached from Protestant pulpits makes it seem that the knowledge of God and the service of God would be easier if everyone lived in the country or in a small town. Protestant preaching, said one denominational leader, is not merely suburban but anti-urban; for we have so glorified the virtues of the supposedly simple life and have so denounced the wickedness of the city that the positive values of urban living have little or no place in Protestant ethics and preaching. Regardless of how one evaluates life in an American suburb—and those who live in them, as well as those who have stayed behind, both confess to a certain amount of ambivalence—it should be possible for Protestantism to meet the needs of the urban man as well as the suburban man.

If this is not possible, then Protestantism will be obliged to revise its estimate of the role it wants to play in American life. In large measure the question of an urban ministry for Protestantism hinges upon a settlement of the racial struggle now going on in many Protestant parishes. Each settlement in the direction of "separate but equal" Protestant churches weakens the Protestant message in its witness to the universality of the gospel. There is no great danger in the immediate future that American Protestantism will become an exclusive club for white Gentile commuters, but there is enough of a trend in

233

that direction for Protestant churches to plan their future strategy more carefully. Recent meetings and decisions in several Protestant denominations suggest that their leaders are aware of this danger and determined to develop a truly urban ministry for their churches. If they do, it seems safe to predict that such a ministry will include more "catholic" elements than it now does.

A Living Tradition

Can Protestantism find devices for symbolizing and carrying the living tradition of the Christian past that are truly meaningful to the general church public?

The challenge of Roman Catholicism is the challenge of a living tradition. The converts of whom we spoke in Chapter XIV often describe the sense of belonging to a tradition as one of the most rewarding experiences in their conversion. Although this has always been true of Roman Catholicism, it has acquired new relevance in modern times. For today the Christian church is one of the few cultural forces that can unite us with our living past. Political, social, and even educational life have lost much of their touch with the tradition. The church is still one place where people can acquire a sense of belonging to a lineage. Now that the Protestant churches have been in existence for a while, they too have developed traditions— or "usages," as some of them prefer to term them—which are hallowed by age and which give the members of the church this sense of belonging. Each such tradition or "usage" raises anew the challenge of Roman Catholicism, for it makes ridiculous the Protestant objections to any tradition simply on the grounds that it is tradition. The churches which rejected the introits and graduals as too static are now using a "call to worship" that sometimes does not vary from year to year.

All too often, however, Protestant efforts to recover a sense for the living traditions end up by losing all touch with their own tradition. The various high church movements in several Protestant denominations often superimpose alien forms upon a church life that is not ready for them. Russian Orthodox chants in a Baptist church or the introduction of "the daily sacrifice of the mass" in a Methodist church are exoticism, not living tradition. In this respect the ecumenical movement has sometimes done a disservice to the churches, for it has enabled some churchmen to go around their own traditions rather than through them to the living tradition of the church. Thus the richness and variety of the Christian tradition has often given way to a passion for uniformity which is not traditional at all. The liturgical scholars of Rome have begun to recover some of that richness and variety as they have given more attention to the Eastern traditions. Behind this is a sound theological principle, which we must extend not only to Roman Catholicism and to Eastern Orthodoxy, but also to the several Protestant traditions. If they take the measure of their own heritage, they will discover a living contact with the catholic tradition. This contact will help them to see how catholic they are in the true sense of the word, and it will point the way for a recovery of a deeper catholicity that is nevertheless germane to their own special heritage.

The only alternative to tradition, then, would seem to be bad tradition. As Protestantism faces the challenge of Roman Catholicism, it must seek devices for symbolizing the living tradition. Open as it has been to influences from the world of culture about it, Protestant thought should be able to adapt some of the devices now being used to symbolize and carry our cultural heritage. For example, some Protestant congregations have experimented successfully with a "Great Books" discussion of selected writings by church fathers. In such a discussion the lay members of these congregations have found an affinity with the fathers that they have never dreamed could exist. A Protestant who reads Irenaeus' *Proof of the Apostolic Preaching* or Augustine's *Enchiridion*—both of them available in modern English translations, with helpful notes and introductions—will learn that he has a greater claim upon the living tradition of catholic Christianity than he would ever have supposed. The hymns of the church are another way of symbolizing the tradition, as is the recovery of the historic creeds in worship. Protestantism can meet the challenge of Roman Catholicism if it uses its own creative power in discovering and then refashioning the symbols of the catholic tradition in which it stands. In the process it may provoke the Roman church into a reappraisal of its own tradition in the light of the greater catholic tradition in which it also stands.

A Sacramental Worship

Can Protestantism meet man's need for sacramental worship without losing itself in either superstition or rationalism?

In the doctrine of the Lord's Supper, says Schleiermacher, there have been two extremes, "the one ascribing a magical value to the sacrament, the other depressing it into a bare sign." [6] The former danger continually haunts Roman Catholic sacramentalism, as we have seen in Chapter VIII; the latter danger easily besets Protestant theology and worship. The presence of Roman Catholicism therefore challenges Protestantism to produce an approach to the sacraments that will avoid both superstition and rationalism. Such an approach does appear within Roman Catholicism, even though the danger of magic is never far away. Sacramental teachings like those of the liturgical movement or of the French theologian de Lubac certainly show that within the limits of Roman Catholic orthodoxy (though just within the limits) it is possible to assert a sacramental presence which does not fall either into fetishism or into abstract philosophical discussions of substance and accident.[7] In other words, the sacramental doctrine of contemporary Roman Catholicism may still tip in the direction of magic, but it does manage to extricate itself from that extreme.

Can the sacramental doctrine of contemporary Protestantism extricate itself from the opposite extreme? All indications suggest that the difficulty will be great. Instead of challenging Protestantism to produce sacramental worship and sacramental teaching, Roman Catholicism has often succeeded in frightening Protestants away from both. Rare indeed has been the Protestant liturgy or the Protestant

236

theology that has not been formulated primarily in antithesis to Rome. Very early in the development of Protestantism, the doctrine of the Lord's Supper became a matter of bitter controversy; current ecumenical conversation has shown that it still is. There has, however, been comparatively little effort to rethink the meaning of the Lord's Supper in the light of the Scriptures and of tradition, and even less effort to express that meaning in forms of worship that truly symbolize the faith of the church. On no doctrine is there a greater hiatus between the systematic theologians and the expositors of the Scriptures, or between all the theologians and the piety of the people. Yet any experience in the parish ministry will convince a man that the piety of the people craves sacramental worship. The ceremonies, good and bad, that have attached themselves to weddings and funerals indicate that people need more than words to express their deepest feelings; and many a Protestant pastor has had to devise forms and formulas to meet man's need for sacramental worship.

Recognition of this need has come hard for some Protestants, but it has come. Now it should be possible for Protestant churches to restore the Lord's Supper to its central position in the worship of the Christian community. The catholic intuition of an extremely Protestant brotherhood, the Disciples of Christ, has caused them to make the communion central in their worship and to celebrate it every Sunday. In the tradition of most Protestant denominations there is a higher estimate of the sacraments than their present liturgies and theologies manifest. The rationalism of the eighteenth and nineteenth centuries has corroded much of the catholic substance in these denominations, but they can still recover it—and they can do so without relapsing into the uncritical patterns of thought that preceded rationalism. For it is by the discoveries of critical historical study that we have been forced to recognize the importance of sacramental worship for our understanding of the early church. Thus historical study and contemporary developments both prompt us to accept the challenge of Roman Catholicism and to recover the sacramental emphasis of our living tradition.

A Policy for Reunion

Can Protestantism formulate a policy for reunion with Rome that will clarify the terms and requirements of a settlement short of unconditional surrender?

Other issues may be peripheral in a consideration of the challenge of Roman Catholicism, but the issue of reunion is central. Has the ecumenical movement moved far enough to be able to speak of reunion with Rome? This is the problem to which all of Part Three has been devoted. Leaders and founders of the ecumenical movement like Archbishop Nathan Söderblom (d. 1931) realized that if the Protestant churches ever begin to speak to one another, they will also have to speak to and about Rome. From the changes within modern Roman Catholicism about which we have been speaking throughout this book, it is evident that some of the historic antitheses between Protestants and Roman Catholics no longer apply. The developments within Protestantism have made some other antitheses obsolete. On still other antitheses, Rome may be prepared to make concessions. Lecturing at St. Mark's, a Protestant church in Stuttgart, the Roman Catholic theologian Karl Adam felt authorized to promise that if Protestants returned to Rome, they would be granted a vernacular liturgy, a married clergy, and the chalice in the Lord's Supper.[8] All three of these are matters of church law, not of divine law, and could be changed.

All three of these are matters on which most Protestants have strong feelings; for some Protestants they would even constitute the chief obstacles to reunion with Rome. Yet Rome could change all three of them and still remain Rome! What it could not change without difficulty are the postures it has felt obliged to take since the Reformation. Even if the current reinterpreters of Trent are right— and they do seem to stretch the decrees beyond the breaking point— the Council of Trent still remains an insurmountable barricade; the Vatican Council, the immaculate conception, and the assumption likewise. Protestants must begin to study these barricades and to formulate an interpretation of them that will draw the line beyond which we are not prepared to yield. Is there, for example, any sense

238

at all in which Protestants are ready to say that a man is justified by faith and works, or that Scripture and the traditions belong to the corpus of Christian authority? And if there is a sense in which such an "and" is permissible, does it correspond to Trent? Or what is the basic difference between the assumption of Mary and the ideas about the ascension of Enoch and of Elijah that formed part of orthodox Protestant theology for centuries and still belong to the faith of many believers? If the latter have room within Protestantism, must a doctrine of the assumption of Mary be ruled out as not only unscriptural but antiscriptural?

I do not presume to answer these questions for the Protestant churches, but to raise them for myself and for the Protestant churches. Whether or not Protestant churchmen go to the new "ecumenical council," Protestantism will have to become much more explicit about what it would demand, and what it would concede, in discussions pointing toward reunion with Rome. For the time may well come—perhaps in the twentieth century, more likely in the next— when Protestantism will be faced with alternatives more terrible than reunion. Under the oppression of National Socialism, Lutherans, Reformed, and Roman Catholics in Germany were beginning to learn the meaning of the *Una Sancta*, the one, holy, catholic, and apostolic church of which we spoke in Chapter XIII. Then came the collapse of the Nazi regime, the tightening of Roman Catholic lines, and a new era for Protestantism. Still the memory lingers of a Christian understanding and concord unknown since the sixteenth century. Such a time may come for Protestantism in other lands too. When it does, Protestants should be able to give an answer to the question of why they are not Roman Catholics. In the words of Bishop Lilje, "each generation of Protestants must re-think the decision of the sixteenth century." Unconditional surrender would be easy; but as we said in Chapter XIV, this would be a denial of the whole Protestant heritage and a disservice to Roman Catholicism as well. It is harder, but it is also more honest, to formulate a policy for reunion.

Then Protestantism may be able to face the challenge of Roman Catholicism and to probe the riddle of Roman Catholicism. For then

239

it may recognize in the church of Rome a fellow pilgrim on the journey to the Heavenly City, whose builder and maker is God. Under God, Protestants and Roman Catholics can begin to face one another across the great divide, to pray for one another if not with one another, and to live out their lives of service and faith in the church of Jesus Christ on earth—

> Till with the vision glorious
> Her longing eyes are blest
> And the great church victorious
> Shall be the church at rest.

240

NOTES

In a book like this it would be possible to provide documentation for almost every sentence. Instead, I have noted those books from which I quote directly or to whose authors I refer by name, and I have added the titles of some books which seem to me unusually helpful or authoritative. Most of them contain bibliographies for further reading. Although I have tried to cite English books as much as possible, it has been necessary to mention some titles in other languages. An asterisk (*) before an author's name indicates that he is a Roman Catholic.

There are two collections of official statements and sources which are indispensable to any student of the Roman church. One of them has been translated into English (but not very well): *Henry Denzinger, *The Sources of Catholic Dogma*, translated by Roy J. Deferrari. Because it is a standard work and has now become accessible in English, I have referred to it wherever I could, even when I have altered the translation in the interests of style. The other sourcebook, unfortunately, is not available in English: Carl Mirbt, *Quellen zur Geschichte des Papsttums und des römischen Katholizismus* (4th ed.; Tübingen, 1924). It contains many materials which round out the somewhat one-sided picture one could gain by reading only Denzinger. The fifteen volumes of *The Catholic Encyclopedia* contain material on most subjects touched on here, and I have consulted it throughout. The brief history of American Catholicism by *John Tracy Ellis (Chicago: University of Chicago Press, 1956) provides a great deal of information and bibliography for the general reader. Probably the most able defense of Roman Catholicism available in English is that of *Karl Adam, *The Spirit of Catholicism*, translated by Dom Justin McCann; it deserves the attention of any serious student of the Roman communion.

CHAPTER I

1. Thomas Babington Macaulay, "Milton" (1825), *Critical and Historical Essays* (Everyman's Library ed.; London, 1924), I, 173.
2. Winston Churchill, *Blood, Sweat, and Tears* (New York: G. P. Putnam Sons, 1941), p. 173.

3. Paul Tillich, *The Protestant Era*, tr. James Luther Adams (Chicago: University of Chicago Press, 1948), p. 194.
4. *Time*, August 26, 1957, p. 54.
5. Friedrich Heiler, *Der Katholizismus* (Munich, 1923). In a revised and expanded form, it has appeared under the title, *Die katholische Kirche des Ostens und Westens* (Munich, 1937-1941), but this has not been completed.

PART ONE

1. *Karl Adam, *The Spirit of Catholicism* (Garden City, N.Y.: Doubleday and Company, Image Books edition, 1954), p. 2.

CHAPTER II

2. Rudolf Sohm, *Wesen und Ursprung des Katholizismus* (2nd ed.; Leipzig, 1912), p. 13.
3. Aleksiei Khomiakov, *O tserkvi*, ed. by A. P. Karsavin (new ed.; Berlin, 1926), pp. 23-24.
4. Adolf Harnack, *The Constitution and Law of the Church in the First Two Centuries*, tr. by F. L. Pogson and H. D. A. Major (New York: G. P. Putnam's Sons, 1910), p. 253, note 1. Harnack does go on to say: "But yet this cannot be taken to mean very much, for the Catholic elements do not constitute the essence of primitive Christianity. It would therefore be misleading to call primitive Christianity 'Catholic.' Even for the post-apostolic age it is better to avoid this name."
5. Adolf Harnack, *The Mission and Expansion of Christianity in the First Three Centuries*, tr. by James Moffatt (2nd ed.; London, 1908). Kenneth Scott Latourette, *The First Five Centuries, A History of the Expansion of Christianity* (New York: Harper and Bros., 1937), I, 66-170.
6. The first instance of the name is in Ignatius' letter to the Smyrneans, 8, 2 in Cyril Richardson (ed.), *Early Christian Fathers* (Philadelphia: Westminster Press, 1953), p. 115.
7. Augustine's letter to Severinus, Epistle 52, 1, *Patrologia Latina*, 33, 194.
8. The catholic ideals abroad in the Roman world have been excitingly summarized by Rudolf Bultmann, *Primitive Christianity in Its Contemporary Setting*, tr. R. H. Fuller (New York: Meridian Books, 1956).
9. The reader can learn the basic issues in the controversy on the ministry by studying books like K. E. Kirk (ed.), *The Apostolic Ministry* (New York: (Morehouse-Gorham Company, 1947), or the fine summary by John Knox, *The Early Church and the Coming Great Church* (Nashville: Abingdon Press, 1955), pp. 119-28.
10. John 20:21-23 and John 21:15-17. Also Matt. 28:19-20, and Mark 16:15-18, "the long ending of Mark," which was probably a later addition.

11. I Tim. 4:14; II Tim. 4:6; Tit. 1:5-6. The meaning of these passages is discussed in Burton Scott Easton, *The Pastoral Epistles* (New York: Charles Scribner's Sons, 1947), pp. 173-79.

12. Tertullian, "On Prescription against Heretics," 37, *The Ante-Nicene Fathers* (Buffalo: The Christian Literature Publishing Company, 1885), III, 261.

13. Two outstanding studies are Joachim Jeremias, *The Eucharistic Words of Jesus*, tr. Arnold Ehrhardt (New York: The Macmillan Company, 1955), and Hans Lietzmann, *Mass and Lord's Supper*, tr. by Dorothea Reeve (Leiden, 1953 ff.).

14. André Benoit, *Le baptême chrétien au second siècle: la theologie des pères* (Paris, 1953).

15. Ignatius' letter to the Ephesians, 20, 2, *Early Christian Fathers*, p. 93.

16. Frank E. Brightman, *Liturgies Eastern and Western* (Oxford, 1896); Gillis P. Wetter, *Altchristliche Liturgien* (2 vols.; Göttingen, 1921-1922); *Johannes Quasten, *Monumenta eucharistica et liturgica vetustissima* (Bonn, 1935-1937).

17. Cyprian, "The Lapsed," tr. *Maurice Bevenot, *Ancient Christian Writers* (Westminster, Md.: Newman Press, 1957), 25, 13-42 and the accompanying notes. My discussion here is based upon Hugo Koch, *Cyprianische Untersuchungen* (Bonn, 1926), pp. 221-85.

18. This process of purgation is beautifully described by *G. K. Chesterton, *St. Francis of Assisi* (New York: Doubleday and Company, Image Books edition, 1957), pp. 19-37.

19. Emil Brunner, *Revelation and Reason*, tr. Olive Wyon (Philadelphia: Westminster Press, 1946), pp. 389-90.

20. Clement of Alexandria, "The Stromata," I, 5, *The Ante-Nicene Fathers*, II, 305.

21. Origen, *Contra Celsum*, tr. Henry Chadwick (Cambridge: Cambridge University Press, 1953). The differences between Clement and Origen are carefully traced in Richard P. Hanson, *Origen's Doctrine of Tradition* (London: Macmillan and Company, 1954).

22. J. N. D. Kelly, *Early Christian Creeds* (New York: Longmans, Green and Company, 1950) supplants all previous literature on this subject.

23. Adolf Harnack, *Lehrbuch der Dogmengeschichte*, I (5th ed.; Tübingen, 1931), p. 395, note 3.

24. The backgrounds for the establishment of this *modus vivendi* are well summarized in Robert M. Grant, *The Sword and the Cross* (New York: The Macmillan Company, 1955).

CHAPTER III

1. Irenaeus, "Against Heresies," III, 12, 5, *The Ante-Nicene Fathers*, I, 431.

2. See pages 77-80.

3. These references from early Christian literature have been collected and translated in James T. Shotwell and Louise R. Loomis, *The See of Peter* (New York, 1927), pp. 235-85.
4. Hans Lietzmann, *Petrus und Paulus in Rom* (2nd ed.; Berlin, 1927); Oscar Cullmann, *Peter, Disciple—Apostle—Martyr*, tr. Floyd V. Filson (London: Student Christian Movement Press, 1953).
5. Charles Norris Cochrane, *Christianity and Classical Culture* (New York: Oxford University Press, 1944), pp. 27-113.
6. Tertullian, "On Prescription against Heretics," 36, *The Ante-Nicene Fathers*, III, 260.
7. As reported in the Acts of the Council of Chalcedon in Ed. Schwartz (ed.), *Acta Conciliorum Oecumenicorum* (Berlin, 1933), II-1, 277.
8. *Hugo Rahner, "Leo der Grosze, der Papst des Konzils," in *Aloys Grillmeier and *Heinrich Bacht (eds.), *Das Konzil von Chalkedon* (Würzburg, 1951), I, 328.
9. Hippolytus, "The Refutation of All Heresies," IX, 2, *The Ante-Nicene Fathers*, V, 125.
10. *K. G. Preysing, "Echtheit und Bedeutung der dogmatischen Erklärung Zephyrins," *Zeitschrift für katholische Theologie* (1928), LIII, 225-30.
11. Adolf Hamel, *Kirche bei Hippolyt von Rom* (Gütersloh, 1951), pp. 113-14, note 1.
12. The best discussion of Honorius in English is that of *John Chapman, *The Condemnation of Pope Honorius* (London, 1907).
13. *Thomas Owen Martin, "The Twenty-Eighth Canon of Chalcedon: A Background Note" in Grillmeier and Bacht, *Das Konzil von Chalkedon*, II, 433-58.
14. Nicholas' letter to Emperor Michael (865), Epistle 86, *Patrologia Latina*, 119, 948.
15. Nicholas Zernov, *The Church of the Eastern Christians* (London: Society for Promoting Christian Knowledge, 1942), p. 13: "The split was brought about, not by quarrelsome theologians or ambitious prelates, as is usually suggested, but by the greed and lust of those men who, in the name of the Prince of Peace, had embarked upon a war of aggression and conquest."
16. *Otto G. von Simson, *Sacred Fortress* (Chicago: University of Chicago Press, 1948) expounds this theme in the art of Ravenna.

CHAPTER IV

1. Quoted in *Karl Adam, op. cit., p. 184.
2. Martin Luther, "Dictata super Psalterium" (1513-1516), *Werke* (Weimar, 1886), IV, 165.
3. *Henry Denzinger, *The Sources of Catholic Dogma* (St. Louis: B. Herder Book Company, 1957), pp. 347-54 (nn. 1351-1451).

4. The phrase comes from Max Weber, *The Protestant Ethic and the Spirit of Capitalism*, tr. Talcott Parsons (London: George Allen and Unwin, Ltd., 1930), pp. 95-183.
5. Johann Gerhard, *Confessio Catholica* (Frankfort, 1679), II, 5, 4, 735-36.
6. A good discussion of Luther's view of the church is that of Gordon Rupp, *The Righteousness of God* (New York: Philosophical Library, Inc., 1954), pp. 329-43. The most authoritative presentation of Calvin's view is by Josef Bohatec, *Calvins Lehre von Staat und Kirche* (Breslau, 1937), pp. 267-380.
7. *Canons and Decrees of the Council of Trent*, tr. *H. J. Schroeder (St. Louis: B. Herder Book Company, 1955), pp. 29-46.
8. *Denzinger, *op. cit.*, p. 303 (n. 995).
9. Jaroslav Pelikan, "Tradition in Confessional Lutheranism," *The Lutheran World*, III-3 (December, 1956), pp. 214-22, is a summary of Chemnitz' case against Trent.
10. Current reinterpretations of Trent by Roman Catholic theologians are discussed by *George Tavard, "The Catholic Reform in the Sixteenth Century," *Church History*, XXVI (1957), pp. 275-88.
11. Stringfellow Barr, "The Duty of a Christian in the Modern World," *Toward a Better World*, ed. William Scarlett (Philadelphia: The John C. Winston Company, 1946), p. 183.

CHAPTER V

1. Carl Becker, *The Heavenly City of the Eighteenth-Century Philosophers* (New Haven: Yale University Press, 1932).
2. James Hastings Nichols, *Democracy and the Churches* (Philadelphia: Westminster Press, 1951).
3. *A. D. Sertillanges, "A quelles conceptions et a quelle structure sociale se rattachent les enseignements de l'encyclique 'Rerum novarum'" in *Il XL anniversario della enciclica "Rerum novarum"* (Milan, 1931), pp. 455-69. The entire volume—with essays in English, French, German, Spanish, and Italian—provides a helpful commentary on *Rerum novarum*.
4. This has been carefully described by *Henry J. Browne, *The Catholic Church and the Knights of Labor* (Washington, D.C.: Catholic University of America Press, 1949).
5. *Claire Huchet Bishop, *France Alive* (New York: McMullen Books, 1947) is a glowing description of this movement.
6. George de Santillana, *The Crime of Galileo* (Chicago: University of Chicago Press, 1955) has rummaged through the evidence once more and has come up with some startling conclusions.
7. The response of the Pontifical Biblical Commission on the historicity of Genesis is reprinted in *Denzinger, *op. cit.*, pp. 545-47 (nn. 2121-28).
8. It is so in the anti-modernist oath which every priest must swear, reprinted, *Ibid.*, pp. 549-50 (n. 2145).

9. H. Richard Niebuhr, *Christ and Culture* (New York: Harper and Bros., 1956), pp. 116-48.
10. *Evelyn Waugh, "The American Epoch in the Catholic Church," *Life* (September 19, 1949), XXVII-12, 144.
11. John T. McNeill, *Unitive Protestantism* (New York: The Abingdon Press, 1930) recounts a large part of the story.
12. *James Brodrick's *The Life and Works of Blessed Robert Francis Cardinal Bellarmine* (London, 1928), I, 119-94, is a witty and learned account of the biographical, though not of the theological, aspect of Bellarmine's career as a polemicist.
13. *Donald Attwater's chapter on "Reunion with the East" in his *The Christian Churches of the East* (Milwaukee: Bruce Publishing Company, 1948), II, 259-72, is a good example of how irenically a Roman Catholic can treat the churches of the East.
14. *Ronald Knox, *Enthusiasm* (Oxford: Oxford University Press, 1950) is a biased, but eminently readable account of Jansenism.
15. *Denzinger, *op. cit.*, pp. 316-17 (nn. 1092-97).
16. James Hastings Nichols, "The Dilemma of the Free Church Liberal," *The Christian Century* (1953), LXX, 1074-76, argues this way about the difference among Protestants; his argument would apply even more to the difference between Protestantism and Roman Catholicism.
17. *Pius X, *Pascendi* in *Denzinger, *op. cit.*, p. 539 (n. 2105).
18. The text of the dogma appears in *Denzinger, pp. 455-57 (nn. 1832-40). See the recent account by Geddes MacGregor, *The Vatican Revolution* (Boston: Beacon Press, 1957).
19. The Syllabus appears in *Denzinger, *op. cit.*, pp. 433-42 (nn. 1700-80).
20. Gerhard Ebeling, "Zur Frage nach dem Sinn des mariologischen Dogmas," *Zeitschrift für Theologie und Kirche* (1950), 47, 389.

PART TWO

1. An interesting sociological survey of Protestant attitudes toward Roman Catholics in an Eastern city has recently been published by Kenneth Underwood, *Protestant and Catholic* (Boston: Beacon Press, 1957). An important interpretation of these attitudes from a Roman Catholic viewpoint is *John J. Kane, *Catholic-Protestant Conflicts in America* (Chicago: Henry Regnery Company, 1955).
2. The term "evangelical catholicity" comes from Nathan Söderblom, "Evangelisk katolicitet" in E. Lehmann *et al.*, *Enig kristendom* (Stockholm, 1919), pp. 65-126.

CHAPTER VI

1. Cyprian's position is interpreted by *Maurice Bevenot in his introduction to Cyprian, "The Lapsed," pp. 6-8.

2. This was the position taken by Luther at the Leipzig debate in 1519, *Werke* (Weimar, 1884), II, 272.

3. The entire problem of how to interpret these words has been put into a new light by the studies and suggestions of Oscar Cullmann, *op. cit.* *Charles Journet has replied to Cullmann in *The Primacy of Peter*, tr. John Chapin (Westminster, Md.: Newman Press, 1954). Other studies in the history of these verses are: Kurt Guggisberg, "Matth. 16, 18 und 19 in der Kirchengeschichte," *Zeitschrift für Kirchengeschichte* (1935), 54, 276-300; *H. Bruders, "Mt. 16, 19; 18, 18 und Joh. 20, 22 f. in frühchristlicher Auslegung: die Kirche der Donatisten," *Zeitschrift für katholische Theologie* (1911), 35, 690 ff.

4. Ethelbert Stauffer, *New Testament Theology*, tr. John Marsh (New York: The Macmillan Company, 1955), p. 33. More representative of Protestant scholarship is Martin Dibelius, *Jesus*, tr. Charles B. Hedrich and Frederick C. Grant (Philadelphia: Westminster Press, 1949), pp. 91-92.

5. Luke 10:16, as it is cited in the bull *Humani generis* of 1950, *Denzinger, *op. cit.*, p. 640 (n. 2313).

6. *Mystici Corporis, ibid.*, p. 616 (n. 2286). This theme is expounded by *E. Mersch, *Le corps mystique du Christ* (Louvain, 1933).

7. *George Tavard, "Holy Church or Holy Writ: A Dilemma of the Fourteenth Century," *Church History* (1954), XXIII, 195-206, is an enlightening historical account of this issue.

8. See the excerpts from *Divino afflante Spiritu* in *Denzinger, *op. cit.*, pp. 620-24 (nn. 2292-94).

9. Two of the best English translations of the New Testament to come out of this—that prepared under the auspices of the Confraternity of Christian Doctrine (Paterson, 1943) and that by *Ronald Knox (New York, 1945)—are both based upon the Vulgate, but reflect the new concern for the Bible.

10. There is a good summary of the Roman Catholic view of tradition in *G. Gilograssi, "Tradizione divino-apostolica e Magisterio della Chiesa," *Gregorianum* (1952), 33, 135-67.

11. *Canons and Decrees of the Council of Trent*, p. 17. The meaning of this definition has been thoroughly ventilated by *Edmond Ortigues, "Ecritures et traditions apostolique au Concile de Trente," *Recherches de science religieuse* (1949), 36, 271-99, and in the authoritative book by *Hubert Jedin, *Geschichte des Konzils von Trient* (Freiburg, 1957), II, 42-82, with complete bibliographical references on pp. 455-62.

12. *Denzinger, *op. cit.*, p. 303 (n. 995).

13. Otto Baltzer, *Die Sentenzen des Petrus Lombardus* (Leipzig, 1902) gives a competent overview of the problem from the standpoint of Peter Lombard. *F. Stegemueller's careful catalogue, *Repertorium commentariorum in Sententias Petri Lombardi* (2 vols.; Würzburg, 1947) demonstrates

how important Lombard was for the medieval solution of the problem of tradition.

14. *Humani generis* (1950) in *Denzinger, *op. cit.*, p. 640 (n. 2314).
15. Robert L. Milburn's appendix on "The historical background of the doctrine of the assumption" in his *Early Christian Interpretations of History* (London: A. and C. Black, Ltd., 1954), pp. 161-92, gives a good introduction.
16. *Elizabeth M. Lynskey, *The Government of the Catholic Church* (New York: P. J. Kenedy and Sons, 1952) is a readable summary.
17. *Josef Sellmair, *The Priest in the World*, tr. Brian Battershaw (Westminster, Md.: Newman Press, 1954) is a warm and human account of the role of the priest in a modern parish.
18. Written from the standpoint of the political problems in France, E. Faguet, *L'Anticlericalisme* (Paris, 1906) shows what a force this has become in the social life of France since the eighteenth century.
19. *Francis J. Connell, *American Ecclesiastical Review* (1944), CXI, 395.
20. Thomas Aquinas, *Summa Theologica*, II, II, Q. 186, Art. 5.
21. Kenneth Scott Latourette cites the lack of monks as one of the reasons why Protestant churches were not very active in mission work before 1800, *A History of the Expansion of Christianity*, III, 26.
22. There is a negative discussion of this topic in Paul Blanshard, *American Freedom and Catholic Power* (2nd ed.; Boston: Beacon Press, 1958), pp. 160-211.
23. This becomes evident from an examination of the material in Arthur Carl Piepkorn, "The Doctrine of Marriage in the Theologians of Lutheran Orthodoxy," *Concordia Theological Monthly* (1953), XXIV, 465-89.
24. On the "Pauline privilege" see the declaration of Innocent III in *Denzinger, *op. cit.*, p. 158 (n. 405).
25. *Patrick A. Finney, *Moral Problems in Hospital Practice* (St. Louis, 1947) gives a good orientation.
26. The anti-modernist oath in *Denzinger, *op. cit.*, p. 550 (n. 2145).
27. *Humani generis*, ibid., p. 646 (n. 2328).
28. *Francis Betten, *The Roman Index of Forbidden Books* (St. Louis, 1912).
29. *Joseph C. Plumpe, *Mater Ecclesia* (Washington, D.C.: Catholic University of America Press, 1943) traces the evolution of this concept. From the Protestant side, see Gustaf Aulen, *The Faith of the Christian Church*, tr. Eric H. Wahlstrom and G. Everett Arden (Philadelphia: Muhlenberg Press, 1948), pp. 347-50, on the church as mother.

CHAPTER VII

1. Paul Blanshard's books, *American Freedom and Catholic Power*, and *Communism, Democracy, and Catholic Power* (Boston: Beacon Press, 1951), are the most widely read formulations of this point of view.

2. A classic statement of this defense is *George H. Shuster, *The Catholic Spirit in America* (New York, 1927).
3. *John A. Ryan and *Francis J. Boland, *Catholic Principles of Politics* (New York: The Macmillan Company, 1940) is a widely quoted work on these principles.
4. *Denzinger, *op. cit.*, p. 187 (n. 469).
5. *Joseph N. Moody has assembled a huge collection of materials in his *Church and Society* (New York: Arts, Inc., 1953).
6. There is a moving collection of documents published under the title, *Dokumente aus dem Kampf der katholischen Kirche im Bistum Berlin gegen den Nationalsozialismus* (Berlin, 1946).
7. F. R. Hoare, *The Papacy and the Modern State* (London, 1940) describes Rome's defense of these rights.
8. See the handy series of quotations edited by *Francis J. Powers, *Papal Pronouncements on the Political Order* (Westminster, Md.; Newman Press, 1952).
9. *Nicolas Iung, *Le droit public de l'Eglise dans ses relations avec les etats* (Paris, 1948) shows how this policy has become part of the legislation on church-state relations.
10. *Roy J. Defarrari (ed.), *Essays on Catholic Education in the United States* (Washington, D.C.: Catholic University of America Press, 1942) gives a good cross-section of opinion.
11. See the interesting debate between Paul Blanshard and George H. Dunne, published under the auspices of the Harvard Law School Forum as *The Catholic Church and Politics* (Cambridge, 1950).
12. *Jacques Maritain, *The Rights of Man and Natural Law*, tr. by Doris C. Anson (New York: Charles Scribner's Sons, 1943) applies this theory to life in the modern state.
13. Although it has been criticized by some legal historians, Felix Flückiger, *Geschichte des Naturrechtes* (Zurich, 1954), vol. I is the best theological study of this development.
14. The most useful English introduction to the vast literature on canon law is *Amleto Cicognani, *Canon Law*, tr. Joseph M. O'Hara and Francis Brennan (Philadelphia: Dolphin Press, 1934).
15. Thomas Aquinas developed his theory of the state on the basis of this interpretation of law, as *Franz Faller points out, *Die rechtsphilosophische Begründung der gesellschaftlichen und staatlichen Autorität bei Thomas von Aquin* (Heidelberg, 1954).
16. The rational and non-rational foundations for a view of natural law are discussed in *M. Schmitt, *Recht und Vernunft* (Heidelberg, 1955).
17. George Michon has documented this indictment in his collection of sources, *Les documents pontificaux sur la democratie et la societe moderne* (Paris, 1928).
18. The recent book of Edmund A. Moore, *A Catholic Runs for President:*

The Campaign of 1928 (New York: Ronald Press, 1956) is a readable and balanced account of the entire story.

19. *The New York Times*, January 6, 1958, p. 27.
20. *Father John Courtney Murray has made this proposal in a series of essays; taken together these essays represent a serious and thoughtful effort to find the neglected elements in the history of Roman Catholic political thought and to apply them to the American situation: "Governmental Repression of Heresy" (Woodstock, Md., 1949); "Contemporary Orientations of Catholic Thought on Church and State in the Light of History," *Theological Studies* (1949), X, 177-24; "The Church and Totalitarian Democracy," *Theological Studies* (1952), XIII, 525-63; "Leo XIII: Two Concepts of Government," *Theological Studies* (1953), XIV, 551-67; "The Problem of Pluralism in America," *Thought* (1954), XXIX, 165-208.

CHAPTER VIII

1. *Parthenius Minges, *Compendium theologiae dogmaticae specialis* (Regensburg, 1922), II, 76. For this chapter, more than for any of the others, *Denzinger, *op. cit.*, is very useful; his topical index on the sacraments covers pp. 36-46 of the index.
2. I am basing this discussion of baptism partly upon Thomas Aquinas, *Summa Theologica*, III, Q. 66-71.
3. The doctrine of *ex opere operato* was made official at Trent, *Canons and Decrees*, p. 52.
4. These pre-Christian origins and the Christian development have been treated by Archdale A. King, *Holy Water* (London, 1926).
5. The form for this appears in *Denzinger, *op. cit.*, p. 155 (n. 399).
6. This question has been debated by Gregory Dix, *The Theology of Confirmation in Relation to Baptism* (London: A. and C. Black, Ltd., 1946) and G. W. H. Lampe, *The Seal of the Spirit* (London: Longmans, Green and Company, 1951).
7. Yngve Brilioth, *Eucharistic Faith and Practice, Evangelical and Catholic*, tr. A. G. Hebert (London, 1934) is a splendid introduction.
8. This co-ordination of church and eucharist is the theme of a stimulating study by *H. de Lubac, *Corpus mysticum. L'eucharistie et l'eglise au moyen age* (2nd ed.; Paris, 1949).
9. The official definition of transubstantiation at Trent is quite brief, *Canons and Decrees*, p. 75.
10. Trent defined this at its twenty-second session, *Canons and Decrees*, pp. 144-46. *Eugene Masure, *The Christian Sacrifice*, tr. Illtyd Trethowan (New York: P. J. Kenedy and Sons, 1943) is the most careful discussion I know of in English.
11. *Richard Ginder, "Our Catholic Hit Parade," *Catholic Digest* (1948), XII, 9-12.

12. Pius XII in *Mediator Dei* of November 20, 1947. This has been edited with notes by *Gerald Ellard (New York: America Press, 1948).

13. In this discussion I have drawn upon the lifelong researches of *B. Poschmann, which he has now summarized in his volume, *Busse and letzte Oelung* (Freiburg, 1951). Henry Charles Lea, *A History of Auricular Confession and Indulgences in the Latin Church* (3 vols.; Philadelphia: John Joseph McVey, 1896) is learned but uneven.

14. *Canons and Decrees*, p. 91. The meaning of this definition has been expounded by G. J. Spykman, *Attrition and Contrition at the Council of Trent* (New York, 1955).

15. Based as it is upon his many years of study in the history of the penitential system, the evaluation of penance by the Protestant historian John T. McNeill is instructive, *A History of the Cure of Souls* (New York: Harper and Bros., 1951), pp. 112-62.

16. F. W. Puller, *The Anointing of the Sick in Scripture and Tradition* (2nd ed.; London, 1910) is a careful study by an Anglican theologian who is not unsympathetic to the Roman Catholic position.

17. The Latin word *viaticum* meant the provisions which a traveler took along on a trip.

18. The encyclical *Casti connubii* of Pius XI (December 31, 1930) is a full statement of the church's teaching, *Denzinger, *op. cit.*, pp. 582-97 (nn. 2225-50). *George H. Joyce, *Christian Marriage* (London, 1933) can serve as a commentary upon this encyclical and other statements of the church.

19. The Syllabus of Errors of Pius IX, *Denzinger, *op. cit.*, p. 441 (n. 1765).

20. *Ibid.*, p. 441 (n. 1766).

21. *J. Tixeront, *L'Ordre et les ordinations* (Paris, 1924) is an authoritative discussion.

CHAPTER IX

1. Edmund Schlink *et al.* "An Evangelical Opinion on the Proclamation of the Dogma of the Bodily Assumption of Mary," tr. Conrad Bergendoff, *The Lutheran Quarterly* (1951), III, 138.

2. "Mary, the mother of Jesus," *Encyclopaedia Britannica* (1958 printing), XIV, 999-1000.

3. The texts for this development are collected in *Paul F. Palmer, *Mary in the Documents of the Church* (Westminster, Md.: Newman Press, 1952); others appear in Walter Delius (ed.), *Texte zur Geschichte der Marienverehrung und Marienverkündigung in der alten Kirche* (Berlin, 1956).

4. It is interesting to note this in Ambrose's writings (d. 397), whose view of Mary has been studied in detail by *Joseph Hahn, *Das Geheimnis der Jungfrau-Mutter Maria nach dem Kirchenvater Ambrosius* (Würzburg, 1954).

5. Thus German people speak of a *Josephsehe* as a marriage which remains unconsummated because of a previous vow.

6. J. B. Lightfoot, "The Brethren of the Lord," *St. Paul's Epistle to the Galatians* (2nd ed.; London, 1866), pp. 247-81, is a thorough discussion of the problem and of various solutions.

7. See, for example, Luther's comments on John 2:12 in *Luther's Works*, ed. Jaroslav Pelikan (St. Louis: Concordia Publishing House, 1957), 22, 214-15. Horst Dietrich Preuss has studied some of these problems in his little book, *Maria bei Luther* (Gütersloh, 1954).

8. *Ineffabilis Deus* in *Denzinger, *op. cit.*, pp. 413-14 (n. 1641). The development of this doctrine has recently been traced with much learning by *Edward Dennis O'Connor et al., *The Dogma of the Immaculate Conception* (Notre Dame, 1958).

9. The history of the term has been sketched in an essay by *John Henry Newman on "Mary Theotocos," *Selected Treatises of St. Athanasius* (5th ed.; London, 1890), II, 210-15.

10. Paul Tillich's essay on "Nature and Sacrament," *The Protestant Era*, pp. 94-112, is a discussion of such resources.

11. *Chesterton, *op. cit.*, p. 36.

12. *William L. Sullivan, "Adoration," *The Catholic Encyclopedia*, I, 152.

13. A full compilation of such titles and an explanation of each can be found in *Donald Attwater, *A Dictionary of Mary* (New York: P. J. Kenedy and Sons, 1956), a very useful reference book.

14. Augustine, *The City of God*, XXII, 10, in Whitney J. Oates (ed.), *Basic Writings of Saint Augustine* (2 vols.; New York: Random House, 1948), II, 630.

15. The Apostolic Constitution *Munificentissimus Deus* in *Denzinger, *op. cit.*, pp. 647-48 (nn. 2331-33).

16. The evolution of this parallel is the theme of Hugo Koch's brief book, *Virgo Eva—Virgo Maria* (Berlin, 1937).

17. A critical but balanced statement is that of Giovanni Miegge, *The Virgin Mary*, tr. Waldo Smith (Philadelphia: Westminster Press, 1956). More sympathetic but still critical are Raymond Winch and Victor Bennett, *The Assumption of Our Lady and Catholic Theology* (London: Macmillan and Company, 1950).

18. *Karl Adam, *op. cit.*, p. 120.

19. Walther von Loewenich, *Der moderne Katholizismus* (2nd ed.; Witten, 1956), pp. 276-77.

20. *Juniper Carol (ed.), *Mariology* (3 vols.; Milwaukee: Bruce Publishing Company, 1955 ff.) is a good example of such erudition.

21. An older work is W. O. Dietlein, *Evangelisches Ave Maria* (Halle, 1863). Hans Asmussen has recently attempted the same in his *Maria die Mutter Gottes.*

CHAPTER X

1. The best book for the beginning student of Aquinas to read is probably *G. K. Chesterton, *Saint Thomas Aquinas* (New York: Sheed and Ward, Inc., 1933), which, despite its journalistic tone, is a profound analysis. The volume by *Etienne Gilson, *The Christian Philosophy of St. Thomas Aquinas*, tr. L. K. Shook (New York: Random House, 1956) crowns the many years of Professor Gilson's work on Aquinas and forms an excellent basis for extended study; its bibliography is very helpful.
2. Paul Tillich, *Systematic Theology* (Chicago: University of Chicago Press, 1951), I, 6.
3. J. Ramsey McCallum, *Abelard's Christian Theology* (Oxford, 1948) is a serious effort to modify the extravagance of earlier Protestant interpretations of Abelard.
4. See p. 82 and the accompanying note.
5. *Summa Theologica*, I, Q. 23, Art. 5. *Hermann Lais, *Die Gnadenlehre des hl. Thomas in der Summa contra Gentiles* (Munich, 1951), pp. 219-22, defends Thomas' emphasis upon the free will of God against some other Roman Catholic interpreters. See also the brief comment in *Walter Farrell, *A Companion to the Summa* (4 vols.; New York: Sheed and Ward, Inc., 1938-42), II, 426-27.
6. *Summa Theologica*, I, Q. 1, Art. 8.
7. *Daniel A. Callus, *The Condemnation of St. Thomas at Oxford*, "Aquinas Papers," No. 5 (Oxford, 1946) summarizes the attack upon Aquinas by John Pecham.
8. *Etienne Gilson, "Pourquoi saint Thomas a critique saint Augustin," *Archives d'histoire doctrinale et litteraire du moyen age* (1926), I, 5-127, is the fundamental study of this criticism.
9. *Maurizio Flick, *L'attimo della giustificazione secondo S. Tommaso* (Rome, 1947), pp. 54-103 gives a good overview of this and (unwittingly!) shows the difference between Thomas and Trent.
10. I mean "from angels to witchcraft" quite literally. *James D. Collins, *The Thomistic Philosophy of the Angels* (Washington, D.C.: Catholic University of America Press, 1947) shows that the doctrine of the angels is a central element in Thomas' understanding of reality, while Charles Edward Hopkin has assessed *The Share of Thomas Aquinas in the Growth of the Witchcraft Delusion* (Philadelphia: Privately published, 1940). Two decades of work on Thomas are compiled in *Vernon J. Bourke, *A Thomistic Bibliography 1920-1940* (St. Louis: Modern Schoolman University of St. Louis, 1945).
11. For example, *Gottfried Geenan has shown that Thomas was critical and selective in his use of tradition when he came to discuss the doctrine of baptism in Part III of the *Summa*, "L'usage des 'auctoritates' dans la

doctrine du bapteme chez S. Thomas d'Aquin," *Sylloge excerptorum e dissertationibus* (Louvain, 1938), V, 279-329.

12. *James A. McWilliams, *Physics and Philosophy* (Washington, D.C.: Catholic University of America Press, 1945) interprets Thomas' commentary on the *Physics* of Aristotle, especially the idea of motion in the two.

13. *Jacques Maritain and Jean Cocteau, *Art and Faith*, tr. John Coleman (New York: Philosophical Library, Inc., 1948). *John A. Duffy's *A Philosophy of Poetry Based on Thomistic Principles* (Washington, D.C.: Catholic University of America Press, 1945) shows the adaptability of Thomistic theory to contemporary literary issues.

14. *Jacques Maritain, *Existence and the Existent*, tr. Lewis Galantière and Gerald B. Phelan (New York: Pantheon Books, 1948).

15. *Martin Grabmann, *Die Geschichte der scholastischen Methode* (Freiburg, 1909), I, 22, note 2. *Ignaz Baches has shown, for example, that Thomas' doctrine of the person of Christ derives much of its power from the theology of the fourth and fifth centuries: *Die Christologie des hl. Thomas von Aquin und die griechischen Kirchenväter* (Paderborn, 1931).

16. *Walter J. Ong's essay on "The Renaissance Myth and the American Catholic Mind," *Frontiers in American Catholicism* (New York: The Macmillan Company, 1957), pp. 52-85, is a learned and incisive account of the diversity in the history of medieval philosophy, especially in the history of logic.

17. Thomas' handling of the Sermon on the Mount can be judged from his exposition of the Lord's Prayer, as contained in the little volume, *The Three Greatest Prayers*, tr. *Laurence Shapcote (Westminster, Md.: Newman Press, 1956).

CHAPTER XI

1. *Romano Guardini's *The Spirit of the Liturgy*, tr. Ada Lane (New York: Sheed and Ward, Inc., 1940) is a splendid and sprightly statement of the role of the liturgy in the life of the church.

2. Werner Elert, *Der Kampf um das Christentum* (Munich, 1921), p. 3; this is the theme of Elert's book.

3. See p. 67 and the accompanying note.

4. Ernest B. Koenker's *The Liturgical Renaissance in the Roman Catholic Church* (Chicago: University of Chicago Press, 1954) deserves the careful attention of anyone who wants to understand the church of Rome today. His presentation has been the basis for much of this chapter, and his bibliography is far more detailed than any I could have suggested.

5. Paul Tillich, *The Protestant Era*, p. 219.

6. Peter Brunner, "Zur Lehre vom Gottesdienst der im Namen Jesu versammelten Gemeinden," *Leiturgia*, ed. Karl Ferdinand Müller and Walter Blankenburg (Kassel, 1954), I, 168-80.

7. Koenker, *op. cit.*, pp. 153-64.
8. *Florence S. Berger, *Cooking for Christ: The Liturgical Year in the Kitchen* (Des Moines: National Catholic Rural Life Conference, 1949).
9. *Ong, *op. cit.*, pp. 1-8.
10. *Gerald Ellard, *The Mass of the Future* (Milwaukee: Bruce Publishing Company, 1948).
11. The historical backgrounds for this have recently been interpreted by *Thomas T. McAvoy, *The Great Crisis in American Catholic History 1895-1900* (Chicago: Henry Regnery Company, 1957), pp. 354-59.
12. *Edwin V. O'Hara's *The Church and the Country Community* (New York: The Macmillan Company, 1927) was one of the earliest statements of the program, which is now under the capable leadership of Monsignor Luigi G. Ligutti.
13. Gerald Ellard, *Men at Work at Worship* (New York: Longmans, Green and Company, 1940) describes some of this in an interesting and informative manner.
14. Reinhold Niebuhr, "A Theologian's Comments on the Negro in America," *The Reporter* (November 29, 1956), XV-9, 25.
15. An early study by *John T. Gillard collected the fundamental statistical data on the church's record: *The Catholic Church and the American Negro* (Baltimore: St. Joseph's Society Press, 1929). He has brought the record up to date and expanded his analysis in *Colored Catholics in the United States* (Baltimore: Josephite Press, 1941).
16. *Joseph Fichter, the Jesuit sociologist, has discussed "The Structure of Parochial Societies" in his important book, *Social Relations in the Urban Parish* (Chicago: University of Chicago Press, 1954), pp. 154-64.

PART THREE

CHAPTER XII

1. Quoted in Albert C. Outler, *The Christian Tradition and the Unity We Seek* (New York: Oxford University Press, 1957), p. 25.
2. *Ibid.*, pp. 33 ff.
3. Leo XIII in *Apostolicae curae* of September 13, 1896, *Denzinger, *op. cit.*, pp. 496-97 (nn. 1963-66). This is thoroughly discussed in a book by Viscount Halifax, *Leo XIII and Anglican Orders* (London, 1912).
4. This even applies to books like *Marie Joseph Congar, *Divided Christendom*, tr. M. A. Bousfield (London, 1939), and *George H. Tavard, *The Catholic Approach to Protestantism* (New York: Harper and Bros., 1955), both of which are very irenic in tone.
5. Kristen E. Skydsgaard, "The Roman Catholic Church and the Ecumenical Movement," *Man's Disorder and God's Design* (4 vols.; New York, 1948), I, 155-68.

6. See page 70, note 18.
7. *Karl Adam, op. cit., p. 5.
8. G. G. Willis, *Saint Augustine and the Donatist Controversy* (London: Society for Promoting Christian Knowledge, 1950) is competent summary.
9. Optatus of Milevis, *De schismate Donatistarum*, II, 1, *Patrologia Latina,* XI, 941.
10. John Knox, op. cit., p. 30.

CHAPTER XIII

1. Gerhardt von Rad, *Studies in Deuteronomy*, tr. David Stalker (Chicago: Henry Regnery Company, 1953) assesses the role of tradition in the Old Testament. Two basic books on its role in the New Testament are: Martin Dibelius, *From Tradition to Gospel*, tr. Bertram Lee Woolf (New York: Charles Scribner's Sons, 1935), and Rudolf Bultmann, *Die Geschichte der synoptischen Tradition* (2nd ed.; Göttingen, 1931).
2. Oscar Cullmann, "The Tradition," *The Early Church. Studies in Early Christian History and Theology*, tr. A. J. B. Higgins (Philadelphia: Westminster Press, 1956), pp. 57-99.
3. Theodor Ellwein (ed.), *Schrift und Tradition* (Bad Boll, 1956) is the mimeographed record of a theological discussion between leading Protestant and Roman Catholic theologians on the question of tradition, held May 22-24, 1956.
4. *Johannes Quasten, *Patrology*, I (Westminster, Md.: Newman Press, 1951) has more references to Harnack than to any other scholar; *J. de Ghellinck, "Un organisateur des recherches patristiques," *Patristique et moyen-age* (Brussel, 1948), III, 1-102.
5. Jean Danièlou, *Origen*, tr. Walter Mitchell (New York: Sheed and Ward, Inc., 1955); *Henri de Lubac, *Histoire et esprit* (Paris, 1950) is a careful interpretation of Origen's work as a biblical interpreter.
6. *Adolf Herte, *Das katholische Lutherbild im Banne der Lutherkommentare des Cochläus* (3 vols.; Münster, 1943).
7. *Joseph Lortz, "The Reformation," *Eastern Churches Quarterly* (1947), VII, 76-91. He has expanded this material into a little book, *Die Reformation als religiöses Anliegen heute* (Trier, 1948).
8. *Jacques Maritain, *Three Reformers: Luther—Descartes—Rousseau* (New York: Charles Scribner's Sons, 1929).
9. Johannes Ruber, *Bach and the Heavenly Choir*, tr. Maurice Michael (Cleveland: World Publishing Company, 1957).
10. James Moffatt, *The Thrill of Tradition* (New York, 1944).

CHAPTER XIV

1. An interesting comparative study of Newman, Manning, Tyrrell, Knox, and Chesterton is that of Arnold Lunn, *Roman Converts* (London, 1925)

—all the more interesting in view of the author's own subsequent conversion to Roman Catholicism, as recounted in his *Now I See* (New York: (Sheed and Ward, Inc., 1933).

2. *Brother David [Sylvester Edward Martin], *American Catholic Convert Authors. A Bio-Bibliography* (Grosse Pointe, Mich.: Walker Komig, Publisher, 1944).

3. See the collected essays in David Wesley Soper (ed.), *These Found the Way* (Philadelphia: Westminster Press, 1951).

4. *Gerald Shaughnessy, *Has the Immigrant Kept the Faith?* (New York: The Macmillan Company, 1925).

5. *Gerald J. Schnepp, *Leakage from a Catholic Parish* (Washington, 1942) studies the role of nationality, marriage, education, and economics in the losses suffered by a representative church. *Joseph Fichter's chapter on "Dormant Catholics and Leakage," *Social Relations in the Urban Parish*, pp. 68-79, is a good summary of the problem.

6. *Father Fichter's statistics on the problem of nationality in one parish are very revealing, *Southern Parish*, I, *Dynamics of a City Church* (Chicago: University of Chicago Press, 1951), pp. 26-29. For a general survey see *John L. Thomas, "Nationalities and American Catholicism" in *Louis J. Putz (ed), *Catholic Church U.S.A.* (Chicago: Fides Publishers Association, 1956), pp. 155-76, with detailed bibliographical notes.

7. *Ronald A. Knox, *A Spiritual Aeneid* (London, 1918), pp. 240-41.

8. *Louis Bouyer, *The Spirit and Forms of Protestantism*, tr. A. V. Littledale (Westminster, Md.: Newman Press, 1956).

9. *Daniel J. Saunders, "The Psychology of a Conversion" in *John K. Ryan and *Edmond Darvil Benard (edd.), *American Essays for the Newman Centennial* (Washington, D.C.: Catholic University of America Press, 1947), p. 58.

10. Heinrich Schlier, *Christus und die Kirche im Epheserbrief* (Tübingen, 1930); *Religionsgeschichtliche Untersuchungen zu den Ignatiusbriefen* (Giessen, 1929).

11. *Heinrich Schlier, "Kurze Rechenschaft" in Karl Hardt (ed.), *Bekenntnis zur katholischen Kirche* (Würzburg, 1955), pp. 180-81.

12. *Vladimir Soloviëv, *Russia and the Universal Church*, tr. Herbert Rees (London, 1948), p. 14.

CHAPTER XV

1. Products of this discovery were books like *Karl Adam, *One and Holy*, tr. Cecily Hastings (New York: Sheed and Ward, Inc., 1951) from the Roman side; and from the Protestant side books like Heinrich Hermelink, *Katholizismus und Protestantismus im Gespräch zwischen den Konfessionen um die Una Sancta* (Stuttgart, 1949).

2. E. Kristen Skydsgaard, *One in Christ*, tr. Axel C. Kildegaard (Philadelphia:

Muhlenberg Press, 1957), is, in my judgment, the most responsible effort by a Protestant theologian to include Rome in the ecumenical perspective.

3. *Humani generis* in *Denzinger, *op. cit.*, pp. 635-47 (nn. 2305-30).

4. *John M. Todd, *Catholicism and the Ecumenical Movement* (London: Longmans, Green and Company, 1956) makes a real effort to understand and appreciate Protestant theology.

5. Paul Tillich, *The Protestant Era*, p. 226.

6. Arnold Schleiff, *Die Selbstkritik der lutherischen Kirchen im 17. Jahrhundert* (Berlin, 1937). There is an interesting collection of such materials in Ernest Zeeden, *The Legacy of Luther* (London, 1954).

7. *Ong, *Frontiers in American Catholicism;* *John Tracy Ellis, *American Catholics and the Intellectual Life* (Chicago: Heritage Foundation, Inc., 1956).

CHAPTER XVI

1. The best of these discussions is that edited by J. P. v. Groeningen, *Toward a Philosophy of Higher Education* (Philadelphia, 1957).

2. Emil Brunner fired the heaviest volley in this campaign against Schleiermacher in his *Die Mystik und das Wort* (Tübingen, 1924).

3. Karl Barth, *Die protestantische Theologie im 19. Jahrhundert* (Zurich, 1947), pp. 379-424.

4. Adolf Harnack, *Lehrbuch der Dogmengeschichte* III (5th ed.; Tübingen, 1932), p. 903.

5. Will Herberg, *Protestant, Catholic, Jew* (Garden City, N.Y.: Doubleday and Company, 1955).

6. Friedrich Schleiermacher, *The Christian Faith*, ed. H. R. Mackintosh and J. S. Stewart (Edinburgh: T. and T. Clark, 1956), p. 648.

7. Koenker, *The Liturgical Renaissance*, pp. 104-24.

8. Loewenich, *Der moderne Katholizismus*, p. 356.

INDEX

Abelard, Peter 144, 146
Abbey of St. Procopius 180
Adam, sin of 91
Adam, Karl 19, 46, 139, 181, 238
Alexandria, patriarchate of 39, 41
Ambrose, bishop of Milan 32
American Ecclesiastical Review 87
Anabaptists 46, 48
Andrew the Apostle 41
Anselm of Canterbury 146-47
Anticlericalism 85
Antioch, patriarchate of 39, 41
Apologists, of Rome 14
Apostacy 196, 205
Apostolic succession 26, 48, 71, 80
Apostolic witness 188
Apostolicity, criterion of 188
Aquinas, Thomas ....65, 67, 122, 143 ff.
    on grace 147
    on obedience 88
    Summa Theologica of 145
    on the theory of knowledge 65
    on tradition ....143 ff.
Aristotle 64, 117, 145, 153, 154
Artemis of the Ephesians 132
Assisi, Francis of 161
Assumption, dogma of 83, 140
    See also Mary, Blessed Virgin
Athanasius 42
Attila the Hun 32
Augustine 24, 30, 42, 47, 69, 75, 81, 93, 145, 155
    on the church 182, 186, 217
    on grace 158
    on love 75
    on tradition 235
    on unity 47
    on veneration of martyrs 136

Augustinianism, as source of heresy 150
Authority, apostolic 25
   biblical basis in the church 16, 52, 80-81, 83, 87 ff., 96
   of the bishop 84
   centralization of 43
   of the church 12, 85
   of the church fathers 80, 82
   of the pope . . . . 83 ff.
   of the priest 85
   of tradition 81-83
Ave Maria . . . . 128 ff.
Avignon, papacy at 44

Babel, tower of 23
Bach, Johann Sebastian 198
Baptism . . . . 27, 111 ff.
   doctrine of ex opere operato 112
   indelible character of 111-14
   institution of 27
Barr, Stringfellow 57
Barth, Karl 207
Becker, Carl 60
Bellarmine, Robert 68, 218
Berdyaev, Nicolas 139
Bible, authority of 49-50
   infallibility of 70
   worship of 16
Birth control, Roman Catholic legislation on 11, 89, 204
Bishops, power of 26, 84, 124
Bismarck 61
Böhme, Jakob 54
Boniface VIII, pope 95
Bousset 68
Bouyer, Louis 207
Brunner, Emil 29
Brunner, Peter 165
Bultmann, Rudolf 193, 207
Byzantium, See Constantinople

Caesaropapism 43, 59
Cajetan, Cardinal 149
Calixtus 68
Callistus I 40
Calvin, John 46, 50, 117, 221
   on the church invisible 50
   on the debt to the heritage of the church 197
   on the primacy of Scriptures 50
Canon law, obedience to 86
Casuistry 87
Catacombs 161

Catholic Christianity . . . . 19, 21 ff., 24
  elements of 50, 230
  identity and universality of . . . . 162 ff.
  piety of 28
  See also Identity and Universality
Celibacy 15, 123, 130
Chalcedon, Council of 38
Charity, Sisters of 88
Charlemagne 44, 60
Chemnitz, Martin, his interpretation of Trent 52
  as apologete for Protestantism 218
Chesterton, G. K. 134, 208
Christ, doctrine of 38, 48
Church: apostolic 22, 187
  apostolicity of 49
  art in 66
  authority of 25-26, 64
  as body of Christ 80, 84, 185, 216
  catholicity of 21, 22, 50, 55, 184
  divided 53
  fall of 33, 47
  government, episcopal form of 25
  hierarchy of 51
  as holy . . . . 22, 181 ff.
  identity of 22, 184-86
  intellectual leadership of 65
  message of 28, 51
  mission of 23-24
  organization of 15, 25, 32
  its place in culture 32
  responsibility of membership . . . . 183, 215 ff.
  sacraments of . . . . 110 ff., 185
  standards of membership 28, 96, 231
  unity of 22, 178
  as worshiping community 164
  See also Authority, Catholic Christianity, Sacraments
Church and state . . . . 31 ff., 43, 58, 60, 94 ff., 106
Churchill, Winston 13
Citizenship . . . . 102 ff.
Clairvaux, Bernard of 47-48, 54
Clement, of Alexandria 30
Clement XI, pope 47
Cochrane, Charles N. 37
Commonweal 222, 225
Communism 140, 151, 225
  See also Marxism
Concordat, of Roman Catholicism with Nazi Germany 61
Confessional, authority of the 120-21

Confirmation 115-16
Conscience, torture of 121
Constantine, Emperor 60
Constantinople 38, 43
   patriarchate of 42
   Sixth Council of 40
Conversion, as blind alley .... 209 ff.
   as compromise 209
   motives of 206
   as way to unity ....202 ff.
Converts, from Protestantism 14, 66
   from Roman Catholicism 53
Cooking for Christ 167
Creation, doctrine of 29
Creeds, development of 29-30, 130
Crusades, as leading to schism 42
   Cullmann, Oscar 36
Culture, the church and .... 32, 56 ff., 62, 64, 66 ff.
   and cultus ....159 ff.
Cyprian, bishop of Carthage 28, 42, 78

Danièlou, Father 198
Darwin, the Roman Church and 16, 64-65, 175
Decalogue 99
   See also Law
Democracy, and Roman Catholicism ....59 ff.
Descartes, Rene 65
Dibelius, Otto 193
Discipline, of the Catholic church 28
   the power of 84
   in Roman Catholicism 86
Divine law, obedience to 86
Divorce 11, 89, 100
Dominicans 148
Donatists 182
Duns Scotus 149

East Harlem Protestant Parish 231
Eastern Orthodoxy 45, 68, 168
   role in Ecumenical movement 176
   its separation from Rome 43, 68
Ebeling, Gerhard 71
Ecumenical Council of pope John XXIII 16
   the Sixth (680) 40
Ecumenical movement 235
   and conversation with Rome 238
   and the use of the liturgy 200
Education, Roman Catholic authority over 97
   and state responsibility 98
Elert, Werner 160

Ellard Gerald, on the liturgy 169
Ellis, Monsignor 221
Ephesus, Synod of (449) 39, 132
Episcopate, rule of the 25
    sacramental status of 125
Errors, Syllabus of 70, 104
    on marriage 123
Eucharist ....116 ff.
    and doctrine of transubstantiation 117
    as medicine of immortality 27
    and mystery 116
    and sacrifice of the mass 117
Excommunication, as way to silence the critics 224
Existentialism 154
Extreme Unction, and healing 122
    sacramental significance of 121
    Thomas Aquinas on 122
    and the viaticum 87, 122

Faith, justifications by 49
    and reason in Aquinas 146
    unity of 145
    universality of 55
    and works 239
Farrell, James T. 204
Fatima, the Virgin of 136
Feudalism 59, 63, 108
Fox, George 54
France, influence of Roman Catholicism in 107
    See also Gallicanism
Franciscans 148
Free Will, papal attitudes toward 69
    See also Jansenism
Freedom, academic, in Roman Catholicism . . 64-67, 80 ff.
    Roman Catholicism as threat to political . . . 11, 94, 104
    and social responsibility ....94 ff.
French Revolution 60
Fundamentalism 16, 64, 228

Galileo, condemnation of 64-65, 91
Gallicanism 59, 107
    See also France, Kulturkampf
Gerhard, Johann 48, 195, 218
Ghellinck, J. de 195
Gnosticism, gnostics 25, 30, 138, 207
Golden Age, return to 66

Grabmann, Martin 155
Grace 147, 153
  church control over ....21, 110 ff.
  means of ....49, 110 ff.
  miracle of ....49, 110 ff.
  See also Sacraments
Greene, Graham 66, 125, 208
Guadalupe, Our Lady of 15, 136

Harnack, Adolf 22, 24, 31, 70, 195, 230
Heiler, Friedrich, interpretation of Roman Catholicism 15
Herberg, Will, on urban Roman Catholicism 232
Heresy, alliance of church and state against 32
  and primitive church 29
Herte, Adolf 197
Hippolytus, on modalism 40
  See also Zephyrinus and Callistus
Hofbauer, Clemens Maria 46
Holy Orders 124-26
  See also Apostolic succession
Holy Roman Empire 59
  and Holy Rome 56
  as unitive factor in medieval Europe 44, 56
Holy Spirit 14, 16, 26, 28, 35, 145, 181
  and the church 33, 80, 115
Honorius, pope 40
Huss, John 47

Identity and Universality ....22 ff., 162, 186, 207
  in Protestantism 50, 54-55, 184, 229
  in Roman Catholicism 54, 71, 77, 184
  See also Catholic Christianity
Ignatius, idea of universality in 196, 207
Images, worship of 119
Immaculate conception 131, 137-38, 184
  See also Mary, Blessed Virgin
Immigrants 12, 171
  ghetto mentality of 67
  loyalty to Roman Catholicism 171, 232
  reaction against Roman Catholicism 204
  urban settlement of 232
Imprimatur, the 91
Index of Prohibited Books 91
Innocent III, pope 44, 161
Innocent X, pope 69
Inquisition 219
Intolerance, in Roman Catholicism 12, 107
Investiture controversy 44
Irenaeus 29, 35, 196
  on tradition 235

Islam, expansion of 41, 42
Israel, religion of 192

Jeremiah, prophetic voice of 223
Jerusalem, congregation at 35
    destruction of 36
    patriarchate of 41
    as seat of apostolic authority 35
Jesus Christ, the church of 15, 19, 78-79
    the great Commission of 23
    the humanizing of 16, 70
    Mary as witness to his life 131
    as mediator 133
    teachings of 115, 193
    virgin birth of 130
Jesuits 51
    See also Bellarmine, R.
Jansenism 69
John XXIII, pope 77
    ecumenical council of 176
Jurisdiction, of Roman Catholicism ..86, 89, 97, 98, 205
Justice ....100 ff.
    See also Law
Justification, doctrine of..................49, 52, 220
    revision of Tridentine formulation of 52

Kant, Immanuel 65, 149
Khomiakov, Aleksiei 22
Kingdom, doctrine of the two ....95 ff.
    of God 57, 77
Knox, John 187
Knox, Monsignor 206
Knowledge, theory of in Roman Catholicism 99
    See also Aquinas, Thomas
Kulturkampf 59, 61, 114

Labor, Knights of 62, 63
    movement 62
    priests of 63-64
Lateran, Treaty of the 61
Law, in Roman Catholic Church ....99 ff.
    canon ....86, 100 ff.
    civil ....86, 100 ff.
    natural ....86, 99 ff.
    revealed ....86, 99 ff.
Leo, Bishop of Rome 32, 38
Leo XIII, pope 62, 70, 106, 150, 157
    against Latin liturgy for Eastern Orthodoxy 168
Lietzmann, Hans 36
Lilje, Bishop Hanns 14, 239

Liturgical movement ....27, 86, 118, 163-64, 198 ff.
  potential of 199
  as self-examination 221
Liturgy, development of 22, 27, 118
  for Holy Week 113, 163
  in Latin 167
  place of, in life of church ......160 ff., 168, 199, 221
  reform of, in Roman Catholicism 198
  as resource for unity 198
  symbols of 165, 170
  tradition of the ....198 ff.
  in the vernacular 168
Loisy, critical method of 70
Lombard, Peter 145, 146
Lord's Supper, the ....27, 116 ff., 236
  See also Eucharist, Sacraments
Lourdes, shrine of 136
Loyalty, of Roman Catholics to Rome 37, 103
  to the United States ....11, 94 ff., 103 ff.
Luther, Martin 46, 118, 175, 178
  on the church 50
  condemnation of, at Trent 50-53
  debt to heritage of the church 223
  the film 219
  loyalty of, to the church ..46 ff., 54, 93, 118, 212, 223
  on the primacy of Scriptures 50
  Roman Catholic picture of 196

Macauley 12
McCarran, Patrick 62
McCarthy, Joseph R. 62
McMahon, Brian 62
Magdeburg Centuries 47
Magic ....110 ff., 236
  See also Mystery
Marcion 30
Maritan, Jacques 197
Marriage 100, 122-24
  church control over ....15, 89-90, 122 ff., 205
Marxism 62, 140, 151, 175, 225
  See also Communism
Mary, Blessed Virgin 16, 128
  doctrine of Assumption of 71, 83, 129, 184, 239
  as guarantee of Incarnation 141
  immaculate conception of 131, 137-38, 184
  as mediatress ....137 ff.
  as mother of God (Theotokos) 132
  as prototype of the Christian believer 142
  See also Celibacy

Mass 117-19, 124, 166
  as dialogue 167
  lay participation in 163
  worship of 134
  See also Liturgy
Melchizidek 43
Merton, Thomas 12
Ministry, the episcopal 25, 125
  evolution of, into priesthood 27
  the threefold ....26 ff.
Missions, of early church ....23 ff.
  within Protestantism 88
Modalism 40
Modernism 69, 81
  controversy over 81
  encyclical against 92
Moffatt, James 190
Monarchy, and Roman Catholicism ....59 ff.
Monasticism 28, 88, 123, 130, 160
Mussolini, Benito 61
Mystery, and magic ....110 ff.
Mysticism, mystics 54, 166

Napoleon 60
National Council of Churches 200
Nationalism, the Reformers and 56
National Socialism 61, 239
Newman, Cardinal John Henry 93, 203, 207
Nicholas I, pope 42
Nicholas, James Hastings 60
Niebuhr, Reinhold 170-71
North Africa Church, loss of 41
  Novena 119, 163
  See also Eucharist

Obedience, of Roman Catholics 88, 103
  to Christ and Church ....80, 86 ff.
  glorification of ....88 ff.
  to the state ....103 ff.
Ockham, William of 149
Ong, Father, critique of Roman Church 221
Ordination, Anglican 179
  See also Holy Orders
Origen 30, 195, 198
Original sin, doctrine of, in Roman Catholicism 91
Orthodoxy, Eastern 43, 45, 68, 168, 177
  of Rome 39-40
  theological 141
Outler, Albert 177

Paganism 15, 128, 133
Papacy, papal, doctrine of infallibility . . 16, 40, 82, 84, 183
   primacy of 43, 83, 94
   rise and decline of 34, 42-44
Pascal, Blaise 69, 150
Patriarchates, of Alexandria 41
   of Antioch 41
   of Constantinople 41
   of Jerusalem 41
   of Rome 41
Patriotism 37, 56
Paul the Apostle 26, 130, 226
   and apostolic authority 25, 35, 194
   and authorship of Pastoral epistles 70
   and the law 99
   martyrdom of 36
   on Mary as mother of Christ 129-30
   mission of 23-25
   opposition to Peter 24, 188
   on unity 226
Paul III, pope, and church reform 51
Pelagius 146
Penance, sacrament of 120-21
Pentecost, experience of 23, 24
Peter the Apostle 35, 92-93
   death of 36
   on identity and universality 24
   the keys of ....36, 77 ff., 93, 179
   opposition to Paul 24, 188
   primacy of 19, 35, 187
Philosophers, Roman Catholic 65
Photius, patriarch of Constantinople 42
Pietism, within Protestantism 87, 105
Piety, Christian 15, 37
   folk 15, 48, 116, 119, 133
   of Roman Catholicism 22, 119, 140, 163
Pious IX, pope 70, 83, 92, 114, 131, 157
Pius X, pope, against modernism 70
   on biblical scholarship 70
Pius XI, pope 61
   See also Lateran, Treaty of
Pius XII, pope 83, 91, 140
Plato 134
Political theory, of Roman Catholicism 60, 95, 107
Pontifex maximus, bishop of Rome as 38
Pontificial Biblical Commission 81
Pontifical Gregorian University 88
Pontifical Institute of Medieval Studies 15

Prayer 37, 120, 129, 140
  Book of Common 215
Preaching, need of in Roman Catholicism 127
Predestination 146
President, of the United States ....11, 12, 104 ff.
Preysing, K. G. 40
Priesthood 124-26
Protestantism, catholicity of 47, 55, 68, 186
  theology of 157-58

Quasten, Johannes 195
Quebec, influence of Roman Catholicism in 105, 107

Race, and liturgy 170
  problem of, in Protestantism 231
  problem of, in Roman Catholicism ....170 ff., 233
Rahner, Father 38
Reconciliation, ministry of ....200-201, 215 ff.
Reformation 14
  necessity of 45-57
  theology of 15, 47, 49
  witness of 224
Reformers, catholicity of ....46 ff., 53, 197, 223
  polemics against Thomism 148
Relics, of saints 83
Religion, history of, in relation to Roman Catholicism 15
Renaissance 64
Repentance 28, 120-21, 221
  as precondition to unity 184
Rerum Novarum, encyclical 62
  See also Labor
Responsibility, taught in Roman Catholic schools ..90 ff.
  need for awareness of our ......200-201, 202, 215 ff.
Reunion, of Christendom, hope for 179
  policy for ....209 ff., 238
Roman Catholicism, academic freedom in ..64-67, 80 ff.
  authority in ....16, 25, 80-83, 87 ff., 96
  definition of essence of 22
  and democracy ....59 ff.
  and fascism ....60 ff.
  genius of ....15, 75, 159 ff.
  interpretations of 12, 152
  missionary policy of 107
  and monarchy ....59 ff.
  political action of 56, 59, 60, 61-62, 107
  political theory of 60, 90, 107
  and totalitarianism 61
Roman Empire, expansion of 24
Roman See, primary of 19, 35, 179, 187

Rome, congregation at 36-37
  patriarchate of 41
  Protestant picture of 14
  roads to . . . . .202 ff.
Roosevelt, Franklin D. 105
Rosary 126, 163
Rüber, Johannes 198

Sacramental system . . . . .28, 110 ff.
Sacramentals, growth of 113, 119
Sacraments 27, 49, 75, 147
  cental place in Roman Catholicism . . . . .110 ff.
  and holiness 182
Sacred Congregation of the Holy Office 91
St. Anne 137
St. Apollonia 135
St. Crispin 135
St. Jude 128, 136
St. Optatus 182
St. Patrick 135
St. Peter, Church of, in Rome 161
St. Vincent Martyr 135
Saints, communion of 142
  confessions of the 49
  miracles of the 83
  worship of the 11
Savonarola 54
Schleiermacher, Friedrich 229, 236
Schleiff, Arnold 221
Schlier, Heinrich 207
Schlink, Edmund 129
Scholasticism 114, 143, 193
Schools, Roman Catholic position on 11, 12, 90, 97
  parochial 81, 88
  Sacred Heart 88
Scriptures, authority of, in Roman Catholicism 31, 52
  canonization of 31
  as means of identity .31, 191
  renewed interest in . . . . .191 ff.
  Trent and the 52
  and unity . . . . .191 ff.
Secularism 57
Segura, Cardinal 225
Self-examination, need of 220-21
Seneca 25
Separation, the burden of . . . . .214 ff., 226
  loss through 222

Sermon on the Mount, in Thomistic thought 156
   place of in the church 164
   need of in Roman Catholicism 127
Shaughnessy, Gerald, on immigrant faith 204
Sin and grace 47
Sitwell, Edith 66, 208
Skeffington, Frank 103
Smith, Alfred E. 104
Socialism, Christian 63
Söderblom, Nathan 238
Sohm, Rudolf 22
Soloviev, Vladimir, conversion of 208
Soviet Union 13
   See also Communism, Marxism
Spain, Roman Catholic control in 66, 107, 225
Spirit. See Holy Spirit
Stauffer, Ethelbert, on primacy of Peter 79
Stephen (martyr) 35
Strasbourg, Congress of 192
Sullivan, William L. 135
Summa Theologica 145
   See also Aquinas, Thomism
Swedenborg, Emanuel 54

Tabernacle, piety of 118, 163
Temple, Archbishop 177
Tertullian 26, 37, 42, 54
Theodosius the Great 32
Theology, basis of 29
   function of 29
Third Reich 215
   See also National Socialism
Thirty Years War 56
Thomism 65, 67, 88, 122, 143-58
   on faith and reason 65
   the future of 157-58
   and the intellectual ....109, 152 ff., 208
   and philosophy 66
   and tradition 155
   revolt against ....154 ff.
   world view of ....227 ff.
   See also Aquinas
Thorn, Polish Conference of 68
Thompson, Francis 66
Tillich, Paul 13, 144, 165
   in continuity with Schleiermacher 230
   Protestant principle of 220
Tiso, Monsignor Jozef 96
Tolerance, as irresponsibility 218

Tolstoy 208
Totalitarianism 59, 61, 96
Tradition ....50 ff., 82, 145
  hymns as symbols of 235
  pope as living tradition 82-83
  in Protestantism ....193 ff., 234
  in Roman Catholicism ....19, 39, 50 ff., 63,
                       69, 151, 155, 234
  Trent and 52, 82, 224
Trent, Council of ....50 ff., 67 ff., 82, 149, 224
  ambiguous interpretation of 117
  as barrier to reunion 238
  the decrees of ....51, 82, 148 ff., 224
  on justification by faith 52, 69, 149
  on tradition 52, 69, 82
  See also Aquinas, Thomism, Tradition
Trinity, doctrine of ....48, 50 ff., 145

Uniat, or Eastern Church 45, 68, 123, 168, 176
Unigenitus, of Pope Clement XI 47
Unitarianism 215
Unity ....22, 177 ff., 190 ff., 238-40
Undset, Sigrid 66, 208
Urban VIII, pope 69
Urban ministry, Roman Catholic success in ......232 ff.

Vatican, ambassador to 106
  Council of 1870 ....40, 70, 150, 238
Viaticum. See Extreme unction
Virgin Mary. See Mary, Blessed Virgin
Von Loewenich, Walter 139

Wagner, Robert F. 62
Walden 170
Waugh, Evelyn 66-67, 208
White House 104, 106
  See also President, of the United States
World Council of Churches 180, 192-93, 200
Worship, as church renewal 160-72

Zwingli, Huldreich 46, 56
Zephyrinus 40